ORIGINS AND
TA.
LOND

Jean Harrowven

Illustrations by Len Strasman
Wood Engravings for the Cover by John Spencer

THE BORROWDALE PRESS 2000

Also by Jean Harrowven

Origins of Rhymes, Songs and Sayings
Origins of Festivals and Feasts
The Limerick Makers
Riddles and Legends of London Bridge
Sir Richard Whittington's Secret
St. Nicholas, Santa Claus and Father Christmas

Published by
THE BORROWDALE PRESS 2000
17 Dixon Road
Norwich NR7 8QJ
Tel: 01603 419411
Fax: 01603 412195

Contents

Praising what is lost
Makes remembrance dear.

JOHN TIMBS

Introduction

London, the illustrious city, has grown from villages in the fields into a vast place of palaces, parks and ancient monuments, shops, sports and amusements, bound together with the strong gold thread of history and tradition that gleams as brightly as ever in modern times. Set in a world that is constantly changing, our capital city, deeply rooted, has preserved her past and in doing so acts as a magnet to draw thousands of tourists from all over the world. The Venerable Bede writing in the seventh century said 'London is the mart of many nations' – and this has not changed.

To write about London from a new angle has not been easy – so many books have been published on the subject already – and yet I feel that I have contributed, in some ways at least, a new dimension to the basic story of progress and development. The book covers such a wide span of history and acreage that I hope I may be forgiven if I have omitted to mention a favourite place or memorable anecdote. Suffice to say that I have tried to recount historical facts that are not well known to the reader, to answer a few questions that hitherto do not seem to have been answered and to relate stories of the social scene which have remained obscure.

Legends of how London got its name and how indeed it became established were a delight to research – as was the growth of Parliament with special emphasis on the Woolsack. The history of the suffragette movement received a boost when I was given unpublished information about Emily Davison – the lady who spent census night in the broom cupboard of the 'House' and later lost her life for the cause. My detective work has led me to find out the long lost link between Sir Richard Whittington,

Lord Mayor, and a cat, the origin of Downing Street and why Hyde Park is so called. In fact I have taken great pleasure in writing this book and I hope the reader will find pleasure in it also.

My thanks go to my friend and illustrator, Len Strasman, (sadly now deceased) not only for his pictures, produced with flair and accuracy, but for his help and encouragement and his knowledge of London which has been invaluable to me. I would also like to thank John Bridges for letting me use his private collection of ancient books on London.

Jean Harrowven
Norwich

I

Beginnings

There are many stories and legends explaining how and when the earliest settlement of London came into being. In reality it is the tale of two cities – London and Westminster – which when bonded together produced an issue which has grown and developed into the greatest capital city the world has ever known.

Many historians believe as I do, that there were dwellings in the area prior to the Roman occupation. Archaeologically speaking there is not much evidence to support this but a few notable pieces have been found which date before Christ. During recent excavations under Billingsgate market a Greek rhyton dated 200 B.C. and a shallow drinking cup which had been used as a miniature water pitcher dated 600 B.C., have been found. An even older relic was discovered in the footings of the London Wall – that of a bronze figure of an Egyptian god. Of course these treasures may have been brought over by the Romans or later invaders but on the other hand they may be remnants of a civilization that inhabited London long before Britain became the Roman Isle.

The old chronicler, Geoffrey of Monmouth, who in 1152 became Bishop of St. Asaph, states in his 'History of Britain' that there was a king called Belin living in the London area in 400 B.C., and he built a gate at the entrance to what is now Billingsgate and cut a hythe into the riverbank to make a place where fishing boats could moor and unload their catches on the brushwood wharf. He goes on to say that when Belin died his ashes were contained in a brass vessel which was set up on the structure of the gate. Monmouth's writings have been discredited by most historians as being unreliable and fanciful but no one can say for sure that there is no truth in this story.

But one thing is certain and that is that the river Thames was there long before any settlement and even perhaps before man himself inhabited these shores. The Thames rises as several small streams in the Cotswolds at a place named Thames Head, near Cirencester – and this is thought to be the source. The narrow winding river journeys to the sea over 209 miles, as it has done for centuries. On its way it flows through Oxford where it is known as the Isis, probably from the Latin name Tamesis. This may give a clue to where the Thames obtained its name. Isis was the Egyptian goddess of mystery and magic and her husband Osiris was god of the after world. In any event the name Thames is thought to be very old indeed, perhaps as old as the Beaker folk who came from North Africa and preceded the Celts. One theory is that the Beakers were responsible for naming not only the Thames, but the Tyne, Towy and Tees also.

Norse, Greek, Egyptian and many other ancient civilizations are rich in stories explaining how man came to be on their particular corners of the earth. Sadly, Britain has missed out on this, although we do have one or two surviving legends which are worth repeating. One concerns a king in Europe named Diocletian, who had thirty-three daughters. His armies had conquered all the lands he required but his heart's desire was to see his daughters happily married. They were obviously unattractive but at last by means of bribes and promises he managed to find thirty-three husbands. But the sisters were unhappy with their spouses and on a certain night the thirty-three brides cut the throats of the thirty-three husbands. Diocletian was furious and ashamed, and threatened to have his daughters executed – for what was their future to be now? He called a council of ministers and the idea was put forward that the sisters should be deported – put to sea in a ship without a crew, but with half a year's provisions, to drift at the will of the winds and the tides, expelled from their homeland for ever. This was done and after a few weeks of relatively calm weather the ship grounded on the beach of an uninhabited island. The women alighted from their craft and the eldest, named Dame Albyne, declared that the island should be their own and that it should be called Albyne after her. Albion – the ancient name for Britain so the story goes – derived its origin from this. Albion in Welsh is Y Wen Ymys and means White Island

and so it is possible that the sisters landed on the Welsh coast.

After a time the ladies became tired of their own company and longed for male attention. Like the giants and creatures fashioned from rocks and icebergs in Greek and Norse mythology, giants came to life in Britain created out of large rocks and boulders, at the will of the sisters. Their offspring were themselves giants whose leaders were Gogmagog or Goemagot and Caugherin. When Brut, or Brutus, the Trojan conquered Albion he slew all the giants, including Caugherin, but kept Goemagot to fight his younger son Corineus. The giant broke two of Corineus's ribs and at this the human became enraged and with great strength and courage tackled Goemagot and threw him over the cliffs at Totnes where the creature was dashed to pieces on the rocks. To this day a place called Lam Goemagot or Goemagot's Leap can be seen at this spot about twenty miles from Plymouth. Brutus and his army were delighted with their victory and two effigies were made representing the fallen enemy and the name Goemagot was split into two. Thus Gog and Magog came into being and after being paraded around the countryside – there are two hills in Cambridgeshire called Gog and Magog – the emblems of victory were finally brought to London for permanent exhibition. Models of the giants have been destroyed and rebuilt throughout the centuries – the last time was during the Blitz – but now two modern editions can be seen at the Guildhall, London.

An old verse entitled the Oracle of Diana remembers the conquering of this island by Brut and his army and in translation reads:

> Brute – past the realms of Gaul, beneath the sunset,
> Lieth an island girt about by ocean,
> Guarded by ocean – erst the haunts of giants
> Desert of late, and meet for this thy people.
> Seek it! For there is thine abode for ever.
> There, by thy sons again shall Troy be builded;
> There, of thy blood, shall kings be born
> Hereafter sovran in every land the wide world over.

It is said that Brut, or Brutus, the Trojan gave his name to Britain and that he founded London and called it Caer-Troiau. His eldest son Lud, who became king after Brut's death, changed the name to Lud-din (Lud's city) and that is one story as to how London acquired its name. Geoffrey of Monmouth records that Lud-gate was built in 66 B.C. to commemorate the death of King Lud and was a river gate, marking the entry from the west of the river Walbrook, into the city. The river flowed between two hills and it was here in the bed of the Walbrook that the Roman Temple of Mithras was discovered earlier this century. Most of the city gates were prisons in the ensuing centuries and I delve into their histories in a later chapter on the police and prisons. The story of Ludgate ties up with the origin of Billingsgate as previously explained and does seem to indicate that there was a thriving settlement in the area which we now know as the City of London long before the Roman invasion.

There are many more theories as to how London got its name but everyone will agree that it does not have a Latin derivation, although it was dubbed Londinium by the Romans, probably because it was already known as that. I favour the idea put forward by Michael Harrison in his book *London Beneath the Pavement* – that London was in fact at one time a river dwelling, that is to say it was built on piles driven into the river and was joined to the bank by a gangway which could be raised if invaders were near. Villages of this nature still exist in the Far East where the ground is swampy and unsafe – as was the land around the Thames in early times. This would explain why archaeological remains pre-dating the Roman period are scarce as they would either have been washed away in the swiftly flowing river or buried deep in the mud of the riverbed. If this was the case then the word London could have stemmed from Llin-din, meaning city of the lake. Llin or Llyn is the Celtic word for lake and din or dun means city or hills. London had all three – a settlement, a river lake and two hills, Cornhill and Ludgate, which stood out against the skyline as unmistakable landmarks.

When the Romans conquered Britain in the first century they saw the strategic value of the river village and increased its importance by building the first London Bridge – a wooden structure which was a superb piece of engineering. It is thought that at first a small fort roughly 200 yards square was built and used as a garrison guarding the bridge which was the main link with the invading armies. It may also have been a mint as many early

Roman coins have been found in the area. At this time Londinium was not the principal Roman city in Britain – but the new lords had a set-back when Boadicea attacked the settlement and razed it to the ground. This came about as follows. When the Romans initially invaded they made a pact with Prasutagus, the husband of Boadicea, promising not to invade his lands in East Anglia and so avoid a bloody conflict with the tribe of Iceni, who were under his command. In return Prasutagus, who had his head-quarters in Colchester, allowed the Romans to use it as their administrative centre, and gave help and advice where needed. Before he died he left half his fortune to Nero, hoping that this would protect his family. It did not, and after his death the Romans confiscated his palace, wealth and property, stripped and flogged his wife and raped his daughters. Queen Boadicea, a lady of great spirit, vowed that these actions should not go unavenged. She summoned up her great Iceni army and many thousands of well trained warriors marched on Colchester and St. Albans, which they destroyed completely. She then set her sights on London and this settlement met the same fate. Before she could be captured she took poison and so escaped torment by her enemies. There is a bronze statue of Boadicea in her chariot near Westminster Pier.

After this experience the Romans thought it prudent to build a wall around the river stronghold. The settlement was extended to cover about 330 acres and the wall was built out from the original fort from the lower western corner and the upper eastern corner and eventually enclosed an area about the size of Hyde Park. The eastern wall borders on to the walls of the Tower which was built, we presume, later. There were seven main gates in those days which are remembered in street names in modern times. These were Aldgate (the oldest of all), Bishopsgate, Moorgate, Cripplegate (this had an underground passage where late travellers could pay a toll to gain entry to the City after sundown. Cripple is derived from an old English word meaning underground), Ludgate and the London Bridge Gate – which had taken the place of the first Billingsgate.

Before the Romans became Christians it is thought that a temple dedicated to Diana was built on the site where now stands St. Paul's Cathedral. During excavations the head of Diana was found and is preserved in the Goldsmith's Hall. After the Great Fire Wren had the task of rebuilding St. Paul's and during excavations found many Roman and Saxon remains including burial urns and sacrificial vessels – but nothing to convince him that a pagan temple to Diana was once built on the spot. However he did believe most wholeheartedly that St. Paul himself had visited these islands on his many journeys and had come to consecrate the ground where he said that a church should be built bearing his name. There is no mention in the Scriptures of St. Paul visiting these islands but the legend of the settling of Joseph of Arimathea in Glastonbury is well known. There is another story concerning Suetonius, the early Christian Roman leader, who, while in Wales killing off the Druids, learnt some Welsh words, and on his return to London named the early church built on the site of St. Paul's 'Llanden', which is Welsh for Church of Diana, and this could also be interpreted as yet another derivation of the word London.

During the Roman occupation London thrived as did all Roman communities in Britain. Temples, houses, roads, offices were built with expertise and craftsmanship far beyond the level of civilization at that time. When the Romans left, London, like all the rest, was disorganized and unready for the Saxon hordes which had been awaiting the opportunity to attack and conquer the island which they regarded as a rich prize. London was reduced to a primitive dwelling place. The Saxons were pagan and nothing was sacred. Roman sculpture, pillars, cornices and all magnificent works of art were pulled down and used as common building stone. Soon not a piece of Roman architecture survived above the ground except the London Stone set up by the Romans as a milestone measuring distances from the City. It can still be seen today above the pavement in Cannon Street.

Linking up with the story of Suetonius we have another tale which relates that in the second century King Lucius, also a Christian, introduced two missionaries from Rome who consecrated the temple of Diana and also built a place of Christian worship in a small suburb to the west of the settlement – on a peninsula called Thorney Island. Sporely, a Saxon monk and chronicler, writes that this community at Thorney slipped back into paganism with the Saxon invasions and the church was converted to a temple dedicated to Apollo. Another monk, John

Flete, writing at an earlier date confirms this and says that in early Saxon times Londoners worshipped Diana and the suburbs of Thorney offered incense to Apollo.

When Christianity again came to Britain through the ambassadors of Rome in the form of missionary bishops, the development of London progressed quite quickly. After the Saxon conquest London was known by various names such as London-Byrig, Lunden Ceaster, Lundain, Lunden Wye, Lunden-Barb or Lunden-Burg. Early imports included salt, earthenware, brass, polished bone, horse collars, glass and amber. Exports were cattle, horses, corn, dogs which were trained in hunting and slaves. The story that children with fair hair and complexions were seen by Pope Gregory may well be true. When asked where they came from he was told that they were Angles. His reply was that they looked more like angels. This incident is supposed by tradition to have prompted the Pope to send missionaries to this country and St. Augustine and his party landed on the south-east coast and set up a monastery at Canterbury – later to become a cathedral. He was appointed Archbishop of England by the Pope in A.D. 600. The Venerable Bede writing in the seventh century tells us that a church named St. Paul's had been built in London and this is the earliest record we have which mentions the church by name. It was built by Ethelbert, King of East Kent. Mellitus, bishop of the East Saxons who was ordained by the Pope, became its first bishop, and a monastery was set up there.

Later, Sebert, King of the East Saxons and nephew of Ethelbert, not to be out done built, we are told, a Christian church on the island of Thorney where a Roman temple sacred to Apollo stood. This was of course the beginnings of St. Peter's cathedral and the Minster in the West which we know as Westminster Abbey. From this day forward a friendly rivalry existed between the two ecclesiastical houses as we shall see later.

The most famous of the early bishops of St. Paul's was St. Erkenwald, who with his twin sister ran ecclesiastical houses. They were the children of Offa, king of the East Angles, and the sister was the Abbess of a convent at Barking. The stories about St. Erkenwald are many and one relates that when out driving a rough cart to a place where he was to preach the gospel to a group of woodmen, one of the wheels of the cart came off.

Erkenwald took no notice and left the wheel lying in the road, and the vehicle ran on, perfectly balanced. One day when visiting his sister at Barking he collapsed and died. He was so highly thought of that the monks of Chertsey and the monks of St. Paul's nearly came to blows as to which establishment should house his remains. The monks of the two sees marched on Barking in haste to claim the body. The St. Paul's contingency arrived first and snatched Erkenwald, much to the distress of the Barking nuns. The Chertsey party were in hot pursuit and caught up with their rivals when they came to a halt on the banks of the river Lea and had no means of crossing it. There was a fight – but when things had calmed down a little a pious onlooker suggested that both parties should relax and look for a sign from God to tell them what to do. The group from St. Paul's sat on the grass and sang a litany. When lo and behold, so the story goes, the waters of the Lea parted and the Londoners were able to walk across the river-bed in comfort, carrying the precious body of St. Erkenwald, and so made their way to St. Paul's. The Chertsey monks accepted the decision from God and went home. The clergy at St. Paul's were overjoyed at their victory as they knew very well that the remains of the revered saint would increase the revenue of the church. Pilgrims would journey from all over Europe to worship at the shrine of St. Erkenwald.

Meanwhile, things had been happening west of the early settlement of London. The story that a temple dedicated to Apollo was built on the site that now houses Westminster Abbey has been dismissed by historians as hearsay as no remains have been found to support this theory. One bishop explained that the temple was destroyed by earthquakes and therefore all evidence was lost. This may be true as in the early days London was subjected to quite severe earth tremors. In any case Westminster Abbey has never been entirely rebuilt, as was St. Paul's, so no one has had the opportunity of excavating beneath the footings of the building. For all we know there may be ample evidence lying beneath the vaults and crypt of the great Minster to justify the story of the temple of Apollo.

The peninsula which jutted out into the swiftly flowing Thames was covered with thorn bushes at the time of the building of the first church. But it was composed of firm gravel soil which compared favourably with the marshy land that surrounded it. It was called an island because in the twelfth century a small tributary of the Thames broke away from its natural course and ran across the neck of the peninsula thus severing the Abbey from the mainland and providing a welcome natural moat which was ideal for the protection of the building and gave a feeling of detachment and sanctuary necessary for the people who lived and worked there. The old boundaries of the island can be seen from aerial photographs.

After the building of the first church by Sebert in A.D. 616 with the blessing of Mellitus, bishop of St. Paul's, the story goes that on the eve of consecration the place was visited by St. Peter who made himself known to a fisherman casting his nets in the river at dusk. St. Peter requested that the man should row him over to Thorney island so that he could enter the church. The fisherman agreed and watched with incredulous eyes for as the saint entered the church it was illuminated with a bright light and he heard the sounds of a heavenly choir coming from inside. He knew then without a doubt that the church was being consecrated by St. Peter himself. After a while the singing died away, the light faded and the saint came again to the fisherman and told him to drop his nets into the water. This he did and when he pulled in the nets a few minutes later they were crammed full of the finest salmon. St. Peter is reported to have said that all the fishermen of Westminster could fish in the river every day except Sunday and all they caught would be theirs except a tenth of the catch which was to be paid as toll to the clergy of St. Peter's. The fisherman went to Mellitus and King Sebert the next day and told them of the miracle that he had seen. They hastened into the church and saw that it was true – the burnt out tapers and the chrism bore the distinguishing marks of the consecration. A celebration Mass was then held and everyone gloried in the happening. The fish tithe was paid to the Deans of Westminster for centuries after this and in the Chapter House and elsewhere in the Abbey there are tiles inscribed with the shape of a salmon which can still be seen. Up to the close of the fourteenth century fishermen were allowed to bring their offering of salmon to the high altar and then enjoy the privilege of sitting with the monks and partaking of a meal.

Up to the Norman conquest London and many other cities suffered heavily at the hands of pagan invaders who wanted to rule 'this precious isle'. Christian places of worship were burnt down again and again but somehow London survived and flourished. A monk named John Brompton writes in 971 about 'Blynesgate' and how King Ethelred had made laws to widen the harbour so that the dock could take much larger sailing ships. King Alfred at this time had succeeded in banishing the Danes for a while and set up monasteries and schools within the city of London and also gave money for the restoration of St. Peter's. At that time there was only a single sandy track winding its way along the riverbank linking the City with Westminster and this was commonly known as the Strand – which means beach.

Alfred was very keen to protect our shores from invaders and built a large navy for that purpose and has been known since as the Father of the English Navy. He also built a large number of merchant vessels which he leased out to merchants trading with the Near East and the Levant. He recognized the need to increase imports and exports and it is known that he was desperate to acquire precious jewels with which to embellish the crown and other regalia. It is thought that Alfred was the first to divide the City of London into wards and this has been dealt with later on.

In 951 St. Peter's church was once more in ruins and King Edgar directed St. Dunstan to rebuild it and set up a monastery. St. Dunstan collected twelve Benedictine monks and made Wulsinus, one of his favourites, the Abbot. The church still was small and insignificant and had not achieved the fame and stature to which it was entitled considering St. Peter himself had consecrated it. In 1013 Edward the Confessor was preparing to take over the monarchy of Britain but had to flee to the Continent because the Danes, under the leadership of Canute, had once more overrun the country. While Canute reigned the city was attacked by Norsemen who sailed silently up the river in their long boats and demolished London Bridge. It is said that they threw long ropes around the piles of the rickety structure and then rowed with great strength backwards, pulling the ropes as they went. The bridge collapsed. Some of the folk on the bridge were taken by surprise and had to run for safety to the south works of fortifications on the south bank and this is where the ward of

Southwark got its name. The raid was under the command of
Olaf the warrior and here is an old verse entitled Heimskringla
by Ottar Svarte which records the event:

> London Bridge is broken down
> Gold is won and bright renown –
> Shields resounding,
> War horns sounding
> Hildur shouting in the din,
> Arrows singing,
> Mail coats ringing
> Odin makes our Olaf win.

After Olaf was crowned King of Norway he became a Christian
but was murdered by his subjects. He was eventually canonized
and the people of London built a church dedicated to him and
named it St. Olaves – and there was a church near the site of
Southwark Cathedral which bore this name and pre-dated the Fire
of London. Incidentally, St. Saviour's, Southwark, was a parish
church for 360 years before being made a Cathedral in 1905. Before
the Dissolution it was known as St. Mary Overie and belonged
to the great Augustine Priory established in the area during the
twelfth century. The legend of this church goes back to Saxon
times when London Bridge had 'fallen down' and the ferryman
named John Overs had sole right to carry people over the water
at this point. Although he was wealthy he was also extremely
miserly and it is said that he feigned his death so that his family
and friends would be forced to fast for one day. When lying in
his coffin he heard the revelry going on in the room next door;
everyone eating, drinking and enjoying themselves on his funeral
day. He was so angry that he arose from his coffin and confronted
the gathering in his burial attire. One of the guests, thinking he
was a ghost, struck him a severe blow from which he died. His
daughter, Mary, pious and good and overcome by grief, devoted
her father's fortune to the foundation of a house of sisters by
whom the ferry was maintained – which was named St. Mary-
over-the-Rie. Later St. Erkenwald, the Saxon, bishop consecrated
the nunnery in 666.

Meanwhile Canute had become a Christian and having taken
a liking to Thorney island had built himself a palace opposite

the small church of St. Peter. The Thames is and was a tidal river and the story telling that Canute ordered the tide to turn at his command has been applied to the banks of Thorney island where it is said that the king sat, issuing orders to the waters to turn back but getting swamped in the process to teach his fawning subjects a lesson. He set out to prove once and for all that he was not God – only a mere mortal and as such could not perform the miracles that his courtiers believed.

In the last years of his life Canute laid down that every citizen should be treated fairly and not taxed too heavily. To the citizens of London he promised that every vassal who had resided in the City for a year and a day without being claimed by his master, should receive his freedom. This was the first gleam of liberty that the mass of the population had experienced throughout the gloom and oppression of the Dark Ages. The City of London received the distinguished title of 'The Free Chamber of the King' – and this was the basis of the independence that the citizens of London have nurtured throughout the ages. Canute died before he could carry out these vows but Edward the Confessor who succeeded him endorsed these Christian principles.

While Edward was on the Continent he vowed he would make a pilgrimage to Rome as thanksgiving if the English Crown was offered to him. His prayers were answered and he was able to return to England and was duly crowned. Mindful of his promise of a pilgrimage he sent an envoy to Rome to confer with the Pope about this matter. The Pope graciously said that instead of making the journey to Rome he was to use the money to embellish a church dedicated to St. Peter. This seems a strange and convenient coincidence but what was more surprising was that at the same time Abbot Wulsinus had a dream in which St. Peter visited him and told him to tell Edward that he wished the church of St. Peter – his namesake – to be restored in all the glory that could be mustered. Between the two of them Edward and Wulsinus convinced the populace and barons alike that it was God's will that an abbey – the best in Europe – was to be built on the site of St. Peter's. Thus Edward the Confessor spent the last years of his life collecting money to build this wondrous abbey and designing it on such a sumptuous and grand scale as had never been witnessed before. When it was finished many more monks were ordained and the lands and property belonging to the monastery were increased to cover a large area. A set of relics was incorporated into the building that was destined to make a fortune and was the envy of every ecclesiastical house. Supposedly, there was part of the manger in which Christ had been laid, some of the frankincense offered to Him by the Magi, parts of the garment which Christ wore on the Cross, pieces of the sponge, lance and scourge with which He was tortured, fragments of the sepulchre and the cloth that bound His Head, and so on.

The Confessor built the abbey on Norman lines, having spent much time in Normandy and being very impressed with the French style of architecture. It was in fact the first Norman building in the British Isles. At last it was finished and Edward, suffering failing health, had the church hallowed in the presence of nobles and clergy, some from overseas, on Holy Innocents' Day – 28 December 1065. On 5 January a few days later he lay on his death-bed in his home across the road – the dwelling place that most probably housed Canute, and now houses the Palace of Westminster. The story goes that attended by his wife, Queen Editha, he was visited by Harold and his brothers who pleaded with him to name his successor to the throne. It is said that Edward with his dying breath said 'Harold, take it if it be thy wish but the gift will be thy ruin. Against the Duke and his baronage no power of thine can avail thee.' The Duke to whom he referred was the Duke of Normandy – William the Conqueror to whom Edward had already promised the throne after his death – or so many think.

Edward gave many treasures to be used in coronations in the Abbey and endorsed the coronation procedure as introduced by St. Dunstan. He was the first king to be buried in the Abbey and this was in accordance with his wishes. The use of the Great Seal was introduced during his reign and the original can be seen in the British Museum. He was patron saint of England up to the thirteenth century when St. George superseded him. There are over twenty churches dedicated to him in England. The death and burial of Edward the Confessor is worked into the Bayeux tapestry, a replica of which can be seen in the Victoria and Albert museum. Edward was the first king to be touched with the King's

Evil, a disease called scrofula – a kind of skin tuberculosis – the last monarch being Queen Anne.

Harold was the first king to have the honour of being crowned in the Abbey and this too, is immortalized in the Bayeux tapestry. His glory was short lived for whilst he was fighting a successful battle against the Norsemen at Stamford Bridge, William of Normandy was preparing to cross the Channel with a small but highly organized invasion force – to land somewhere near Hastings. When Harold heard the news he was flushed with victory over the Norsemen and without giving his men time to recover ordered a forced march south. The English troops were in an exhausted state when they reached the battle area and the fate of the future of England was soon sealed. William then marched on London, desecrating everything in his path. He was met by the leading merchants at the City gates and was given the keys of the City in total surrender. The citizens of London were tired of continued attacks on their lives and property and hoped that from now onwards they would have security and prosperity under the leadership and protection of William. And they were right. Ruthless he was, but as long as the Saxons did as they were bid William treated them fairly and from that time in 1066 London grew and developed into the great metropolis that we know today.

2

Westminster Abbey,
St. Paul's Cathedral
and the City Churches

WESTMINSTER ABBEY

Continuing from the previous chapter the story of the Abbey,
which by now had the official title of the Collegiate Church
of St. Peter in Westminster, William I was crowned king of
England in this building on Christmas Day in 1066. For William
the dream of a lifetime had come true. Earlier coronations had
taken place at Kingston-upon-Thames, Bath and Winchester –
the Confessor being crowned in the latter place. Before Edward
died he had applied to the Pope for permission for all future kings
of England to be crowned in the Abbey, and this was granted.

It was St. Dunstan who had introduced certain rituals into the
coronation service, first carried out at the coronation of King
Edgar, that are still performed today. The investiture with the
sword, sceptre and the rod of justice, the playing of a traditional
anthem, the Archbishop's consecration and anointing, and the
shout of recognition from the assembled lords are all rituals which
are still carried out in present times. The idea of patriotism was
first introduced at the crowning of the king as his followers saw
their leader as a national figure. The Saxons witnessing the crowning of William were familiar with the procedure and gave a joyful
shout when the king had the crown placed upon his head.

The Norman soldiers on the other hand, inside and outside
the Abbey, were ill at ease and expecting trouble. Legend has
it that when they heard the cry of acclamation from the Saxons

they thought it was the sign of a rebellion against their leader and immediately ran into the Abbey to save William or went about setting fire to the houses adjacent to the Minster. The ceremony which up to then had been going smoothly came to an abrupt halt as the English rushed from the building to save their families and properties from being burnt. The Conqueror was left alone except for a few priests and he sat shivering with fear and unprotected, expecting a Saxon mob to enter the Abbey at any minute and slay him. This did not happen and after a while he ordered the inauguration ceremony to proceed and added an extra promise that he would treat the English commoners as well as the best of the Saxon kings had done. When the ceremony was over William went out into the streets to organize the fire fighting and stop the plundering of houses by his own soldiers.

Although William was crowned in the Abbey he was not buried there, but there is a story that King Sebert's remains are in a tomb near the gates of the South Ambulatory.

At the time of the coronation of Richard I feelings against the Jews were running high. They had come over and settled in London at the express wish of William the Conqueror – mainly to look after his finances. Their business acumen soon made them unpopular with the citizens of London. Richard forbade Jews to enter the Abbey or join in the feasting and merry-making after the coronation. Some of the more zealous Israelites thought that if they gave rich gifts to the king they would at least be allowed to attend the ceremony. The king was greedy so gave his permission, and all might have gone well if a sharp-eyed Christian had not spotted the group of Jews laying gifts at the feet of the king during the inauguration. This sparked off a fight actually within the Abbey which afterwards developed into a purge of Jews in general. They were killed in the streets by the mob, their houses were burnt and when the women and children were forced to come out of the smoking buildings they were raped and murdered.

The king was told of this while he attended the coronation banquet, and he commanded his minstrels to play louder so as to drown the screams and cries of the poor wretches being put to death outside his door. So much for his promise to do right by his people which he had solemnly given at the ceremony.

Richard, like so many monarchs, probably had debts piling up with the Jewish money lenders and was relieved to see them liquidated as were many of his courtiers. The king had two of the murderers hanged just to give the appearance of upholding the laws of justice – but that was all.

King John lost all the coronation regalia in the Wash, including the crown, and his son, Henry III, was crowned with a plain circlet of gold. He was only ten years old at the time so probably did not have much say in the matter. He grew up to be a pious king and devoted much of his life and all his money to restoring the Confessor's shrine and other parts of the Abbey. To raise money he organized a fair in Tothill fields near by and ordered that all profits were to go into the restoration fund. He commanded that all shops and markets be closed so that citizens were forced to buy goods at the fair. But it rained so hard and for so long that the whole thing was a wash-out. Henry was so poor that he had to pawn the jewels intended for Edward's tomb and on more than one occasion had to ask himself and his family out to dine with rich merchants because his cupboard was bare. In the end his efforts were rewarded and in 1269 the new shrine was consecrated and the body of the founder of the Abbey was placed in it. Henry died in 1272 and his body was buried in a magnificent tomb studded with precious jewels, in the shrine which he himself had created. But his heart, as he had promised, was sent to the Abbey of Fontevrault in France where Richard Coeur de Lion and his grandfather Henry II were buried. In fact many of the earlier kings were buried in France.

The Coronation Chair was created for the coronation of Edward I. The chair is made of hard wood and the sides were formerly painted in gilt and enamelled in various colours. The feet of the chair consist of four small carved lions, but it is the stone that is slotted underneath the seat that has the more interesting history. It is a rough looking sandstone measuring 26 inches in length, 16¾ inches in breadth and 10½ inches in thickness and could be seen in the Confessor's shrine. It is of course still used at coronations. There is a tradition that the stone originally came from Ireland and was brought there by the Scythians. It was said to issue sounds resembling thunder whenever one of the royal Scythian race seated themselves on it for inauguration and that he was only crowned king if the stone groaned or 'spoke'. It was brought from Ireland to Scotland by Fergus the first king of Scotland and he was crowned king seated on it in roughly 330 B.C. It was used from that time onwards at all coronations of the Scottish kings at Dunstaffnage and Scone. It was carried to Scone by Kenneth II when he united the territory of the Picts and the Scots in the ninth century, where it remained until the thirteenth century. The stone became an emblem of national independence for the Scots and it is said to have borne a verse upon it in Latin in those early days, which in translation read:

> Except old saws do fail,
> And wizards' wits be blind,
> The Scots in place must reign,
> Where they this stone shall find.

In 1296 Edward 1 of England overran the Scots and took the Scone stone – 'The stone of destiny" – to Westminster and had it placed underneath his new coronation chair. In the eyes of the proud Scots he had committed the worst outrage imaginable. According to Fordun, the Scottish chronicler, they would gladly have exchanged Baliol, the Scottish king at the time, for the honoured Scone stone. From that time onwards the Scots consoled themselves with the thought that perhaps one day a Scottish king would rule Britain and indeed this did come true. Mary, Queen of Scots' son, James VI of Scotland, was asked to become James 1 of England on the demise of Elizabeth 1. Today the Stone has been returned and can be viewed at Edinburgh Castle.

When Edward I died he was buried in the Abbey with much pomp. The body was dressed in expensive velvet and lace and the whole tomb decorated inside and out with precious stones. It was not until some time afterwards that the jewels were found to be faked – just paste and glass.

Following this many kings and queens were buried in the shrine including Henry V, a popular hero after the Battle of Agincourt. He died when he was 33 from a mysterious illness whilst campaigning in France and was given one of the most spectacular funerals ever witnessed. The procession started from Vincennes, proceeded to Paris, crossed the Channel and continued up to London. The cortège was met by all the English bishops and the clergy chanted untiringly, holding 1,400 lighted candles. When the procession reached the Abbey the three chargers that had belonged to the king bearing his armour, saddle, shield and sword were led right up to the high altar. Some of these relics can still be seen over his tomb today. His young and beautiful queen, Catherine de Valois, later married Owen Tudor, founder of the Tudor House. She died in childbirth in 1487 and her effigy can be seen in the Abbey Museum. It was the fashion in those days to create effigies of dead royalty and other important people and many of them have survived and have a fair likeness to the persons they represent. Catherine was buried in the Lady's Chapel which was later pulled down during the reign of Henry VII to make space for his own chapel. The remains of this lady were found and covered with loose boards. Clergy charged a shilling a time for commoners to take a look at the dead queen and Samuel Pepys recorded in his diary in 1669 that he had seen the body of Queen Catherine de Valois and had taken up the upper boards and kissed her face. He was very proud of the fact that he had kissed the face of a queen – but one cannot imagine what the actual remains looked like!

Henry V's son was the youngest monarch ever to be crowned in the Abbey. He was only eight months old when he was carried on his mother's lap in an open chariot through the City to West-minster where he was duly crowned as Henry VI. He was raised to assume the throne under the protectorship of his uncles, the Dukes of Bedford and Gloucester, until he came of age and his accession was recognized.

At the Dissolution of the Monasteries the Abbey did not suffer as badly as did other places of worship. Henry VIII honoured its ties with royal burials and coronations and this saved it from destruction. The monks were sacked, of course and the land con-fiscated, much of it going to the Crown, including Hyde Park which we shall hear more of later. The Royal Treasury was established here at this time in the Chapel of the Pyx – the oldest remaining part of the building still to be seen in modern times. As the seat of government was at Westminster, this too protected the Abbey from desecration. When the child king Edward VI, son of Henry VIII and Jane Seymour, was crowned the service was shortened because of his youth, and the way from Whitehall

Palace to the Abbey was covered with blue cloth. The Minster was carpeted with red and its walls hung with gold trappings. There was a raised dais at one end so that the crowning ceremony could be seen by the maximum number of people.

This venerable building can be roughly divided into three main sections: the Confessor's shrine, now old, pitted and dank, containing the massive tomb of Edward the Confessor and the Coronation Chair; the Commoners' Abbey; and Henry VII's Chapel. The roof of the Commoners' Abbey is high and remote and is reminiscent of the French cathedrals of Rheims and Amiens and contrasts greatly with the miscellany of statues, epitaphs, monuments and so on that meet you at eye level. I will not attempt to describe these monuments as any guide book will do that for you but I would like to mention Thomas Parr who has a memorial tablet in Poets' Corner, although why it is here I do not know, for he was not a poet. Thomas Parr was supposed to have lived to be 152 and because of his great age was buried in the Abbey. He was born, so it is recorded, in 1483 and lived through the reigns of nine kings and queens – Edward V, Richard III, Henry VII, Henry VIII, Edward VI, Mary, Elizabeth, James I and Charles I. He died in 1635. Parr went blind in his old age and employed a jester, so we are told, to tell him what was happening and to amuse him. Because of his great age he was exhibited at fair grounds, and people paid to go into his tent and have the privilege of speaking to him. Apparently he was married at 80 and at the age of 105 did penance in a white sheet at a village church in Gloucestershire, where he lived for most of his life, for 'naughty' behaviour with a lady named Katherine Milton. His wife died when he was 112 and at 120 he married again. He had but one tooth left at the end of his life. In September 1635 he was presented to Charles I who asked him what he thought contributed to his great age. He replied 'I did penance at a hundred'. He died in November of that year and William Harvey, who discovered the circulation of the blood carried out a post mortem. Harvey reported that Parr's organs were very healthy and attributed his death to the change from the pure air of Gloucestershire to the polluted air of London. After his demise pills called Parr's Pills were on sale and it was stated that Parr had taken this medicine while he was alive and it was responsible for his great age. Although this was treated as rubbish by his family, who had never heard or seen the pills before, the person who promoted them did a very good trade!

Longevity in those days was very rare and was treated with respect. Another centenarian buried in the Abbey was Ann Birkhead who died in 1568 aged 102. Camden the chronicler gives this inscription which he says was once on her tombstone:

> An auncient age of many years
> Here lived Anne thou hast,
> Pale Death hath fixed his fatal force
> Upon thy corpse at last.

Henry VII's Chapel is laid out tastefully and is well preserved in contrast to the Confessor's shrine. It was built on the site of a house where Chaucer once lived and the memorial to the 'Father of Poets,' erected in 1555 can be seen in Poets' Corner. Strangely enough it was Edmund Spenser who was first to be buried in Poets' Corner and not Chaucer. Leading out of this Chapel is a smaller Chapel dedicated to the Royal Air Force. The black and white diamond patterned floor, covering the whole area gives a pleasing effect.

The museum of the Abbey is well worth a visit as it houses an assortment of treasures. The effigies of Henry VII and his Queen, Elizabeth of York, can be seen here. It is known that playing cards were introduced to England at about this time and the broadish face of the queen was copied and portrayed on the cards which have remained more or less of the same design ever since. The hair-style of the men of this early Tudor era was long and curled in a roll on the shoulders and this is depicted on the kings and jacks.

General Monk, famed for the part he played in the Civil War and after, is to be seen here in effigy form. He is resplendent in full armour with a white neckerchief. Frances Stuart, a beauty in the reign of Charles II and probably one of his mistresses, has her place in the museum. She posed as Britannia to be stamped on our old coinage (pennies). She died in 1702 and her parrot died a few days after her and was stuffed. It is also on display and is believed to be the oldest stuffed creature in existence.

Reproductions of the crown jewels used at rehearsals are to

be seen in the museum and the cameo ring which Elizabeth I gave to the Earl of Essex, whom she loved deeply, is also on display. The story goes that he was to send it to her if ever he needed help. When he was imprisoned in the Tower he sent the ring to the Queen but jealousy at court prevented her receiving it. He was executed in 1601 and the ring was at first set in Elizabeth's tomb in the Abbey but in 1964 it was removed to the Museum for safe keeping after an attempt had been made to steal it.

Oliver Cromwell's effigy was once housed in the Abbey but at the restoration of the monarchy it was taken out and hung by the neck from a window in Whitehall – near the place where Charles I was executed. Afterwards it was torn to pieces by the mob.

A well-dressed model of Nelson can be seen here: James Lock, the hatters of St. James's, made his hat and Gieves the tailors made his uniform. Both these firms were still trading up to the mid twentieth century.

The cloisters, where once most of the domestic life of the monks was spent, is now an area of grass surrounded by old walls and pillars many of which commemorate the dead. The South Walk was thought to have housed a barber at one time and on the east side the Abbot is said to have performed Maundy services, giving gifts and washing the feet of the poor before these duties were taken on by the monarch himself.

The Chapter House, the common room of the monks and also the meeting place for the House of Commons from 1250 until the end of the reign of Henry VIII, is a well preserved airy building with seats around the walls. The floor was tiled by Henry III and is a wonderful muted green colour. There is a central column which holds a vaulted ceiling and the whole place, having six large windows, has a sense of space and light. The echo gives a kind of ethereal quality.

The Chapel of Pyx is the only part of the building which dates back to the original as built by the Confessor. As stated it became the Treasury in Henry VIII's time and it was here that standard pieces of gold and silver were weighed to test the current coinage for the correct weight and metal content.

Westminster School, housed in one of the buildings adjoining the Abbey, was founded by Elizabeth in 1560 and is one of the greatest public schools in England. The open stairway to the library is named after one of the school's best remembered head-masters – the flogging headmaster – Richard Busby.

William Caxton was the first to introduce the art of typography to this country – he was in fact the first English printer – and had strong links with the Abbey. Caxton was a native of Kent and was born in the year 1410. Having served his time as a mercer he went abroad as an agent for the Mercers' Company and after-wards was taken into the suite of Margaret of York, wife of the Duke of Burgundy. Whilst residing in Flanders he acquired a knowledge of the art of printing and translated in that country the *Recuyell of the Historyes of Troye*. He returned to England in 1472 and brought with him this and other printed books as speci-mens of his skill. Under the patronage of Thomas Milling, Abbot of Westminster at the time, he established a press in the Almonry where he produced in 1474 a small book translated from the French entitled *The Game and the Playe of Chesse*. This was the first book ever to be printed in England. Caxton printed and published about fifty works – some of them large volumes and many of them his own production. He died in 1491 working to the last.

At the coronation of our own Queen in 1953 one of the attractions to be seen at the Abbey was the collection of the Queen's beasts. These animal models, some six feet tall, repre-sent all the former royal houses in the line of the monarchy. There is the Lion of England, the Unicorn of Scotland, the Falcon of the Plantagenets, the Griffin of Edward III, the Welsh Dragon, the Greyhound of the Tudors, the Bull of Clarence, the White Lion of Mortimer, the Yale of the Beauforts and the White Horse of Hanover. They can now be seen at Hampton Court.

ST. PAUL'S CATHEDRAL

St. Paul's Cathedral is the national monument of the City of London, seat of the Bishops of London and Parish Church of the Commonwealth. In June 1957 the Queen approved that St. Paul's should become the Church of the Order of the British Empire.

As stated previously, in 604 King Ethelbert built the Church on the Hill, the first St. Paul's, and Mellitus was appointed from Rome as its first Bishop. In 959 St. Dunstan became Bishop of London before being made Archbishop of Canterbury. The Cathedral was burnt down at least three times before the great Gothic building of the Middle Ages was erected during the twelfth century.

In 1193 Richard I was on the throne but spent his time fighting in the Crusades and only resided in England for two brief periods during his reign. When returning through Austria from one of the Crusades he was seized by the Holy Roman Emperor and thrown into prison. The Emperor demanded 100,000 marks for his release. His mother, Queen Eleanor, set about collecting the money from every source she could think of. Churches sold their valuables, people were taxed heavily and laymen were ordered to part with a quarter of their possessions. A trouble maker in the City by the name of William FitzOsbert stirred up angry passions at St. Paul's Cross – an open-air meeting place for commoners and clergy alike outside the choir stalls in St. Paul's Churchyard. He argued that the collection of taxes had not been fair as the poorer classes had been asked to pay as much as the rich merchants and traders in the City. For a while the Bishop and his men did nothing, waiting and hoping that the matter would subside and peter out. But FitzOsbert was persistent in his accusations and in the end the Archbishop of Canterbury ordered his arrest. Getting wind of this, FitzOsbert took refuge in the church of St. Mary-le-Bow with his mistress and some of his followers. He killed one of the clergy in the process. Action was then taken and although the troublemakers were hiding in the tower of the Church and had sought sanctuary, this was ignored and the process of smoking out the rebels began. Unfortunately the whole church was burnt down. FitzOsbert was hanged in chains at Smithfield and afterwards his followers tried to make a martyr of him, claiming that even the very chains that killed him had magic healing powers. The clergy, always on the lookout for ways to make money, encouraged this and a shrine was erected to the dead man in the crypt of Old St. Paul's. Many revered relics were 'obtained' – such as the Magi casket, the arms of St. Mellitus, a knife used by Our Lord and so on.

As with other shrines the relics attracted pilgrims from Britain and Europe and helped to swell the coffers of the Cathedral, not to mention the pockets of the clergy.

It is interesting to note that this was the first recorded incident involving St. Paul's Cross although it is thought that it had existed for many years previous to this. Incidentally Richard I was rescued at last and the ransom paid. He returned to England in 1194 but did not appreciate the sacrifices that had been made on his behalf and soon went to live in his French lands, dying there a few years later.

Old St. Paul's was built on a design closely resembling Norwich Cathedral which can still be seen today in all its glory. St. Paul's was subjected to many fires during the centuries and the money to repair such a large building was not always forthcoming. As we have seen Henry III spent much of his time and all his money rebuilding Edward the Confessor's shrine in Westminster Abbey and therefore the rebuilding and repair of St. Paul's was neglected. But the King knew it was important to gain the respect and loyalty of the people of London, both for him and for his son, later to be crowned Edward I. So he feasted fifteen thousand poor citizens of London in the Cathedral grounds. He had not sufficient money of his own so the bill was paid out of the coffers of the Cathedral, which he was able to do as there was no Bishop of London at that time. He also addressed the crowd at St. Paul's Cross from time to time during his reign to endorse support and allegiance to the Crown for the rest of his life and that of his son afterwards.

An amusing story concerning shoe fashions is connected with the place of oration in St. Paul's Churchyard. In the fifteenth century Anne of Bohemia, Richard II's queen, introduced shoes with long pointed toes – so all the wealthy fashion-conscious women of the age followed suit. Clergy preached sermons at the Cross denouncing this mode of footwear, reasoning that ladies wearing this kind of expensive shoes could not kneel down and pray in the proper manner for fear of ruining them. Therefore prayers were excluded by the female aristocracy of the time from its timetable. The Pope suggested that a tax on the shoes might deter ladies from buying them, so a levy of 20 shillings per pair was imposed by Parliament and a law was passed that no shoe toe should exceed 2 inches. But by all accounts nothing could change the fashion and the ladies continued to wear pointed shoes for as long as the Queen did.

A Bishop's palace was added to the nave of St. Paul's at an early date and in the fourteenth century a double-storied cloister was built – the first of its kind in the country.

St. Paul's School was founded in 1509 by Colet, the son of a city mercer and the eldest of 22 children. He became Dean of St. Paul's in 1505 and one of his first tasks was to open a school for 153 boys – the number of fishes found in St. Peter's net when he was fishing in Galilee. The school building cost £4,500 and was paid for by the sale of property in Buckinghamshire owned by the Cathedral. The children had to be able to read and write and recite the catechism before being admitted. Colet appointed members of the Mercers' Company to be governors because in his opinion they were the most honourable band of men he knew. Dean Colet banned cock-fighting and other equally obnoxious sports from the school on the grounds that they were unethical. The cemetery was the boys' only playground. In 1884 the school was moved to Hammersmith.

The main event at St. Paul's during the sixteenth century was the marriage of Prince Arthur, eldest son of Henry VII, to Catherine of Aragon. Amid much splendour the couple were married on a specially designed and decorated dais erected in the Cathedral so that the maximum number of people could witness the ceremony. The Archbishop of Canterbury officiated, attended by no less than nineteen bishops and abbots. Alas, in a few weeks the young Prince was dead and Catherine later married Arthur's younger brother Henry, Duke of York, who became Henry VIII.

According to John Hearsey in his absorbing book *Bridge, Church and Palace*, when Henry petitioned for a divorce from Catherine to marry Anne Boleyn, who he hoped would present him with a male heir, he had high hopes that the Pope would grant his wish without any problem. This was because a few years previously the Pope had graciously granted Henry's sister Margaret a divorce with no strings attached. But Catherine's nephew was Charles V, Holy Roman Emperor, who at that time held the Pope as his prisoner. The Pope was ordered to refuse permission for the divorce. Charles's ageing aunt had given the best years of her life to Henry and to be disowned as queen and ejected from court and the life she had been accustomed to would be more than she could bear or deserved. His Holiness had no alternative than to turn down Henry's request. The King as we all know was not a man to be thwarted and he then ordered the liquidation of all Catholic establishments in this country and appointed himself head of the Protestant Church and Defender of the Faith. Thus the Dissolution of the Monasteries came about during which they were sacked, pillaged and burnt. The Catholic clergy were either forced to recant or were murdered. The lucky ones escaped to the Continent. The Act of Supremacy was rushed through Parliament and gave authority to Henry's commands. The preaching of Catholicism at St. Paul's Cross or anywhere else in the country was banned on pain of death. During the rest of his reign, and that of his son, Edward VI, the desecration of St. Paul's and most other churches and monasteries in the land was almost complete. Henry seized the wealth of the church and the lands it had owned and used the money to help pay for an expensive war which was being waged on the Continent. In Edward's reign the Manor of Paddington, belonging to Westminster Abbey, was transferred to Old St. Paul's and thus came into being the saying 'Robbing Peter to pay Paul'.

Since early times it had been the custom for folk to use the inside of St. Paul's Cathedral as a market and meeting place and even at times as a gambling den. Throughout the centuries various people had tried to stamp out this malpractice but with little success and in the sixteenth century it was as bad as ever. Horses, oxen and other beasts were led through the nave on their way to market – or were even sold in the aisles. In Elizabeth's time many of the treasures removed in the Dissolution had been restored to the Cathedral but much of the building stone had been carted away to be used elsewhere – it is said that Somerset House was built mainly from St. Paul's stones. An old nursery rhyme tells us more:

> Upon Paul's steeple stands a tree,
> As full of apples as it may be,
> The little boys of London town –
> They run with hooks and pull them down;
> And then they go from hedge to hedge
> Until they come to London Bridge.

The rhyme must have preceded the burning of the steeple in 1561 and tells at first hand the state of St. Paul's at that time. There were no funds available for complete repairs. After the fire Queen Elizabeth gave a generous sum to help renovate the badly damaged building but the money ran out before completion, and the steeple never materialized. When news of the defeat of the Armada reached our shores the Queen attended a service of thanksgiving at St. Paul's amid much rejoicing and excitement.

After the discovery of the Gunpowder Plot four of the culprits, Digby, Grant, Winter and Bates were hung drawn and quartered in the Churchyard. Later Garnett, a Jesuit priest, was accused of being one of the plotters and he too was executed here.

The commoners continued to use the Cathedral as a meeting place and market as well as a short cut from one street to another. The nave was known as Paul's Walk and the south aisle as the Duke of Humphrey's Walk, getting the name from a tomb thought to belong to that gentleman. The Duke of Humphrey was at one time an important person in London who owned Castle Baynard, but he was buried elsewhere and where the connection stemmed from is a mystery. Discredited army men, banished courtiers and others who were once important met here to 'dig the dirt'. Often grievances talked over in the aisle were later aired publicly at St. Paul's Cross. As mentioned earlier the Cross stood in the churchyard and according to Colin Clair in his book *St. Paul's Cathedral*, it was built of stone steps and had a wooden pulpit with a stone and lead covering. It is known to have been standing in 1241 – but in 1643, in an act of violence, it was pulled down by the mob. It was not until the last century that a new cross was erected on the site, built with a legacy from H. C. Richards, MP.

Before the Civil War Inigo Jones, having the task of renovating Old St. Paul's, used Portland stone to reface much of the stonework to good effect. The dignified uplifting of the Cathedral was short lived and all the money and time spent on it wasted when the Civil War broke out. Parliamentary soldiers raped the inside and took all valuables to supplement their pay. Even the scaffolding still standing for the repair work was pulled down and sold and part of the building collapsed as a result. The army used the building as a barracks and its degradation seemed complete. It is said that the poor people of London were so short of fuel to warm themselves at this time that they dug up the dried horse manure which clogged the aisles.

After the war the people looked again at their beloved Cathedral and plans were made to repair the place. The first thing to be done was to remove all shops from inside – and Christopher Wren was asked to report on the old structure. His report was not favourable. Nevertheless it was decided to try and patch up the old building once again and work was started which continued intermittently through the plague of 1665, But in 1666 came the Great Fire and the fate of Old St. Paul's was settled once and for all. The people of London Town, seeing their homes in flames, put all their belongings into the great Cathedral in the belief that the stout walls were indestructible. This was not to be: the extreme heat turned the great bells into molten metal which ran down the walls into the streets so that even the pavements glowed red. Great slabs of masonry crashed down killing anyone in the way, and everything was lost. The tower and ruins stood for twenty years before Wren was given permission to rebuild. His earlier plans were rejected – his first being approved by the King but turned down by the chapter and clergy. He then submitted a second design which has been called the 'nightmare design'. The King approved once more and gave him a free hand to make what alterations he chose. When Wren had his chance to design with a free hand the plan which we now have came into being – and the clergy could do nothing but grumble. The work of building new St. Paul's was begun and in the same year Christopher Wren received his knighthood. There is an interesting story connected with the rebuilding. When the site was being cleared for the footings a labourer was asked to bring a stone to act as a marker for one of the surveyors. The man brought the first flat stone that he could find and it happened to be part of an old monument with a single word left inscribed upon it – '*Resurgam*' – which means 'May I rise again'. Wren, so we are told, was so taken by this 'sign' as he called it that he resolved to build the greatest Cathedral the world had ever known. The word '*Resurgam*' can be found over the south portico and is illustrated by a phoenix rising out of the fire.

The building is the work of a genius and the construction of the dome is unique. It is in fact made up of two domes – one inside the other. The outer one measures 145 ft in diameter. Between the two domes there is a brick cone which takes the weight. The brick work is hidden by clever design and an iron chain girds the bottom of the dome to prevent the structure bowing outwards. Wren was hauled up in a basket to look at the progress of the work. He was 36 when the building first started and 78 when the last stone was laid by his son, in the lantern of the cupola, while the architect waited below. During this time Wren's salary was cut by half because the work was taking so long to complete, and he lost favour with the court and clergy. The authorities wanted to erect a balustrade which they believed would improve the building. Wren was bitterly opposed to this alteration of his conception but nevertheless they had their way and the balustrade can still be seen today. On completion of the building Wren was dismissed from his office of Surveyor of Works and he retired to his house at Hampton Court where he spent the last five years of his life. He was content, knowing that however people treated him in his old age his life's work had been completed.

The Cathedral was opened for public worship on 2 December 1697. The Mayor and Aldermen of London attended and the service was conducted by the Bishop of London. The King, William III, attended a private service in his own Chapel.

Wren died in 1723 and for nearly 150 years after there was no memorial to him in the glorious building that he had created. Only his epitaph was allowed in a dark corner of the crypt – written by his son in Latin. According to Colin Clair in translation it reads:

> Underneath lies buried the builder of this Church and City, Sir Christopher Wren, who lived for more than ninety years, not for himself but for the public good. Reader if you seek a monument look around you.

Early in the nineteenth century a memorial stone was erected to him on the front of the organ gallery and today, after the bomb damage suffered during the last war, Wren's memorial can be seen and immediately recognized in the pavement directly underneath the dome.

There is a hidden gallery upstairs which contains Wren's death mask – his nose is said to resemble a bird's beak – along with his penknife and measuring stick with the words 'Surveyor to the Fabrick'. The public is unaware of the mysterious galleries and spiral stairways hidden in the thick walls of the structure. These are the back stairs by which the workmen deal with internal repairs and look after roughly two and a half acres of lead roof. The workmen are also responsible for the safety of the external statues of St. Paul and the Apostles in the portico facing Ludgate Hill. The circumference of the stone gallery is more than the whole height of the building from the pavement to the cross. The circular balcony at the top of the dome holds a lantern bearing the orb and the cross. The gold cross on the pinnacle, weighing $1\frac{1}{2}$ tons, is set in a sleeve which allows it to move a foot in the wind – if it was rigid it would snap off. The gilt orb weighs $2\frac{1}{2}$ tons. St. Paul's is continually shifting on its bed of moist clay and the cracks in the stones open and shut according to the weather: the sun expands the stone and the cracks close and when cold and damp descends the reverse happens.

The quarry from which Portland stone is cut, from which many buildings are constructed in London and elsewhere, lies in the peninsula of Portland in Dorset – once an island. Inigo Jones used Portland stone with satisfaction when repairing the banqueting hall at Whitehall, the Tower and other prominent buildings. It was used extensively to repair Exeter Cathedral in the fifteenth century. But it was Christopher Wren who started to use the stone on a grand scale, he had a great many buildings to redesign after the Great Fire and Portland stone seemed to have all the qualities that a master mason looks for. The stone is a marine deposit of the Jurassic period – it is fossilized limestone and the fossil shapes and imprints can be clearly seen on the freshly cut whitbed stone. The facing of St. Paul's on the south parapet bears traces of fossilization and the plinth of King Charles's statue at Charing Cross also shows similar patterns. As James Bone remarks in his book *The London Perambulator* it is fitting that with the glorious naval history of Britain some of her most famous buildings should be formed out of sea creatures. It is as if the sea was paying back a debt.

The weathering of the stone is fascinating. It washes itself clean and the composition is very suitable to our variable climate and the inevitable pollution. The tops of the buildings are clean and white and the bottoms grimy, and when the crust of grime reaches a certain thickness it cracks under its own weight and falls off, leaving the stone as it was. It is then washed by rain and dried by wind and becomes the grey ashen colour in which lies its beauty. True, it powders off after a certain time, but this it does uniformly so that the whole surface sustains a flatness which is remarkable.

Nicholas Stone, a quarry man and stonemason of Portland, was probably responsible for introducing the building material to Wren. Stone obtained shares in the quarries of Portland through his marriage – his father-in-law had money and probably invested some of it in the quarries on Stone's behalf. The quarry men of Portland are a closely knit community and take their work very seriously. Most families have been stonemasons for generations and the surname of Stone is very common. They are proud that most of the London monuments are built of the stone from Portland. Wren built the Cathedral, over fifty churches, part of Greenwich Observatory, the Towers of Westminster Abbey, the Monument, parts of Chelsea Hospital, Marlborough House and many more buildings including some of the Companies' Halls. Gibbs, Hawsmoor, Kent, Chambers and Robert Adams followed in his footsteps.

The petrified garden of Portland, as it is called, is scored with cuts small and large where the stone has been quarried for some building or other. Some quarries are named after the great buildings they provided with stone. One is still called St. Paul's, and Wren's special mark – a 'Y' or a wine glass – can be seen engraved on the walls. One quarry, a small excavation, provided the cenotaph and has been left alone since as a sign of respect. Robert Harvey, a surveyor of St. Paul's obtained the Portland stone he wanted for repairs only 100 yards away from Wren's main quarry.

The guide books tell us that there is plenty to see inside the Cathedral and I shall not go into all the details. The carver's shop just off the crypt is worth a visit and a master carver, Tony Webb, who learned to carve like Grinling Gibbons, restored Wren's Great Model – one of his earlier designs which was turned down. It is so big that if you bow your head you can walk inside. The lifts in the Cathedral have unique buttons with markings such as W.G. for Whispering Gallery and C for Crypt and so on.

Old St. Paul's possessed a great curfew and passing bell which was tolled when a member of the royal family or a prominent citizen died. There are now two bell towers, one housing the clock and the other Great Paul, the biggest bell in the country, weighing 17 tons. It tolls for five minutes at 1 p.m. to tell city workers that it is time for a break. The cables are still there which two men used to work manually but now the bell is electrically operated. St. Paul's did not possess a peal of bells until the seventeenth century. The Society of Bell Ringers called 'The Ancient Society of College Youths' was founded in 1637 and is still in operation. The fact that the old Cathedral had no steeple for much of its life explains why there is no mention of the peal of bells from St. Paul's in the old nursery rhyme 'Oranges and Lemons'. Most of the City churches, prior to the fire, had their own special verses interpreted by the public to fit in with each distinctive peal of bells.

St. Paul's has its own government and about 150 people are employed in running the place. The Lord Mayor's jurisdiction ends at the great West Door. The Dean and his Chapter of four canons hold power inside the Cathedral and their collective word is law. But like so many other ecclesiastical houses, St. Paul's **is broke. The expense of its upkeep is enormous, and a charge is made for entry. The public enjoys the sights and history of the Cathedral and now has to pay for them.**

It is fitting that Prince Charles and Lady Diana Spencer chose this lovely Cathedral for their wedding. For the story which we remember and like to believe in is the one that says the Church of Diana once stood on the site, many, many centuries ago.

CITY CHURCHES

The number of churches in the City must have been quite bewildering to visitors to London in medieval times. In fact before the Great Fire there was a common saying that anyone throwing a stone in the City would hit either a church or a prison, so great was the density of buildings and population. William the Conqueror was a religious man and encouraged the building of places of worship he could call his own in the city. Many of the ancient churches, now long forgotten, were erected and paid for by well-to-do merchants who wanted to leave a memorial to their family in the City. Thus quite a few churches were named after individuals such as St. Benet Fink, St. Martin Orgar, St. Margaret Moses. These were burnt in the Fire and never rebuilt. Other places of worship were sponsored by the Companies or Liveries of the City and adopted as their own and of course these were restored after the Fire. In 1666, 87 London churches were destroyed; 51 were rebuilt by Wren during the following thirty years. The blitz during the last war destroyed or damaged quite a few and only those with special historical links were rebuilt.

St. Helen's of Bishopsgate, often called the Westminster Abbey of the City, escaped the Fire and now houses many of the relics rescued from churches that were not so fortunate. St. Helen's has a long and interesting history and is said to be associated with Constantine, the first Christian Emperor of Rome. His mother Helena, who was converted to Christianity when he was born, was the daughter of Coel, King of the Trinobantes, who had strong links with Colchester – he is believed to be the original Old King Cole of the nursery rhyme. Constantine, so the story goes, built the church and dedicated it to his mother – hence the name St. Helens's. The remains of a Roman arch and a Benedictine nunnery were found during excavations in 1210 and the parish church was extended at that time to provide a private chapel for the nuns, and this explains why the church has two naves. It appears that the nuns were a worldly lot for they had the reputation of going out into the streets and kissing any young men passing by who took their fancy! In fact it was said that at Christmas time in 1432 the Mass was shortened in order that the nuns might indulge in long sessions of dancing and celebrating in ways that were not in keeping with their order.

The church contains a monument to Sir Thomas Gresham, who built the first Royal Exchange during Elizabethan times. Sir John Crosby, a notable Lord Mayor who was knighted by Edward IV in 1471, has his monument here also. Crosby was a wool stapler and obviously very rich as he built Crosby Place in Bishopsgate Street, the biggest and most beautiful of all the London residences at the time. After his death his widow let it to Richard III but his stay was short-lived. In the 1670s Crosby House ceased to be a home, having been lived in by many men famous in the City. For different periods it was put to a variety of uses, a restaurant being the last enterprise on the Bishopsgate site. In 1908 the Great Hall was carefully taken down and rebuilt in the garden of Sir Thomas More's house on Chelsea Embankment where today it can be seen virtually the same as when Sir John Crosby built it. The lease was bought by the British Federation of University Women in 1922. There is a carving in the church of Martin Bond, captain of the trained bands at Tilbury when the Armada was expected. He is shown sitting in his tent with sentries on the alert. He died in 1643.

Sir Andrew Judd, a Lord Mayor who died in 1558, is remembered by an epitaph inscribed on the wall – telling of his travels in his year of office. Obviously he could not have spent much time carrying out civic duties as it reads:

> To Russia and Muscovai
> To Spaine, Germany without fable –
> Travelled he by land and sea,
> Both Mayor of London and Staple.

The reference to the Mayor of Staple reminds us of the wool staple market at Westminster and its connections with the Woolsack in the House of Lords, which will be dealt with later.

St. Sepulchre's, now the largest parish church in the City, has incorporated parishes of churches that have been lost for one reason or another. It was originally dedicated to St. Edmund the Martyr, of East Anglia, but changed its name during the Crusades. According to Richard Tydeman in his *Guide to St. Sepulchre's* its position outside the north-west gate of the City corresponds almost exactly to the position of that Jerusalem church built over the site of the Sepulchre at Calvary – the 'Green Hill without a City Wall'. It was from St. Sepulchre's that the knights of the Crusades set out to free the Holy Sepulchre from the Saracens. There was a tavern named the Saracen's Head adjacent to the church for many hundreds of years. The benefice of the Church of the Holy Sepulchre was granted by Rahere, the Prior of St. Bartholomew's, to one Hago, the Clerk, in 1137. Rahere's deed is on a scroll with two seals in the British Museum. For a time the church was known as St. Edmund Sepulchre and now as St. Sepulchre. Pepys referred to it as St. Pulchre. Since the Dissolution the patronage has been in the hands of the President and Fellows of St. John's College, Oxford.

There is not enough space to mention all the attractions of this church, but in the nave there is a list of all Vicars and Rectors since 1249, which is rather unusual. One of these was John Rogers – the first Protestant to be executed in Queen Mary's reign, at Smithfield. He was also known as Matthew and helped Tyndale to translate the Scriptures published in England which are known as the Matthew Bible. The church has strong links with Newgate prison and the Old Bailey (Old Bailey Court was the street in which it was housed). In the tower the peal of bells was responsible for the line 'When will you pay me say the bells of Old Bailey' in the old nursery song. It is worth mentioning that it was indeed the bells of St. Sepulchre's and not the bells of Newgate in Old Bailey Court – the prison did not possess bells. In the old days the clerk of the church had certain unpleasant duties to perform. On the night before condemned prisoners were to be hanged he had to proceed, with the execution hand bell, along a tunnel leading to the prison and to recite a verse which was supposed to purify the souls of the miscreants. This is how it went:

> All you that in the condemned hole do lie,
> Prepare you, for tomorrow you shall die.
> Watch and pray – the hour is drawing near
> That you before the Almighty must appear.
> Examine well yourselves, in time repent,
> That you may not to eternal flames be sent,
> And when St. Sepulchre's bell in the morning tolls
> The Lord have mercy on your souls.

The tunnel entrance has been bricked up but the execution hand bell can be seen in the church. When the criminals were in the carts on their way to Tyburn it was customary to stop at the door of the church and be given a nosegay. One of the last to receive this was highwayman John Rann who wore the posy in his buttonhole and went jauntily to the gallows, as if he was going to a wedding. He was gay and flippant and not the penitent man that many would have wished!

The church was gutted in the Great Fire but later rebuilt. In the last war it was damaged and repaired except for the peal of bells. At present only two bells hang in the tower until further money is forthcoming.

The particularly fine organ was originally built by Renatus Harris in 1670. Under the pipe-work can be found the carved initials 'C.R.' which mean 'Carolus Rex' and refer to Charles II. Among other esteemed musicians to have played the organ are Handel and Mendelssohn. Sir Henry Wood learned to play on it and at the age of fourteen was appointed assistant organist. When he died in 1944 his ashes were buried beneath the central window which contains the image of St. Cecilia, the patron saint of music, and around this the Musicians' Chapel was formed.

The front pew on the south side is occupied by the Lord Mayor on State occasions, the great sword being placed in the iron sword stand which bears the arms of the City – the red cross of St. George with the sword of St. Paul. There are eight kneelers for the Lord Mayor and the Sheriffs, four with the shield of the City and four bearing the crest. The Livery Companies, or guilds originating in medieval crafts, have strong connections with most City churches. St. Sepulchre's is supported by several Companies.

The Worshipful Company of Cordwainers, a body of men who made shoes from the finest Cordovan leather and became known as Cordwainers, holds an annual service here in accordance with the bequest of James Shawe in 1630. The Worshipful Company of Cutlers has its hall within the parish and annually attends the church when a new Master is elected each June. As well as cutlery, surgical instruments are made by this Guild. Stationers' Hall is also within the parish and its members meet at the church. The Company of Stationers insists that its members are connected with the 'art or mastery of a Stationer or Newspaper Maker'. Books may still be registered at Stationers' Hall. The rector of St. Sepulchre's is chaplain to the Worshipful Company of Feltmakers – those employed in the making of hats, mainly at Luton in modern times.

The church is renowned for its embroidered samplers, kneelers and so on and it is fitting that the Worshipful Company of Broderers should attend here and the Company's arms are embroidered on the kneelers. The arms of the Musicians' Company are presented at the annual festival of their patron St. Cecilia. Also at St. Sepulchre's can be found the banner of the Worshipful Company of Parish Clerks, showing their patron, St. Nicholas. The arms of Christ's Hospital and of St. John's College, Oxford, are embroidered on some of the kneelers, and the boys of the Blue Coat School, which first stood in Newgate Street, come up from Horsham where the school is now housed and attend a service in the company of the Lord Mayor, who afterwards entertains them at the Mansion House.

St. Andrews's Undershaft church was so named because it stood in the shadow of a tall maypole erected on a permanent site in the Strand. This church houses a monument to John Stow built of Derbyshire marble and alabaster. Stow was the great Elizabethan historian, a tailor by trade whose great delight was writing about London and its history. He was born in 1525 and died in poverty in 1605 although his books were by then well known and appreciated. The monument, on the wall of the north aisle, shows Stow, writing a book with a feather quill in his hand. It was restored by the Merchant Taylors' Company in 1905. A commemorative service is held every year on the Sunday nearest 5 April – the date of his death – and a wreath of flowers is laid before the monument. For many years people took away the quill pen as a souvenir thinking that it was the original one used by Stow.

The monument to John Speed, whose writings on London followed Stow's, can be found in the church of St. Giles Cripplegate. He also was a tailor. He lived at Moorfields and had eighteen children to support. His most successful work was *Historie of Great Britaine* which he wrote in Latin. His patron was Sir Fulke Greville and when Speed went blind in later years his patron stood him in good stead and he died in better circumstances than did Stow.

Another good, but unknown, man is remembered in St. Giles Church – one Charles Langlie, an alebrewer who was buried on 8 June 1602. As his epitaph relates he gave generously to the poor:

> If Langlie's life thou liste to know,
>   reade on and take a viewe,
> Of faith and hope I will not speak,
>   his work shall shew them treue.
> Whoe whilst he lived, with counsaile grave

ye better sorte did guid
A stay to weake, a staffe to poore,
    without backbite or pride,
And when he died, he gave his mite,
    All that did him befall,
For ever once a yere to cloathe,
    St. Giles poore withall,
All Saints he pointed for the day,
    gowne's XX: redie made
With XX: shirtes, and XX: smock.
    As they may best be hadd,
A sermon Eke, he hath ordayned,
    that God might have his praise
And others might be wonne thereby,
    to follow Langlies waies.
On Vicar and Churchwardens the,
    His trust he hath reposed:
And they will answer him one day,
    When all shall be disclosed.
Thus being deade, yet still he lives,
    Lives never for to die:
In heaven's blysse, in worldes fame,
    And so I trust shall I:

This was written by the Vicar, Launcellott Andrewes, later to become Bishop of Winchester, who died at the Bishop's Palace, Southwark in 1626.

In this church also, Busbie, another 'do-gooder' has his epitaph, and it is only right that the good unknown should be recognized and remembered once in a while. The wicked and thereafter infamous find their way into the history books easily enough.

Not all citizens were of such good intentions. One left in his will a large sum of money for the burning of heretics in the parish of All Hallows the Great. The bequest was designed to purchase faggots and in more recent times the money was used to buy fuel for those in need at Christmas.

The origin of St. Clement Danes (ancient name Ecclesia Clementis Danorum) in the Strand dates back to Alfred the Great, who on his victory over the Danes showed clemency to

Danish men who had married English women, by letting them settle outside the City walls, where they built a church and called it St. Clement Danes. There is also a story that after the Battle of Hastings, Harold and his brother, both Danes, were buried in this church. The clergy claim that this is indeed the church of St. Clements which rung out the first famous line of 'Oranges and Lemons'. A custom which I recently read about in *The Great Metropolis* by Thomas Holmes published in 1850, seems to bear this out. Apparently, up to the late eighteenth century there was a tradition that annually on 1 January the porter of St. Clement's Inn near the church presented the people residing at the Inn with an orange and a lemon each and in return expected to receive a half-crown. In the old days before the river was used as a sewer the fruit was brought up in barges from ships moored on the Thames and carried by porters through the Inn to Clare market. The residents were disturbed by this early morning bustle and decided to charge a toll, and fruit was given in payment. In 1920 the rector of St. Clement Danes, the Reverend W. Pennington, arranged for the nursery rhyme melody to be played on the bells of the church and inaugurated a children's service to be held annually. On leaving, each child received an orange and a lemon. In 1939 the tradition carried on and during the war, when the church lay in ruins, the service was still held. Only about 26 children attended during wartime – the rest having been evacuated and only oranges could be given at that time because of food shortages. The tradition is still continued – the service being held on a Sunday in March.

St. Mary-le-Bow, the church of Bow bells, is probably one of the most famous churches in the world. Both Saxon and Norman architecture can be seen in the crypt, which was arched in Saxon times and gave the church its Saxon name of St. Mary of the Arches. In fact some historians believe that this church was built on the site of a Roman Court of Justice or Basilica – a building which was fashioned with arches in accordance with the Roman style.

Bow church, with its Latin name of Sancta Maria de Arcubus, was built in the Cheap market and the special relationship that was built up with the City of London was through its great bell which tolled out the curfew first introduced by William I. In time

Bow bell and its sound defined the City boundaries, and the saying that anyone born within the sound of Bow bells is a true Cockney, must be quite ancient. Incidentally the derivation of the term 'Cockney' is an interesting one. As the townspeople thought the country yokels slow and dull witted, so the country-folk thought the antics and quick speech of the City dwellers peculiar also. They dubbed them cock-ney, meaning a cock's egg. Ney is an old English word for egg and of course a cock's egg was an impossible inexplicable thing – which summed up the opinion country people had of their cousins in the City.

The church of Bow has had a chequered existence, being ravaged by fire many times, or simply collapsing for want of repair often killing and injuring people close by. A story of a happening in 1284 tells us that a certain Lawrence Duket, goldsmith, wounded another in a fight and then took refuge in the church. During the night the wounded man's friends broke into the church and hanged Duket, making the death look like suicide. A boy who witnessed the hanging told the authorities and Edward I, who was in Wales at the time, was informed of the occurrence. He sent word that the miscreants were to be tried and dealt with severely for their deed. The privilege of sanctuary must be upheld said the King. So sixteen men connected with the incident were tried and hanged and a woman named Alice was burnt. The doors and windows of the church were stopped up with thorns until it was thought that the church was cleansed of the foul deed that had taken place inside its walls.

After 1472 the Bell of Bow also woke people every morning at 5.45. John Donne left a legacy to maintain this custom and it continued until 1874. Up to the Great Fire the Court of Arches was held in the church; lawyers and judges conducted trials in Latin which was beyond the comprehension of the layman. Samuel Pepys once visited a sitting, he tells us, and was thoroughly bored – not understanding a word!

After the Fire, which burnt out the church, Sir Christopher Wren designed and rebuilt it on the plan of the ruin of the Basilica of Constantine near the Colosseum in Rome. He followed up the legend that a Roman basilica was once built on the site – perhaps because he found remains of a Roman wall in the crypt. On top of the tower Wren built a weathercock in the shape of a griffin or dragon with the cross of St. George on its outspread wings. The dragon was 8 ft 10 ins long and was probably chosen to represent the arms of the corporation of London.

Bow church was the most costly of all Wren's churches and most people will agree it was the best. The tower, built of Portland stone, was one of his strokes of genius. A church in New York, Trinity, was allowed by special charter from William III to be built on the same lines as Bow.

The church was ruined by bombs during the last war and the bells crashed down and were smashed to pieces. The metal was carefully collected and at the end of the war melted down to make new bells which were recast by Mears and Stainbank of White-chapel. The recording of Bow bells was used as a freedom signal to those in occupied Europe during the Second World War, but it was not until 20 December 1961 that the actual bells of Bow were set ringing once again from the restored belfry by the Duke of Edinburgh. The restoration of the church started in 1956 after a world-wide appeal for funds, and it was rebuilt as close to Wren's design as possible.

A piece on the City churches and their histories would not be complete without mention of the story of the Fatal Vespers. After the Dissolution of the Monasteries devout Catholics had a hard time. They were forced to hold services in secret and the venues were hard to come by. The surviving buildings of Blackfriars monastery were assigned to secular lords and one such house belonged to Henry Carey whose title was Baron Hundson – thus the house was named Hundson House. Later, in 1623, when feelings were running high against the Catholics after the discovery of the Gunpowder plot, this house was owned by the French ambassador. The building was in a dilapidated condition and he allowed Catholics, for whom he had some sympathy, to hold meetings there. On Sunday 23 November, three hundred people climbed the rickety stairs to assemble in the large attic of Hundson House for worship. The room was 40 ft wide and 17 ft long and as space had to be made for the vestry, the congregation was packed very tightly indeed. After the preliminary prayers and vespers had been said the priest began his long and boring sermon. The congregation became inattentive and children whispered and shuffled their feet. The constant movement proved too much for the rotten timbers and suddenly there was a loud crack and the main beam snapped and the whole of the floor plunged into the room below which in its turn collapsed down to ground level. Men, women and children were thrown into the pit and those standing by the edge had to balance themselves so as not to follow suit. The only way to get out of the room was to cut holes in the surrounding walls with knives and scramble through to adjoining rooms. In vain the rescuers dug and tried to pull the victims free – but over a hundred lost their lives; many were suffocated or died of their wounds. Many more were horribly maimed for life. The Puritans had no pity on their religious rivals and said that it was the vengeance of God that had caused this tragedy to happen. Strangely enough many Catholics believed this too – although some of them accused the Protestants of making the accident happen by sawing through the beams beforehand.

In days gone by, churches had emblems to mark the boundaries of the parish and these were usually to be found on the walls of buildings. Some of them can be seen in City museums; St. Mary-le-Strand and St. Martin-in-the-Fields are two examples.

St. Mary-le-Strand

St. Martin in the Fields

As the living population in the City fell with the centuries passing, the need for so many churches lessened. Many were pulled down to make way for new development. The cemeteries and graveyards of these ancient sites were converted into children's playgrounds or small public gardens during the Victorian and Edwardian eras. These patches of green, with grass and shady trees, provided oases for the poor of the East End. They had not the means to visit the large parks in the West of London. When the General Post Office was built, the cemetery of St. Boltoph's Aldersgate became a stretch of green known as Postman's Park. The Red Cross opened some gardens in Southwark which were greatly appreciated by the residents. Sometimes ponds and fountains were constructed and swings and play areas introduced. The City Companies contributed much money for these schemes and gradually the quality of life for the slum-dweller of the East End began to improve.

3

The Palace of Westminster and Whitehall

THE PALACE OF WESTMINSTER

To write a history of the Palace of Westminster is to write a history of England, for many great names, whether esteemed or infamous, have had a hand in moulding and developing the 'Mother of Free Parliaments'. As a secular building there is nothing to compare with it as regards antiquity amongst the great non-religious houses of the western world. It had been a royal residence five hundred years before Catherine de Medici laid the foundation stone of the Tuileries and even the Vatican did not come into being until two hundred years after Edward the Confessor first held his court at Westminster, in fact the Vatican has only been recognized as the official residence of the Pope for the last five hundred years. It is thought by many that Canute had built a palace on the island of Thorney and Edward lived in the building for convenience as it was directly opposite the Abbey.

As we have seen, Edward died a week after the hallowing of the Abbey in the presence of his nobles and clergy, and we are told by Ailred, Abbot of Rievaulx, who attended the ceremony, that the effort to be present cost Edward his life. After the interview with Harold, Queen Editha mourned over her dying husband but was reassured by him that he was not going to die but to live in the great Abbey that he had created.

William the Conqueror was crowned in the great Minster a year after Edward's death in front of the revered tomb. We are told that he began to live in Edward's house and to improve and develop it. Old chroniclers tell us that Elfric, Abbot of Peterborough, was tried before him and great councils were held at Westminster Palace, as it was now called, in the years 1074 and 1076. This was the beginning, when the seeds were sown of the judicial and legislative systems which throughout the succeeding centuries were to blossom and bear fruit. William Rufus, son of the Conqueror, was the instigator of the Great Hall at Westminster which gave it the hallmark of a royal residence. Successive Norman kings added their contributions and ideas and the palace grew in size and importance. According to A. Wright and P. Smith, in their book *Parliament Past and Present* (1908), it was Stephen who built the first chapel which was destined to become the home of the House of Commons in the centuries to come. The Painted Chamber was first built by Henry II and Henry III, a room steeped in history and one of the most famous of all the rooms in the Palace, with murals which portrayed the battles of the Maccabees and scenes from the Scriptures.

In Edward I's reign the building was burnt down and Edward, great castle-builder that he was, had no problems in the rebuilding. He included the Princes' Chamber and the Parliament Chamber as well as restoring the Painted Chamber. As it was the place of his birth he took a special interest in the design. During Edward's reign we have the first graphic description of a Parliament in sitting. The picture is a copy reproduced by my illustrator, Len Strasman, of an ancient drawing formerly housed in the College of Arms. It represents a young-looking Edward sitting on the throne with Alexander, King of Scotland, on his right on a lower seat and Llywelyn, Prince of Wales, on his left. Below Alexander sits the Archbishop of Canterbury and below Prince Llywelyn is the Archbishop of York. In the centre of the picture is a woolsack on which sit four figures; the Chancellor, the two Chief Justices and the Baron of the Exchequer. Two other woolsacks are placed each side of the central one and on them sit the Judicial bench – four persons on each. Two other persons with documents in their hands are thought to be clerks – standing without hats behind the woolsacks with their faces to the King. Behind the clerks sit seven men, all with hats, facing the throne. All are robed but the right-hand man appears to be seated higher than the rest and has a chain about his neck. These are described as 'the faithful commons' and the one with the chain 'the Speaker'

The Parliament of Edward I

– collecting ideas and votes from the other six and speaking for them – in the same way as the foreman of a jury does today. In fact some historians believe that this picture not only shows the beginnings of the House of Commons but also the start of the judicial system as we know it. The word 'court' in ancient times meant quite simply a meeting of the monarch and his ministers – or in loose terms, his friends. Nowadays of course it describes a place where criminals are tried and justice is believed to be done – the jury having an important say in the matter. The

Great Hall of Westminster apart from being used as a banqueting hall was also used as a court room where prisoners of note were tried as we shall see later.

To continue with the description of the picture: each side of the room contains two benches at right angles to the throne. On the left there are two bishops and five peers on one seat and in front at the upper end sits Prince Edward, son of the king, later to become Edward II. On the other side mitred abbots sit with six more bishops.

Prince Llywelyn and the King of Scotland were obviously on friendly terms with Edward at that time. This state of affairs did not last long for Edward was a warring king and set out to conquer both Scotland and Wales, which he did successfully. He built a ring of castles around Snowdon which can still be seen today. After enjoying the privilege of sitting in an English parliament, Prince Llywelyn is reputed to have made the unfortunate remark that one day he would return and be crowned king in Westminster Abbey. His refusal to pay proper homage to Edward could only result in war. During the battles in Wales the Prince was captured by English troops in 1282 and beheaded. Edward ordered his head to be brought to Westminster Abbey and displayed there, crowned with a garland of flowers. This shows the sadistic humour of the king, in keeping with the mode of the day.

I have said earlier that Canute became a Christian before he died and also did much to increase foreign trade with Britain during his reign. The Woolsack, I believe, has strong connections with the wool market or staple at Westminster which had been thriving from the mid-Saxon era and increased in importance under the influence of Canute. The word 'staple' has a Danish derivation and as Canute's father was King Sweyn of Denmark it seems quite possible that the term staple and the idea of grading, measuring and weighing goods was introduced by the Dane. For example the rule of staple was applied to the length and quality of wool strands. The Dane ruled England by what is known as 'Canute's code' – a collection of laws largely based on earlier Saxon customs – and probably improved on this by introducing a fairer way of selling goods according to quality and quantity. The goods not only included wool, but tin, lead, leather and wool-fels (skins), in fact the most important exports of England at that time. The

Wool Staple, as recorded by Charles Knight in his book entitled *London*, was 'The last relic of the old monopolising principles of business which confined certain advantages to certain places'. It seems very probable therefore that the Woolsack, now in the House of Lords, has strong links with the Woolstaple and is in fact an emblem, confining 'certain advantages to certain places', namely the Palace of Westminster. Whoever sat on the wool sack, or sacks, as there was more than one in early times, held a position of power in the realm, controlled the purse strings of the nation and answered only to the monarch himself.

The wool merchants of Westminster were rich and it is said that they built the church of St. Margaret near the Abbey as the parish church of Westminster. A mayor and two councillors were appointed to be responsible for the Woolstaple and to ensure that the rules of the market were adhered to. They, in their turn, were directly under a person described as a law merchant, who acted for the Crown. This may well have been the Chancellor who sat on the Woolsack. The jurisdiction of the Woolstaple stretched from Holborn bars to the actual gate of the Wool market. In 1353 a tax of threepence was levied on every sack of wool and every three hundred wool-fels and other commodities carried by land or water to the Staple of Westminster. As the traffic had increased considerably and the roads were in a bad condition, the tax money was spent on improving and repairing the highways leading to the market. House owners along the routes were also required to pay a certain amount of tax for road repairs.

The ancient nursery rhyme 'Baa, baa, black sheep' is said to have close connections with the wool tax levied at this time. It is my idea that it may also refer to the Woolsacks which featured so prominently in Court sittings. The lines 'three bags full' and 'one for my master, and one for my dame, but none for the little boy that cries down the lane' may well identify the Woolsacks as being tokens of the rich – the poorer classes not being allowed a share of the takings.

Stow, the Elizabethan historian, writing about the Woolstaple had this to say: 'It seemeth that the merchants of the Staple be the most ancient merchants of this realm and that all commodities of the realm are Staple merchandise by law and charter, such as wool, leather, wool-fels, lead, tin and cloth.' The Staple was held, according to Stow, the day after the feast of St. Peter Vincula, which links it once again with Westminster.

When Westminster bridge was being planned in the mid-eighteenth century it was agreed to build it from a place called Woolstaple near Westminster Palace, over the water to Lambeth on the south bank of the river. At that time the old gate of the Woolstaple was still standing and had to be taken down to make way for the bridge construction.

Nowadays the Lord Chancellor, holding the highest position of law in the land, sits on the Woolsack in the House of Lords and the term to 'get the Woolsack' simply means to be appointed as Lord Chancellor. The Woolsack is a large square couch without arms, stuffed with wool and covered with red cloth. In early times it was usually the higher ranking members of the Church who had the privilege of the Woolsack but as the Church became less rich and powerful the Chancellor's duties became more judicial, and it was generally accepted that his most important job was to play the part of the king's conscience and make sure that organizations, such as hospitals, schools and monasteries, enjoying the King's patronage were taken care of. Many Lord Chancellors met untimely deaths in the turbulent history of our country. Thomas à Becket was one and another was Cardinal Wolsey, who died on his way to the Tower – after the Dissolution of the Monasteries. Sir Thomas Moore held the position until he lost the King's favour and also his head.

It is interesting to note that there never was such a Woolsack in the House of Commons – not even when the first Chancellor of the Exchequer was appointed.

The Staple Inn, Holborn, dates from the fourteenth century and it got its name from the merchants of the Staple who used it as a hostelry and possibly as a place where wool was weighed and excise duty collected. A wool pack, the emblem of the Staple, could be seen up to the mid-twentieth century on the wrought-iron gate of the garden. This seems to endorse the theory that the Woolsack in the House of Lords was an emblem of the Wool Staple at Westminster in the early days. The Benchers of Gray's Inn bought the building in 1529 and added a quaint overhanging façade, which until the middle of the last century was the oldest form of Elizabethan domestic architecture in London.

During the Middle Ages Westminster Palace was not the only royal residence in London. The Tower was used as a royal home at one stage, then St. James's Palace and then Whitehall. Westminster was generally used for meetings of the Court which were sometimes held in Westminster Hall, a room large enough and grand enough for the occasion. One of the first important Parliaments, as we know them today, was held in the Hall in the reign of Henry III. He was an irresponsible king and was taken to task by the people for not keeping to the clauses of the Magna Carta signed by King John at Runnymede. Parliamentary reform took place after which the people had more representatives, who were summoned from various walks of life to take part in parliamentary sittings. Knights represented counties and cities and burgesses represented towns and boroughs. The City of London sent four members and has enjoyed this arrangement until modern times. The gathering sat in one chamber and it became known as the House of Common Talk – hence the name House of Commons.

In Edward III's reign a disagreement broke out between the Commons and the Lords and in 1337 the two sections split up and the Commoners were allowed to meet instead in the Chapter House of Westminster Abbey. This was mainly because the Commoners felt that they had no say in the assembly and therefore left for a venue which offered more freedom of speech. From that time onwards the Hall of Westminster was not used as a meeting place for Parliament but for judicial matters or banquets for the pleasure of the monarch.

For two hundred years the Commons met in the Chapter House and enjoyed free speech and as the Chapter House was also the common room for the priests they enjoyed talk with the monks. The Commoners could talk as much as they pleased but of course their departure gave the monarch and his ministers more freedom than ever when it came to ruling the country. It is thought that the Lords met in the Painted Chamber at this time. The last sitting of the Commons in the Chapter House occurred on the day Henry VIII died. The members, so we are told, created such a noise and general rowdiness that the Abbot turned them out saying that never again would they have the privilege of meeting in the Abbey as such a rabble could not be tolerated in a House of God.

St. Stephen's Chapel in the Palace, which had been desecrated and stripped of its valuables during the Dissolution, was then given to the Commons to be used as a meeting place after their ejection from the Chapter House and it was later converted into St. Stephen's Hall. Thus the Commons and the Lords were housed once again under one roof, during the reign of Edward VI. When attending a full meeting of Parliament the Commoners were not allowed to advance beyond a certain point into the room and were prevented from doing so by the Bar of the House. They were only allowed to speak by proxy and towns sending representatives to Westminster had to pay them wages as it was not considered an enviable job. Many towns received charters from the king which freed them from attending Parliament: a privilege that the citizens treasured! Later it was fashionable to be a member of Parliament. Rich squires and country gentlemen sometimes spent fortunes in bribing people to elect them and intimidation was rife.

St. Stephen's Chapel from the Thames

Henry VIII was the last king to use the Palace of Westminster as a royal residence for a fire destroyed much of the building during his reign. He built St. James's Palace but did not reside in it for long as he had his eyes on Whitehall, of which we shall hear more later. Westminster was repaired and retained as the meeting place of Parliament although the legislature moved with the King to Whitehall where it has remained ever since. Elizabeth enjoyed making speeches in Parliament and even had apartments there, although her main palaces were at Whitehall and Greenwich.

The most famous scene in the House of Commons must surely be the entry of Charles I demanding that five members be taken and thrown into the Tower on the charge of treason. The men were Pym, Hampden, Hazlerig, Holles and Strode. Goaded to show his authority by his eccentric French wife, who hated the Commons, Charles marched from Whitehall to the House accompanied by a contingent of soldiers. Leaving the troops in Westminster Hall he went boldly into the Chamber and asked the Speaker, William Lenthall, whether he could borrow the authority of his chair for a few minutes. He then addressed the House and demanded that the five members show themselves and go with his troops. The five had been warned a few minutes previously and had made their escape across the river. When Charles realized that the birds had flown he said that he meant them no harm, and that they should have a fair and legal trial.

Then Lenthall went on his knees before the King and made a memorable speech: 'I have neither eyes to see nor tongue to speak in this place but as the House is pleased to direct me, whose servant I am here: and I humbly beg your Majesty's pardon that I cannot give any other answer that to what your Majesty is pleased to demand of me.' Members of the House shouted 'Privilege, privilege' to remind the King that they had certain rights within the House. The King turned on his heel and strode out of the room in a furious temper. The clerk of the House had recorded all that had been said and Charles sent for the script the next day and made corrections. Meanwhile the five members had taken refuge in the City and were granted protection by the citizens. Charles marched to the City gates and demanded that the five men be given over to him but this was refused and he returned to Whitehall empty handed.

Later he moved to Hampton Court as feeling was running so high against him in London that he feared for his life. However he continued to collect ship money from people living on the coasts. This money was supposed to go into a fund for building ships to defend our shores but of course it went to pay for the Royalist army that Charles was raising in preparation for the battles he knew were to come. In 1643 the Royalist army met the Parliamentarian troops at Edgehill and the Civil War had begun.

Parliament was dissolved by Charles from 1629 until 1640 as the members would not carry out his wishes. Since that time the sovereign of Britain is the one person who is not allowed in the House of Commons. When the monarch opens Parliament he or she sits on the throne in the House of Lords and orders Black Rod, a messenger, to tell the members in the Commons that everything is ready for the ceremony. Black Rod then knocks at the door leading to the Commons and it is opened and then shut in his face to indicate that the monarch shall not enter. The Commons then file into the Lords and witness the speech of the monarch as Parliament is opened for the ensuing session.

It is a curious fact that women were considered an essential part of early Parliaments – in fact ladies holding high offices in the land were thought to be an important part of the assembly. Westminster Palace, being the home of the monarch for over 500 years, housed his wife, children, relations and probably his mistresses also. It would have been very difficult therefore to exclude the queen and her ladies in waiting from attending meetings held in her own house, and often they were allowed to be present, bringing perhaps a little light relief to the affairs of the day. In the reign of Edward III a writ was issued summoning a number of ladies of high birth to attend the meeting in the National Council Chamber. Among them were Mary, Countess of Norfolk; Anne Despencer, Countess of Pembroke and Matilda, Countess of Oxford.

As the years went by and the Commons divided from the Lords the inclusion of females for the sittings fell out of favour and although no bill was actually passed it became a gentlemen's agreement not to appoint women to represent the country and for centuries the Free Mother of Parliaments became a closed shop to the fair sex. True, ladies with fire in their blood petitioned the House on one cause or another. The members treated their appeals with patronizing amusement and usually let them have their way. Later, ladies were barred even from the Strangers' Gallery and therefore had no access to the House at all. Naturally they objected to this, especially the wives of the members and on more than one occasion women banded together and stormed in through the doors to sit with their respective husbands on the benches. Some ladies of high birth once went to the House of Lords and sat on the steps of the throne or hid in Black Rod's box. The men just sat in silence until the female contingent became tired of waiting after a few hours and went home. To prevent further such invasions the watch on the doors of the House was intensified and ladies had to resort to more subtle means to gain an entrance. Many dressed in male attire and sat in the public gallery. The Duchess of Gordon was one such lady and another was Mrs Sheridan, who did it frequently in the late eighteenth century and afterwards let the papers know what she had been up to.

In desperation the House of Lords passed a Bill in 1822 excluding ladies from the House and instead letting them view the proceedings from a garret directly above the Chamber – through a ventilator shaft to be exact. Of course this proved so uncomfortable and degrading that it was totally unacceptable – especially so because almost nothing could be seen of the House through the shaft at that angle. It was dubbed 'the dog hole' by the women who had seen it. After the great tally stick fire of 1834 when most of Westminster Palace was burnt down, the plan of the new building included a special grilled gallery for 24 ladies at a time in the Strangers' Gallery. Even this idea received opposition from some quarters. For instance, Lord Brougham said at a meeting of the building committee: 'I think ladies would be better employed in almost any other way than attending Parliamentary debates'. And the Marquis of Lansdowne said: 'Ladies are not mentioned in the report, and, as far as I can prevent it, never shall be.' I think these narrow-minded gentlemen would turn in their graves if they knew that we have had a lady Prime Minister.

In 1900 Mrs. Garnett Fawcett formed the National Union of Suffrage Societies, and the fight by the suffragettes to procure the right for women to vote was launched. The efforts of Mrs. Emmeline Pankhurst and her daughters, Christabel and Sylvia, and many other women, and what they endured in the cause of freedom for women, are well known. Years ago I received a letter from a lady named Madame Marie Stuart De Baecker, who lived in Paris, and who was in fact a neice of Emily Davison, the woman who lost her life when she threw herself in front of the king's horse on Derby day in 1913 at Epsom. The background of this lady is not well known and I have great pleasure in supplying a few details as given to me by Madame De Baecker. Emily Davison was a clever and cultured woman. She graduated with honours at London University and then took first class honours at Oxford in English Language and Literature. Afterwards she took up a post preparing pupils for the Cambridge Higher local examinations. She was on the Executive Board of the Marylebone Branch of the Workers' Educational Association. She was keen on literature and music, wrote verses and was religious. She was a strong swimmer, good looking, with a mass of auburn hair, and she enjoyed life to the full with very high spirits and a maximum of perseverance and dedication to the cause of obtaining civic rights for women. As a child Madame De Baecker would listen to her aunt when she came to stay. She would explain to the family: 'Women must obtain the right to vote not because they must take men's places, but because their own jobs as women, wives, mothers give them enormous responsibilities in the Nation's existence.'

In those days women had no rights; the man in the family was allowed a free pass into any club or institution but the woman was allowed nothing and the law ignored the female sex. They could not enter the Law Courts as public citizens nor even the House of Commons. Emily Davison was imprisoned more than once and in 1909 went on her first hunger strike because she was not treated as a political offender. She fasted for over 124 hours. In Strangeways prison she barricaded herself in her cell and to break her spirit a hose pipe was directed on to her. The cell was flooded but she did not give up. In 1911 there was a census and Emily Davison went to the House of Commons in a party and somehow contrived to be left behind and spent the night in 'Guy Fawkes' cupboard along with the brooms. She was discovered the next morning and had the satisfaction of knowing that it was recorded that a woman had spent census night in the House of Commons. Her point was: Why should a woman be included in the census if she had no civil rights? In 1912 she spent six months in Holloway prison and was forcibly fed. In protest she managed to escape from the room and threw herself down ten feet of stairway. The authorities were perturbed by what she might do next and released her. Then came the climax. On 4 June 1913, Derby day, Emily Davison went to Epsom intending to make a protest and deliver a blow for the suffragettes. According to her niece she did not intend to kill herself as she had her return ticket in her pocket. At the critical moment she crept underneath the railings and stood on the race track with arms outstretched, facing the oncoming racers. She stopped the king's horse but was knocked down and rolled over, unconscious. She lay for four days in Epsom hospital in a coma before dying on 8 June, aged 40. On 14 June 1913 the most remarkable funeral procession that had ever honoured a woman commoner moved through London. Traffic stopped completely and thousands of mourners, mostly women, lined the streets in silence. The procession of mourners was over two miles long. It started at Victoria Station and ended at King's Cross at the wish of her sister, Madame De Baecker's mother. Emily was buried in the family grave at Morpeth in Northumberland.

A memorial service was held on the same day as the funeral at St. George's Church, Hart Street in Bloomsbury. It is rather ironical that the text of the sermon should read 'Greater Love hath no *man* that this, that *he* lay down *his* life for *his* Friend.' Unfortunate wording to say the least and obviously chosen by a male!

Emily Davison loved London and wrote a verse about the City when away in the country in 1906:

> Oh London, how I feel thy magic spell
> Now I have left thee, and amid the woods
> Sit lonely! Here I know I love thee well,
> Conscious of all the glamour of thy moods,
> But it is otherwise amid thy bounds!
> Thou art an ocean of humanity,
> Embarked on which I lose my soul, in sounds

That thunder in my ear. The vanity
And ceaseless struggle stifle doubt and fear
Until I cry, bemused by the strife,
'The centre of the universe is here,
This is the hub, the very fount of life'.

Miss Davison's motto was 'Deeds, not words'.

She did not die in vain and at last public opinion turned in
favour of civil rights for women but it was not until after the
Great War that women received the right to vote. A commemorative service was held in the House of Commons in June 1963 to
honour the sacrifice made by Emily Davison fifty years before.
Madame Stuart De Baecker was invited to attend and read out a
statement about her aunt during the service.

As previously mentioned Westminster Hall was not used for
politics again after the two Parliamentary Houses in the Palace
of Westminster split up during the reign of Edward III. Instead
it served as a banqueting hall and court room where prisoners
of note were tried. The trial of Guy Fawkes and some of his fellow
conspirators was held here. They received traitors' punishments –
being hung, drawn and quartered opposite the very place they
had tried to destroy – in the Palace yard facing the House. Sir
Walter Ralegh was tried and beheaded here in 1618, facing death
with brave words, but the most important trial in our history
must surely be the trial of Charles I after his capture during the
Civil War. It is said that during his appearance in court there
was constant hustle and bustle among the laymen. The cracking
of nuts, swigging of ale and eating of victuals created a disturb-
ance that was so loud it drowned, at times, what the lawyers were
saying. Smoking, too, was commonplace although decrees had
been passed banning this because of the fire hazard, but it seemed
to make little difference to the habits of the onlookers.

During the seventeenth century and after, the Hall became an
inside market. Samuel Pepys often went there to buy books and
look at the stalls selling baubles and ribbons, gloves and so on.
Vendors even called out their wares, while at the same time on
the other side of the room the lawyers were trying to do business.
Legal matters, decrees, and the buying and selling of property
were dealt with, and often the law men had to shout for silence

amongst the vendors in the market. This unsatisfactory state of affairs continued until the Law Courts were removed to the Strand.

As there were no kitchens in the House in early days, eating places, taverns and coffee houses sprang up in the Palace yard for the convenience of members of Parliament, and in fact the whole area degenerated into a common street market. The great tally stick fire which burnt down the Palace of Westminster in 1834, altered this and the new buildings, planned by Sir Charles Barry, housed adequate kitchens and dining rooms. Bellamy, a cook who had provided meals for the members before the fire, was asked to take over the supervision of the new kitchens, which he was very pleased to do. Westminster Palace became the most exclusive club in London in Edwardian times.

New Palace Yard

St. Stephen's Chapel, the home of the Commons, had to be enlarged at various times during the past centuries to accommodate the growing number of members of Parliament. In 1800 walls had to be pulled down once more to make room for 103 Irish members as a result of a Union with Ireland. The walls were found to be four feet thick and in the course of demolition many old paintings came to light dating back to the reign of Edward III in the fourteenth century. The paintings were in oils and well preserved and therefore must be some of the rarest frescoes in existence. The Chapel was pulled down when Barry built the new structure.

It would take too long to describe the present layout of the Houses of Parliament but I cannot resist mentioning that from the Central lobby a flight of stairs leads to the rebuilt Stephen's Hall. Brass knobs in the floor indicate where the Speaker's Chair used to be and it was here that Speaker Lenthall barred the way of Charles I when he came to arrest five knights. During the Second World War the House of Commons debating chamber was demolished and the Commons sat in the House of Lords: the Lords used the Prince's Chamber. The new Chamber of the Commons was rebuilt in 1950 to the plans of Sir G. G. Scott.

The Jewel House which has survived fire and bombs since the time of Edward III is of course the oldest building in the Palace. It was once the treasure house for kings – hence its name – and is now a small museum showing some relics of interest linked with this Palace in the West.

I cannot leave the House of Commons without some words on the history of the Clock Tower and Big Ben. For over six centuries there has been a clock tower at Westminster. It was invaluable to the citizens in early times as clocks were rare and watches unknown. It was good to be able to see the time of day and hear the great bell toll the hours away. The story of how the Clock Tower came into being can be traced back to the Middle Ages when a certain Sir Ralph Heigham, Lord Chief Justice, was found to have altered a court record – thus defrauding a poor man out of his rightful dues. This misdemeanour came to light and the judge was fined eight hundred marks by the king, which was duly paid. The king used the money to build a tower in the Palace yard which housed a clock to remind the judge, and everybody else who had the responsibility of seeing justice done, when hearing the toll of the bells that they should carry out their duties with integrity and impartiality. The inscription on the dial read '*Discite justitiam moniti*' – Here is a monument to justice. The lesson was learnt and it is reported that in Elizabeth's time two judges were overheard discussing whether or not to alter the record for some matter or other. One was in favour but the other refused saying that he did not want to build another clock tower.

The clock was one of the first mechanical striking clocks to come to England and was a very good example of horological science. The earliest striking clock with a dial was made in Italy in 1335. The Westminster clock may well have come from this source. The bell was of great size and weight and its sound could be heard as far as the City if the wind was right. The bell was first christened Edward, after the Confessor, but later, after the Reformation, it was known affectionately as 'Great Tom' because of its deep tone. A happening during the reign of William and Mary involved a sentry on duty at Windsor Castle who was court-martialled for falling asleep during the night. The man insisted that he was not asleep and to prove it he said that the bell of 'Old Tom' had struck thirteen instead of twelve, that night. The court disbelieved this story until several witnesses came forward and said that they too had heard the bell strike thirteen, Whereupon the king granted a free pardon for the prisoner.

In 1698 the old Clock Tower was pulled down because it was in a dilapidated and unsafe condition, and the bell was transferred to St. Paul's, which had just been rebuilt after the fire. The bell weighed over 82 cwt and there was some difficulty in transporting it to the Cathedral. The roads were bad and the bell fell off the cart at Temple Bar with such force that it split into two. It was then recast by Whitman in 1716 and was hoisted into position in the Western Tower, where it remains to this day. The old clock at Westminster disappeared, more's the pity, and for over 150 years there was no clock. After the fire in 1834, Sir Charles Barry was appointed the architect to design the new Westminster Palace and he very aptly included a clock tower reflecting the plan of the old buildings. He designed the two towers, Victoria and the Clock, so that they would be the most prominent features of the new Mother of Parliaments. For years controversy raged as to who should design and build the clock, and when it was decided that a certain Mr. Dent should be given the honour the unfortunate man died – probably from shock! The arguments started all over again but eventually a Mr. Denison and assistant clockmakers were given the task, which proved harder than they had expected. First, the hands which had been made out of cast iron were found to be too heavy to put up then, when they had been made out of gun metal and fixed into position, they fell more than a minute or two every time they reached the vertical position. The bell was cast by bell-founders in Stockton-on-Tees; Messrs Warner and Co., and it was named Big Ben after the first Commissioner of Works, Sir Benjamin Hall – a rather corpulent gentleman. After a stormy sea passage, when the ship carrying the bell to London narrowly missed being wrecked, it eventually reached Westminster where it was hung for testing at the foot of the new Clock Tower in the Palace yard. When it was weighed it was found to be nearly two tons heavier than had been calculated and therefore needed a clapper twice as heavy as the one that had been provided. Day after day crowds were admitted to the yard to see Big Ben and listen to its tone. Many swore that it was 'off tune' and after some months the bell cracked and the critics were justified. There had been a flaw in the casting of the bell and so the first Big Ben was rejected and was then recast by Messrs Mears of Whitechapel. Again the casting revealed a flaw in the metal but this time it was possible to repair it. The renovated bell was at last pulled into position, supervised by Sir Benjamin Hall, and has remained there ever since, with only a few days' silence while repairs have been carried out. The bell weighs 13½ tons and the striking clapper 7 cwt. The four quarter chime bells together comprise nearly 8½ tons of metal. The staircase to the tower is winding and has 374 steps, and an inner gallery runs around the inside of the four faces of the clock. Each face is 23 ft in diameter, the minute hand of each dial is 14 ft long and the minute spaces are a foot square. The huge weights that drive the machine are adjusted by coins, some as small as old halfpennies, to keep the clock accurate: a halfpenny would make the difference of two-fifths of a second each way. Big Ben is the world's most famous clock and during the Second World War its chimes were used to announce news bulletins broadcast to enemy-occupied Europe. The clock has stopped only twice: once in 1928 when the hands became frozen in snow and once in 1957 when a pot of paint obstructed the hands. When a light shines in the belfry at night it shows that the House is still sitting.

Victoria Tower is 336 ft high and 75 ft square. Up to the mid-twentieth century it was the tallest square tower in the world. Over a million documents, including copies of every act of Parliament from 1497 are housed in it, and many of these must have survived the tally stick fire and other conflagrations over the centuries. If Parliament is sitting in the daytime a flag flies from Victoria Tower.

WHITEHALL

During the Middle Ages the land owned by the monks of Westminster Abbey stretched from Westminster to the City gates. John Hearsey, in his book *Bridge, Church and Palace*, states that in 1223 a powerful baron by the name of Hubert de Burgh bought some land along the riverside road to the City, from the Abbey, and there built a mansion. On his death in 1243 the property was transferred to Walter de Grey, later to become Archbishop of York. The barons objected to this appointment on the grounds that de Grey was illiterate and therefore not qualified to hold such an important position. De Grey travelled to see the Pope, who endorsed his appointment, saying it was better to be illiterate than corrupt. Nevertheless it cost de Grey £10,000, money which found its way into the Pope's coffers, before this decision from his Holiness was extracted. De Grey lived in the house and transferred its ownership to the See of York so that it would be passed on to his successors. He renamed the house York Place. For three hundred years it remained the London residence of the Archbishop of York and the Church spent vast sums of money renovating and improving the building until it was a worthy place in which to entertain kings and foreign visitors. The monarchy was often short of money and York Place became a convenient venue for costly ceremonial events and Edward III even opened Parliament there on occasions.

In 1514 Cardinal Wolsey was given the See of York, albeit that he already held three others, and York Place became his property. He set to work to make it one of the most splendid palaces in Europe. He had hundreds of servants who looked after his every whim. There were two kitchens, one to cook the food for him and his family, and one to provide victuals for the servants. The whole place was lavishly furnished with expensive drapes and ornaments of gold, silver and precious stones. Even the plates were made of solid gold. His clothes were magnificent and he spent thousands of pounds yearly on his wardrobe. Whenever he went into a public place Wolsey carried a large orange from which the flesh had been dug out and the inside filled with a sponge soaked in vinegar, spices and herbs, which he constantly sniffed, hoping to ward off any pestilence which might be around at the time. He was a haughty, ambitious man, who thought he would be appointed Pope in due course. He was also two-faced and wasted money on his high standard of living while the poor died from starvation not far from his door. Wolsey imposed heavy taxes on the rank and file which made him very unpopular. And the seeds of jealousy were growing in Henry VIII's bosom when he saw how the Archbishop lived. Wolsey was riding for a fall and his downward trend began when he was asked by Henry to procure for him a divorce from his first wife, Catherine of Aragon. Henry badly wanted a legitimate male heir and saw Anne Boleyn as the means of obtaining one. Wolsey tried to stop the romance by telling Henry of Anne's affair with Lord Henry Percy: an act for which Anne never forgave him. When Anne was Queen, having married Henry in January 1533, when she was already pregnant with the future Elizabeth I, she tried to discredit the Archbishop in the eyes of the King by every means she could. This was not a hard task as Henry had never forgiven Wolsey for failing to obtain papal permission for the divorce.

During the Dissolution of the Monasteries Henry greedily seized nearly all the rich lands and property previously owned by the Church. York Place and Hampton Court, both belonging to Wolsey were commandeered by the Crown. Only Westminster Abbey remained comparatively free from desecration. Wolsey retired to York, where he was still Archbishop, but he was so much hated that a plot was hatched which accused him of treason and he was ordered to stand trial at the Tower. In failing health he began the journey back to London but died in Leicester Abbey with these words on his lips, 'If I had served God as diligently as I have done the king, He would not have given me over in my grey hairs.'

In 1529 Henry took over York Place and renamed it Whitehall. This was a traditional name given to any great hall which served as a meeting place for people of high standing. The King began to make alterations and improvements. He built steps leading down to the river, later known as Whitehall Stairs, for use of royalty only. Then two gateways were built, one on the river side named the King's street gate, and one on the other side of the road named the Holbein gate, mistakenly as it turned out as Holbein did not in fact design it. The two gates supported a convenient footbridge across the road. On the north side Henry began to build his sporting houses; a covered tennis court, with three outdoor ones close by, a cockpit which looked more like a chapter house, a tilt yard and a bowling green. The game of real tennis as played by Henry and his friends was a very different game from the one we know as lawn tennis. Real tennis was played with a hard ball over an iron net against three walls, something on the lines of squash. A real tennis court can still be seen at Hampton Court. A club plays there and can be watched by the public on certain days.

Henry and Anne lived at St. James's Palace for a year or two but soon Henry, in his disappointment at not being granted a male heir, began to look elsewhere for a wife who could perhaps provide him with what he wanted. Jane Seymour became the object of his affections and Anne was sent to the block at the Tower on a fabricated charge of treason. Jane did provide the King with a sickly baby son and died in the attempt. Whitehall came into its own again when Henry returned: a dying man, looked after with devotion until the end by his sixth wife Catherine Parr. He died on 28 January 1547 and his funeral cortège was magnificent and stretched for four miles. A wax effigy of the king lay on top of the coffin with all the royal trappings including the crown and sceptre. According to his wishes Henry was buried at Windsor next to his favourite wife and queen, Jane Seymour.

The boy king, Edward VI, lived at Whitehall and was easy prey to the whims and wants of the lords of Court. It is said that one most notorious character, the Duke of Northumberland, used to go to the boy's bedroom when he was asleep and whisper what he wanted to be suggested at Court the next day. The child, half drugged with sleep, would listen and then present plans indoctrinated by Northumberland, as if they were his own. In those days there was an open air court called Sermon or Whalebone Court outside the council chamber. It was dubbed 'Whalebone Court' because the skeleton of a whale found in the river at Woolwich in 1532 was on display and remained there for over 60 years. In 1522 Edward was so ill with tuberculosis that Parliament had to come to Whitehall for the opening ceremony. Edward died at Greenwich in July of his sixteenth year and Mary his half-sister, daughter of Catherine of Aragon, was crowned queen. She was a devout Catholic and proceeded to try to re-establish the Catholic Church, sending many Protestant martyrs to the stake in doing so. She also made plans to marry Philip of Spain, whom the people did not like for fear that England would become just one of Spain's colonies.

The rebel from Kent, Wyatt, led an army from his home county to London to try and frighten Mary out of this allegiance. When he reached Southwark he found the London Bridge drawbridge had been drawn up and so he marched to Kingston and crossed the river by the bridge there. When he eventually reached Whitehall his followers were tired and drenched to the skin, and so disheartened that they dispersed, leaving Wyatt sitting alone on a log, with his head in his hands in despair. Meanwhile in Whitehall itself soldiers and courtiers alike were in a state of panic. The only one to keep cool was the Queen. When news reached them that the rebellion had petered out, the troops took heart and Wyatt and some of his followers were brought before the Queen prior to being executed at the Tower. Others who had taken part in the rebellion were hung, drawn and quartered and displayed in various parts of the City. The rest were rounded up, a group of about 400 men, chained together in fours with halters around their necks and brought before the Queen in the courtyard of Whitehall. There she pardoned them and their shackles were removed and they were freed. They lay down in the mud before Queen Mary and thanked her for the clemency shown. There have been so many unpleasant tales about 'Bloody Mary' that it is encouraging to find one that had a happy ending.

Queen Elizabeth divided her time between Greenwich and Whitehall. The Banqueting Hall, the only building to survive until this day, was first built in her reign. It was a canvas affair in those days but was later built of brick in the reign of James I. Although Elizabeth was not renowned for her sense of humour legend has it that she fitted the sundial in the gardens of Whitehall with a water spray, so that when guests went to look at the dial they were sprinkled with water. This was done by a series of small jets placed around the perimeter, joined to pipes leading to a water wheel hidden in a summer house. When a gardener saw guests approaching he had instructions from the Queen to turn the wheel and set the jets working.

John Hearsey in his book *Bridge, Church and Palace* tells a story that is worth repeating. In the reign of James I, a lady named Frances Howard, a very beautiful woman and a social climber related to the ill-fated Catherine Howard of the previous century, was betrothed and married at an early age to the Earl of Essex whom she did not love. While it was rumoured that she was the mistress of James's eldest son, Henry, she was infatuated with Robert Carr, the King's closest friend whom he had brought with him from Scotland. She was determined to marry Carr at all costs and wanted a quiet divorce to avoid any scandal. Carr had a close friend in Sir Thomas Overbury to whom he confided everything. Frances realized that if her plan was to succeed she would have to get rid of Overbury who knew too much. First, with the help of her ambitious family, she planted the seeds of jealousy in the mind of James who had homosexual tendencies and wanted Carr for himself. Then Frances persuaded James to offer Overbury such posts abroad as the British envoy to Russia or ambassador to the Hague. Overbury was quite happy in England and refused these offers. He was then sent for by the King, accused of disobedience, and dispatched to the Tower. A wardrobe mistress, a Mrs. Turner in the pay of Frances Howard at Whitehall, was persuaded to let her servant attend Overbury in the Tower. Through the servant a constant supply of poisoned tarts and cakes were fed to Overbury, from which, consequently, he died. Frances Howard obtained her divorce and married Robert Carr. About this time, Mrs. Turner was allowed to introduce a new fashion for women at court in the shape of starched yellow ruffs to decorate a dress. For a while all went well until a servant of the apothecary who had supplied the poison that had killed Overbury, went abroad and became ill. On his death bed he confessed the whole plot and it was relayed post-haste back to Whitehall. Mrs. Turner and her servant were arrested, tried and executed at Tyburn. The Lord Chief Justice objected to her dress fashion, which he thought vulgar, and ordered that she was to be hung in one of her own creations so that the fashion would die with her. Later, when Robert Carr and his wife were taken to the Tower, the Lieutenant of the Tower, Sir Jervis Elwes, lost his nerve and confessed that he too had been involved in the plot. He was executed on Tower Hill bringing much shame to his family. The Carrs were sentenced to death but James stepped in and reprieved them on condition that they never set foot in Whitehall or any other royal residence ever again. This must have been a cruel punishment for the Carrs as they had thrived on royal connections. James meanwhile had turned his affections to George Villiers, Duke of Buckingham, whose family was later to be linked with the building of Buckingham House.

During the Civil War Whitehall was used as a barracks for the King's troops. Its trappings, paintings and other valuables were taken to pay the soldiers' wages, for food and armaments, as the King's coffers were empty. When the war was drawing to a close, Charles was tried at Westminster Hall and heard that his punishment was to be death by the axe. On execution day, the King walked from St. James's Palace where he had been staying, into the Banqueting Hall at Whitehall. A window frame on the first storey had been removed and through this the King stepped on to a dais erected for his execution. The act was watched by thousands of people – men mourning and women crying as they realized too late what a terrible thing had been done.

Cromwell lived in Whitehall for the rest of his life. When Charles II was asked to ascend the throne he, too, made Whitehall his London residence when the plague did not threaten.

It is said that at that time the palace had over a thousand rooms which housed the King, his courtiers, some of his mistresses amongst whom was a French woman named Louise de Querouaille, later to become Duchess of Portsmouth, and his children by them, including his eldest son, the Duke of Monmouth. Nell Gwyn, the people's favourite, and probably Charles's also, lived in a house in Pall Mall. She dubbed the French woman 'Squintabella' as she had a marked squint. Lady Castlemain, probably the most beautiful of all Charles's mistresses, lived at the Palace and mothered at least four of his children. She was, according to Samuel Pepys, the most beautiful creature that he had ever seen! Queen Catherine was barren and was treated very shabbily by the ladies of the court and by the King himself. She lived in poorly furnished apartments, in contrast to the luxurious rooms appointed to the favourites of Charles.

During the Great Plague only two men remained in London in an official capacity to organize the collecting of the dead and the tolling of bells. These two brave men were General Monk and the Lord Mayor of the City of London. In the Great Fire which followed, Whitehall was not damaged. After the death of Charles his brother, James II, came to the throne to rule uneasily at Whitehall Palace. He had a son by his second wife, Mary of Modena, who by rights was the heir to the throne but being a Catholic was prevented by James's daughters, by his first marriage to Anne Hyde, Mary and Anne. Fearing assassination James had a weathercock placed on top of the Banqueting Hall as he knew that when the wind blew from the east it was favourable for William of Orange, husband of Mary, to set sail from Holland to claim the throne with Mary. When news came at last that William was crossing the Channel James evacuated Whitehall via the Privy stairs and was taken across the river to a coach which was waiting to take him to Dover and so to the continent. His queen had already left with her baby son, who would become known as the Old Pretender. The weathercock which played such an important part in the drama can still be seen in Whitehall.

Although William and Mary were crowned at Whitehall, William soon decided to discard this venue as the official London residence of the monarch in favour of Kensington Palace in the extreme west of the City. This was because he suffered from asthma and thought the air would be better for him away from the smoke of Whitehall. In doing so he weakened the legislative ties between Whitehall, Westminster and the Crown. At the end of the seventeenth century an uncontrollable fire destroyed Whitehall, except for the Banqueting Hall, and it was never rebuilt. After a while buildings sprang up on the site which still belonged to the Crown. It was during this time that the old Cockpit chambers were pulled down and government offices such as we have today were erected. This deprived Sir Robert Walpole, first Lord of the Treasury and our first Prime Minister, of his suite of rooms. George II offered No. 10 Downing Street as a personal gift. Walpole was delighted and said he would only accept if it became the hereditary home of all future Prime Ministers. This was granted and from that time onwards with a few exceptions this has been so. Walpole loved the place as did Pitt the Younger.

Downing Street has a long and interesting history. Its name is derived from Sir George Downing, an American colonist who was the first graduate to be sent out by Harvard College in 1642. He came to England and served under Cromwell as a chaplain in his army. After the war Cromwell appointed Downing to be British ambassador in the Hague. While he was there Downing realized that the tide was turning against Cromwell and so he turned his attentions to Charles, whom no doubt he had met in the course of his duties as ambassador. A writer of the day described Downing as 'a sider with all times and changes'. He wormed his way into Charles's favour and when Charles returned to this country and was proclaimed king, Downing was granted a piece of land opposite Whitehall Palace. The King asked him to build four mansions with 'back fronts' facing St. James's Park. He also requested a large terrace walk next to the park. Downing was pleased to do this and erected four handsome brick houses and for many years after this the street became a desirable place in which to live. But towards the end of the century it became crowded with smaller dwellings, many of them inns and lodging houses, and was described by some as 'a mean street'. Boswell lodged here but he did not boast of the fact.

During the nineteenth century the government set about buying up the whole of the property in the street for convenience as well as safety. Gradually the venue was cleaned up, and the lodging houses and taverns disappeared. No. 12 was bought for the Chancellor of the Exchequer. At one time there was a milliner's factory opposite the Foreign Office where a number of attractive young ladies worked. Clerks in the Office, with time on their hands, amused themselves by hanging out of upstairs windows and, with the use of mirrors, reflecting light so that it flashed bright blinding rays on to the workers' faces in the hat factory. The proprietor wrote a letter complaining of this behaviour. Palmerston, who was then Foreign Minister, dealt with the matter with characteristic humour. In the margin of the letter of complaint he wrote: 'Who are the unmannerly youths who have been casting reflections on the young ladies opposite?' He then sent the letter up to the clerks' office for their perusal. The millinery establishment was never troubled again by the apprentices across the street.

The Admiralty, War Office and New Scotland Yard can be found in Whitehall today together with many other government offices. The Banqueting Hall housed the Royal United Service Museum up to 1963. The Horse Guards Parade is perhaps the most interesting sight for the tourist in Whitehall. It was built to William Kent's design in 1750–60. It has an archway and a clock tower and the two sentry boxes house two men of the Household Cavalry. What they guard no one knows but they do play an important part in the ceremonial attractions of London today and this is dealt with in the last chapter.

The Tower of London

4

Palaces and Parks

THE TOWER OF LONDON

The Tower of London must be the oldest and most important secular building in Britain because of its links with the famous and infamous throughout the ages. It has been a palace, fortress, mint, prison and zoo, not forgetting the depository for the Crown Jewels. It has seen the murder of kings and queens and other royalty, and the torture and martyrdom of clergy during the religious turbulence of the past. In fact it can be said that the very walls bear an index of the history of this country. The Tower was built by William the Conqueror, some say to impress the citizens of London, which he probably succeeded in doing. He used the old Roman wall, parts of which had been repaired, to form the mainstay of the Tower. Under the guidance of a monk named Gundulf, who was one of the first stonemasons in this country, the White Tower was built and completed in 1098. Stone from Caen was imported and used for the facing stone and Kent ragstone for the less important interior walls. Inside, the chapel of St. John was built and throughout the centuries has been the place where kings, queens, princes and churchmen have prayed for guidance in their desperate plight. To the Anglo-Saxons, at least, the Tower was a symbol of oppression – those who did not conform were subjected to an untimely and painful end within its walls. It is thought that the Conqueror lived in the Tower and succeeding monarchs also. Henry III, who rebuilt much of Westminster Abbey, spent a good deal of money on the Tower, making it a safer place in which to live. The moat was successfully flooded in his reign and it was Henry who first ordered the central tower to be whitewashed and from that time it has been known as the White Tower. His son, Edward I, dubbed 'the castle builder', reconstructed the Tower in the form that we know today. He built a second great wall and so increased the defence of the building and also introduced Traitors' Gate. It was not used as such in those early days but only as a water entrance to the Tower.

Although the Tower was the official residence of the Crown for many years after the Norman conquest, other palaces and residences in London proved more attractive and comfortable to the royal family. The Savoy Palace was one and Greenwich Palace was another. Many buildings were erected around the Tower at the whim of the reigning monarch, including a splendid palace which was built in front of the White Tower, in which, it is said, the little Princes were murdered. In time these buildings fell into disrepair and gradually a system of towers complementing the White Tower was built. Today there are twenty towers, including the Bloody Tower which is said to have been built on the spot where the two Princes lost their lives. The Lion Tower, in which the menagerie was kept for seven centuries, was pulled down when the animals were finally removed in the mid-nineteenth century to Regent's Park. A curious story concerning April Fool's Day is told in my book *Origins of Festivals and Feasts*. Apparently the first record we have of the custom of playing tricks on the first day of April is to be found in Dawks' Newsletter for 2 April 1698 which states that 'yesterday being the 1 April several persons were sent to the Tower Ditch to see the lions washed.' And again in 1860 it is recorded in *Notes and Queries* that several people bought cards at a penny each from a ballad shop in Seven Dials which they thought would admit them to the Tower to watch the annual ceremony of washing the lions, albeit the menagerie had been removed from the Tower over twenty years before.

Animals had been kept at the Tower since the days of Henry III. An elephant, sent to the King by Louis IX of France, had a special room built to house it. The space was 40 ft long and 20 ft deep and according to Sarah Bailey in her article 'The Menagerie in the Tower' from *Strange Stories of the Tower of London*, people came from all over the country to see this wonderful beast. The conditions must have suited the species as elephants were actually bred in the Tower from time to time. Another attraction was a bear which was allowed to fish in the river Thames, with a long rope attached so that it couldn't escape. During the nineteenth century the menagerie dwindled and many of the animals died – one lion bit a soldier, much to the anger of Arthur Wellesley, Duke of Wellington. He persuaded the Keeper of the Tower to ask the king if the animals could be removed as they had become a danger to one and all. As the Tower served as a barracks the Duke thought it degrading that it should also house wild animals for the entertainment of the public.

Today as always the Crown Jewels are kept in the Tower and attract sightseers from all over the world. There have been many stories concerning the theft of the jewels but none so daring I think as the plan carried out by the notorious Captain Blood. According to Guy Wilson in his article 'Treason! Murder! The Crown is stolen' out of *Strange Stories of the Tower of London*, Blood, dressed as a clergyman and accompanied by a woman who said she was his wife, knocked at the door of Martin Tower, where the jewels were kept at this time. It was an evening in 1671 and the keeper, an old man of seventy-seven hardly equipped to guard such treasure, opened the door and agreed to let the couple see the jewels. While they were looking at the display, the 'wife', according to plan, feigned illness and was looked after by the keeper's wife in an adjoining room. Captain Blood had ample time to view the lay-out of the room and the manner in which the cases could be forced open and the jewels taken. On his next visit he was accompanied by his 'nephew' and they expressed delight at seeing the jewels and also interest in a pair of pistols hanging on the wall. The arms were there to protect the keeper against thieves but he was so bemused by the enthusiasm of his visitors that he agreed to sell them the pistols at a handsome price. On the next visit Blood brought three accomplices and the keeper, not suspecting anything, let them in. This time he was roughly treated and a cloak thrown over his head and he was warned that his assailants were armed. He continued to struggle but was finally knocked unconscious with a mallet and stabbed in his stomach. The thieves broke open the cupboards and one of the men, named Parrot, stuffed the orb down his breeches. Blood had to crush the Crown so that he could hide it under his cloak and another began to file the sceptre into two. By strange coincidence the keeper's son, who had been away fighting in Flanders, returned home on leave that very night and interrupted the thieves. They ran for their lives, taking what they could. When the gag had been removed from the old man he shouted 'Treason, murder – the Crown is stolen'. Blood shot a guard who tried to stop him but the others became too frightened to do anything and all, including Blood, were soon caught. The jewels were mended and restored to their rightful place once again.

The reason for Blood's desperate raid was because he was destitute. He had been a wealthy Irish landowner and fought on the side of Cromwell during the Civil War. For a reward he was richly endowed with Crown properties, which he lost when Charles II was crowned. The King requested an interview with Blood and listened to his life story. Blood was clever. He acknowledged that the punishment for what he had done was undoubtedly death but he said that he could not be responsible for the King's life if he lost his own as his friends had sworn to assassinate the King if he was killed. Blood promised to serve Charles faithfully if he was pardoned. Surprisingly enough Blood was set free and his lands were restored to him and he was even given an annual pension of £500. Perhaps Charles secretly admired Blood's audacity. Whatever the reason for his pardon it will never be known.

In modern times the Crown Jewels are kept in the thirteenth-century Wakefield Tower and it was here that Henry VI was kept prisoner and then murdered. The Bell Tower was the prison of Bishop Fisher and Sir Thomas More. Both were executed, but Elizabeth, who spent some time here, was later released to become Queen of England. It was in Tudor times that the water gate became known as Traitors' Gate, for many passed under it on their way to the Tower to receive the punishment for so-called treason. The Bell Tower is now the home of the Governor and is known as the Queen's House. It was here that Guy Fawkes and some of his conspirators spent their last miserable days, tortured beyond belief before being executed outside the Houses of Parliament – the building that they had tried to destroy. A story linked with the Gunpowder Plot is worth repeating. It concerns a Jesuit priest named Garnett who went into hiding, after

Traitor's Gate

the plot had been discovered, in Hindlip House in Worcestershire. It was a building well known for its hiding places, secret stairs and cupboards. A compatriot had given way under torture and told that Garnett and his friends were hidden in Hindlip House. Sir Henry Bromley was given the task of smoking out these gentlemen but it was many days before he succeeded. The house also gave up quite a few other outlaws. Garnett and his friends had been wedged between two chimney breasts and had been fed liquid by the lady of the house through a straw passed through a crack in the wall beside the mantlepiece. They were suffocating and their limbs had become so swollen that it was impossible to endure the confined space any longer. The traitors were taken to the

Tower where two of them were tortured, but Garnett and his closest companion in the plot, were not. In fact they were treated quite respectably and were given two cells with a communicating door. The warder assured them that they were at liberty to visit each other and talk freely. Of course the whole thing was a trap and a recorder, sitting out of sight, took down all that was said. Soon there was enough evidence on record to ensure their execution. Garnett was tried at the Guildhall and executed in the grounds. There was a strong feeling among the Catholics that Garnett was a martyr, and a strange story stems from his execution which has become known as 'Garnett's Straw'. It is said that as Garnett's head and quarters lay in a basket of straw, one of the straws blew out of the basket and fell at the feet of a man named Wilkinson. He took it to a lady who he knew was a pious Catholic and very grieved over Garnett's demise. She put the straw into a bottle for safe keeping and after a few days showed it to a friend. The friend, after looking at it for a few moments, said that she could see Garnett's face in the bottle. The woman then saw the face herself and soon the news spread that a miracle had occurred. People from far and near flocked to see the face in the bottle. It was then decided by the people that Garnett had been innocent and further stories claimed that the face had a halo above it and a cross on the forehead.

The Ceremony of the Keys has been going on for 700 years and is thought to have been started in Henry III's reign. This is the procedure today as recorded by Chief Warder L. Varley in an article in *Strange Stories of the Tower of London*. The Chief Yeomen Warder leaves the Byward Tower at eight minutes to ten and proceeds to the Bloody Tower carrying the working keys, as opposed to the ceremonial keys, on a red plush cushion and the ornate candle lantern presented by London's Honourable Artillery Company to mark their occupation of the Tower as its garrison in 1915 and 1916 to 1919. The sergeant and two men of the 'Escort to the Keys' line up under the arch of the Bloody Tower. The sergeant and one man are armed and the Chief Yeoman Warden keeps the Keys and gives his lantern to the lantern bearer, who is not armed. They march to the Byward Tower and are met by the Yeoman Warder on Watchman duty. He prepares the West Gate for Locking and the Chief Yeoman

Warder locks the gate by the light of the lantern. The armed guards turn inwards and present arms as a compliment to the Queen's Keys. The procedure is repeated at the Byward Tower but as the company move along Water Lane the sentry at Wakefield Tower (where the Crown Jewels are housed), challenges them.

'Halt.'

The sergeant orders: 'Escort to the Keys, Halt!'

'Who comes there?'

The Chief Yeoman Warder answers: 'The Keys.'

'Whose Keys?'

'Queen Elizabeth's Keys.'

And the sentry replies 'Pass, Queen Elizabeth's Keys. All's well.'

After the sentry has presented arms as a compliment to the Queen's Keys the company moves on and meets the main guard waiting at the Broad Walk. The Escort halts and the main guard's officer commands that everyone should 'Present Arms'.

The Chief Warder steps two paces forward, doffs his Tudor bonnet and shouts 'God preserve Queen Elizabeth', to which the others say 'Amen.'

Behind the main guard the 'drummer' takes his bugle and with the first stroke of ten from the barracks clock blows the first notes of 'The Last Post'. After the call the Main Guard shoulders arms and the Chief Yeoman Warder collects his lantern from the Lantern Carrier and the company then marches to the Queen's House and leaves the Keys in safe custody for the night. Then his Escort and the Main Guard are 'dismissed to its duties'.

The whole ceremony takes ten minutes and is performed almost every night of the year.

THE SAVOY PALACE

Although the Savoy Palace is no more, the Savoy Hotel reminds us of an illustrious medieval building which once stood on the site. The founder was Peter de Savoy, brother to Boniface, Archbishop of Canterbury, and uncle to Eleanor, the queen of Henry III. He was created Earl of Savoy and Richmond and knighted in Westminster Abbey in 1245. By 1328 the Savoy Palace was the most splendid residence in London. When King John of France was defeated at the Battle of Poitiers the Black Prince brought him to London as his prisoner. King John was treated with respect and even reverence by the Black Prince, who allowed him to ride into the City on a magnificent cream coloured charger while he himself rode behind on a small black palfrey. John was given the Palace of Savoy to use as his London residence while the terms of his ransom were being worked out. The King and Queen of England fêted him and sent him presents and never before has a prisoner been so well treated. When the peace settlement was agreed upon John returned to France but to his chagrin his ransom money was not available. To everyone's surprise John turned up later in London, filled with mortification that his part of the bargain had not been kept. He was welcomed with open arms by Edward III and took up his final residence at the Savoy where he died a few months later. His body was conveyed to St. Denis in France.

In 1381 Wat Tyler and a hundred thousand desperate men gathered on Blackheath. They ransacked and burnt many grand houses and the Savoy Palace suffered more than most. Tyler

The Palace of Savoy

ordered his men to pillage and set fire to the building and destroy all valuables such as gems and silver plate. One man was caught trying to steal a silver salver for himself and this caused fury amongst his companions. They threw him screaming into the flames, crying as they did so: 'We are zealous of truth and justice, not thieves and robbers.' Certain barrels of gunpowder were found on the premises and, their contents unknown, were thrown on to the blaze. This resulted in a tremendous explosion which blew up the whole Palace; the miscreants hardly had time to escape the blast. It is said that 32 of the rebels entered the wine cellars and drank until they were besotted. When the explosion occurred they were buried alive under the rubble. Their cries for help were heard for a week but no one came to their aid until they were dead. The Palace remained in ruins until Henry VIII built a hospital on the site, which lasted until Charles II's time when he turned it into a military hospital and garrison. Later it was allowed to fall into disrepair and by the eighteenth century it was only a shell. Due to the reclamation of the river and the building of the Victoria Embankment the Savoy Hotel no longer overlooks the water as did its predecessor but is situated in the Strand.

ST. JAMES'S PARK AND PALACE

Although the Palace of Westminster and the Tower are still official palaces belonging to the Crown, it is many centuries since royalty lived in them. Both these monumental buildings were destined to play more meaningful roles in the history of Great Britain. There remain today three principal palaces in London which are the official town residences of the Queen and her family. These are St. James's Palace, Kensington Palace and Buckingham Palace.

The five central parks, common marshy land in Saxon times, were taken over by the monasteries at an early date. After the Norman invasion the monks grew rich and prosperous, enjoying the protection and privileges that the new regime offered. St. James's Park has links with the church dedicated to St. Peter, later to become Westminster Abbey. Although there was no known charter it was accepted by the populace that this area of land, covering roughly 93 acres, belonged to the mother church.

As there were many pools and small streams the monks founded holy wells and healing waters and the area became consecrated. Villagers treated the land as enchanted and were superstitious about crossing it. This attitude suited the clergy who preferred to keep the area as private as possible and discouraged common rights of way winding across it.

During the mid Saxon period the land was gradually drained by the monks until it became quite a reasonable and useful stretch of arable and grazing country. The pool in the centre was called at first Cowford probably named after a cow that had floundered in it which needed the construction of a ford to help in its rescue.

Under the auspices of the monastery a hospital was set up here by fourteen maidens suffering from leprosy. Six chaplains and two laymen were appointed to look after their wants. The maidens, all virgins, wished to live a life of chastity and devotion to God: to live in fact like the purest order of nuns. This they were able to do for even the pagan invaders who overran London from time to time would not venture near a leper hospital. The ladies studied the Scriptures and adopted St. James the Less as their patron as he spent so many hours each day kneeling or lying in prayer that the skin on his forehead was said to be as tough as camels' hooves! The community grew until in the time of Edward the Confessor the nuns were farming over 160 acres around the hospital. The King decreed that a fair was to be held annually on the Eve of St. James – 24 July – and that all the proceeds should be donated to the hospital. In addition, as was the practice in those days, all shops were ordered to close so that provisions had to be bought at the fair. Apparently there are two St. Jameses, both of whom were martyred, one with a sword and the other with a club. The King confused St. James the Less with St. James the Great and ordered that the fair should be held on the eve of the latter – when in reality the hospital was dedicated to St. James the Less whose saint day was 2 May. But in the long run the mistake was forgotten in the revels of the fair and nobody minded.

The pool and land was given to Henry VII by Abbot Islip at the beginning of the Tudor era. The pool became known as Rosamund's Pond and covered about five acres at the time. When Henry VIII came to power he lived in the Palace of Westminster and was not impressed with the leper hospital virtually on his doorstep and he tried in a subtle manner to have it removed elsewhere. He discovered that the hospital had been granted protection by Eton College and so made arrangements with the governors to have the establishment moved to Chatisham in Suffolk. He then claimed the building and land adjacent to his palace for his own use. After thorough fumigation he ordered the hospital to be pulled down and a royal palace to be built on the site. He had the land walled in and additions such as a bowling alley, tilting yards and cockpits were built. Henry was also fond of hunting and he arranged for the adjoining woods to be stocked with deer. The Palace was intended as a live in bower for Henry and Anne Boleyn and lovers' knots and the initials H.A. were inscribed on the doors and archways.

When James I came to the throne, he too lived at St. James's. He craved for a menagerie to compare favourably with the one at the Tower. Many animals were sent to him from different parts of the world including a leopard, two antelopes, hawks, a wild boar, flying squirrels, crocodiles, ducks and cormorants. It is not known how long these animals lived and it must be assumed that all but the hardy perished in the severe winter frosts. The greatest prize was an elephant costing £273 a year to feed. His keeper insisted that the beast be given a gallon of wine every morning during the cold weather – obviously thinking that alcohol would keep it from catching chills. He was paid well for looking after his charge – £250 per year – a fortune in those days.

A few lines of poetry from *Coryats Crudities* published in 1611 tells about the animals in St. James's Park.

St. James' his guinea hens, the Cassowary, moreover
The beaver in the Park (strange beast as ever any man saw,
Down shearing-willows, with teeth as sharp as handsaw).

The cassowary was explained as being an East Indian bird which could eat coals!

Near the Palace the King laid out a herb garden which he called his physic garden. James was very interested in the use of herbs as medicine. Lavender was also grown to keep clothes sweet. Numerous sprigs were put between layers of garments in chests and drawers – people did not wash clothes in those days. Later the phrase 'to lay in lavender' meant to pawn clothes – the articles being covered in lavender to keep a freshness about them. James also had the idea of keeping silk worms and for this planted mulberry trees. He had a grove of mulberry trees planted just north of Rosamund's Pond – on the present site of Buckingham Palace and there is still a mulberry tree surviving in the Palace gardens to this day. Unfortunately he bought the wrong kind of mulberry trees and the worms perished as the leaves did not suit them.

If the exotic animals died, the ducks did not. They thrived and multiplied and adopted a small island on Rosamund's Pond as their permanent home which came to be known as Duck Island. It became a well-known bird sanctuary and a small dwelling on the island was erected so that bird fanciers could watch in seclusion. Today Duck Island is famous for its starlings which have settled there in their thousands. Evelyn speaks of the pleasures of watching the birds in the Park and tells of a crane which had broken its leg above the joint and had a wooden one made for it by a soldier, The bird managed quite well on its artificial limb and lived for several years becoming a great attraction to visitors to the lake.

The game of 'paille maille' was introduced at this time by James I, the son of Mary, Queen of Scots, and the first alley lay next to the walk in the Park. According to J. M. Scott in his delightful *Book of Pall Mall* the game was a cross between croquet and golf. It originated in Italy where it was called *palla a maglio* and was a game using a mallet and ball. It spread to France and probably Mary Queen of Scots introduced it to Scotland when she returned there after the death of her first husband, the Dauphin. There is a tradition that this lady was the first to play golf in Scotland. According to a Frenchman named Joseph Lautier there were four forms of the game: *au rouet* – singles, *au partie* – two or more players on each side, *aux grands coups* – long driving, and *à la chicane* – in open country, which we may take as the origin of golf. The first three types were played on short, well tended alleys of grass or a surface of powdered sea shells. The boundaries were marked with fences and the balls were made from box wood. Although the size was not regulated they were usually roughly $2\frac{1}{2}$ ins in diameter. The mallets were more like polo sticks and a pair can be seen in the British Museum. The object of the game was to hit the ball from an iron peg at one end of the course and strike the peg at the other end and then back again hitting a central hoop or peg in as few strokes as possible.

During the Commonwealth the Park was neglected and the menagerie allowed to die out altogether. The deer and ducks were poached without mercy. When Charles II came to the throne, although he did not re-establish the menagerie, he did like dogs and had scores of them. He concentrated on improving the Park and employed Le Notre, the man who designed the gardens at Versailles to do the work. Shrubs and trees were planted and a canal was made which was the origin of the present lake. He also collected rare birds which he kept in cages along what is now known as Birdcage Walk. Charles constructed a new paille maille alley outside the walls of the royal park but he and his players had so much trouble with the dust and dirt thrown up by carts travelling on the route to Westminster that he decided to close the route, and allowed the road to run along the old Paille Maille on the north side. The new Pall Mall route did not stretch as far as the highway had done; and it ended abruptly at the corner of Green Park and travellers had to cut themselves a new route to join up with the old one leading out of London. The road was paved after it had been in use for a year and renamed Catharine Street after Charles's wife Catherine of Braganza – but the people of London still called it Pall Mall and it has been known as such ever since.

Soon it seemed every large estate in London had a paille maille alley and there were known to be three in Paris, at the Tuileries, but only London remembers the name of the game in modern times. The game of paille maille was revived with enthusiasm during the American War of Independence when the soldiers at Whitehall used to play it on the drill square in their spare time.

There is a story that when Charles I walked across the Park on his way to his execution at Whitehall, two women who kept a milk stall by the lake gave him a cup of milk. When Charles II came to the throne he rewarded the milk ladies by granting them a charter saying that they and their descendants should be allowed to keep a stall and two cows in the Park for as long as the family wished. The ladies' names were Mother Kitchen and Mother Bury, and it is said that a milk stall was still in evidence in the Park at the turn of the last century and that two cows grazed free of rent. The stall was famous for its syllabub, and the cry of the milk vendors' 'Buy a glass of red cow's milk' was part of the London scene. Morland endowed immortality on these two women when he made a print of them with their cows by the water in the Park.

The Earl of St. Albans and other wealthy men began to buy up property in Pall Mall and grand houses were built. The area was soon to be regarded as the aristocratic part of London. Nell Gwyn had a house here, number 79, and the site is now occupied by two insurance houses. Gainsborough lived in the street and also Admiral Pallister and Lady Emma Hamilton. In 1766 a man named James Christie opened auction rooms in the street. He was born in Scotland and it was rumoured that he was closely related to Flora MacDonald, the lady who helped Bonnie Prince Charlie to escape after the Battle of Culloden Moor. Later Christie moved to a house in King Street and of course Christie's is famous all over the world today. The street was well known for coffee houses and places where good food could be obtained and gradually the exclusive clubs – some of which still survive – came into being. A certain Captain Morris who lived from 1745 to 1838 was a noted high liver and frequented the clubs in Pall Mall. He loved London and wrote a poem of 19 verses about the City. This is the last stanza:

> In town let me live, then, in town let me die:
> For in truth I can't relish the country, not I.
> If one must have a villa in summer to dwell,
> Oh, give me the sweet shady side of Pall Mall.

The Royal Automobile Club, of which we shall hear more later, bought up buildings in Pall Mall in 1908 and 1911 and is still established in the street.

During the Regency period Nash redesigned the Park, making three terraces to flank Birdcage Walk, and built Wellington barracks. The roads were made fit to travel on with comfort. As Wren was to the City, so Nash, with the Prince Regent as his patron, was to the West End – although many of his designs have been destroyed or blatantly pulled down without any regard

94

to their beauty or historic value. Master Edward Storey was appointed the keeper of the King's birds and the entrance from Great George Street to St. James's Park is called Storey's Gate as he had a lodge there. Birdcage Walk was not open to the public until 1828 and the Park not until 1845. Even then the authorities were very particular as to who entered the Park. A workman dressed in his working clothes or a person carrying a parcel were not allowed to enter. It was still a rich man's playground. The blades of the day wore narrow trousers for the first time in the mid nineteenth century when walking down Pall Mall or in St. James's Park and this was considered just another foppish idea but the fashion has stayed until this very day.

'Given at our Court of St. James's'. This statement has been used in Royal decrees since 1697 when the Court was removed temporarily from Whitehall to St. James's Palace after a disastrous fire. It is said that Charles II and his brother James, later to become James II, often walked and talked in the private royal gardens. On more than one occasion James implored the King not to attempt to walk unguarded for fear of being attacked by footpads, The reply was less than gracious:

'Brother James, take care of yourself; no man will kill me to make you king.'

During the mid eighteenth century two gangs calling themselves the Mohawks and the Hawkubites terrorized people in the precincts of the Park. They went around slashing faces with razors, stealing, murdering and overturning carriages. The government was forced by public opinion to offer £100 reward for these criminals. They were eventually caught but justice was not seen to be done as they were found to be the sons of peers and judges and so only had small fines imposed upon them. Soldiers from barracks at Whitehall, when out of uniform, were also guilty of crimes of this sort.

St. James's Park became a quieter place after the opening of the Serpentine in Kensington Gardens. Commoners and gentry alike flocked to enjoy the new attraction. The Park was under the protection of royalty and people sought sanctuary in it – no one could be arrested for bankruptcy or embezzlement while he stayed in the Park. After the demise of William, Mary and Anne, all of whom had lived in Kensington Palace, the Hanoverian

Georges preferred to make St. James's their official London residence. George I could speak no English and there is rather a curious story concerning the customs practised at Lent in those times. Apparently a man was appointed as the King's cock crower and had to crow like a cockerel and pop into the room, like a cuckoo out of its clock in the King's presence at every hour during Lent. At the beginning of Lent on Ash Wednesday, George was sitting down to his evening meal when in burst the cock crower and crowed ten times to remind the King that it was ten o'clock. The King thought he was being made a fool of and was so shocked and insulted that it was with the utmost difficulty that an in-

The Palace Gate 1765, St. James's Palace

terpreter explained the reason for the intrusion. He said that the custom had been acted out for centuries and was to remind the King and his companions of Christ's sacrifice on the Cross. Needless to say the custom was discontinued after this incident. The Georges enjoyed their stay in the Palace and Queen Charlotte was very fond of the gardens. She had a pet swan named Jack which lived to be 70, and which fed every day with fresh white bread. But Jack was very fierce and killed not only other birds but dogs also. One day a pack of Polish geese set on him and pecked him to death – obviously tired of his bullying.

As the centuries passed the Palace was burnt down and rebuilt many times and today only the main gateway with the clock dates back to the original building. During its long history many courts with strange sounding names have been built within the main building. These are Engine Court, Colour Court, Ambassadors' Court and so on and each has its own special story to tell. In days gone by there were numerous rights of way for public use. More recently other additions have been made, such as Clarence House, which is the home of the Queen Mother. State secrets were discussed at the Palace and it became known as the Cabinet of St. James's and this is where the term 'Cabinet' stems from.

Up until 1907 the gentlemen-at-arms at the Palace were splendidly dressed soldiers. They were originally appointed as Henry VIII's bodyguard. In Queen Elizabeth's reign the members had to be very wealthy to be appointed to hold this coveted position – and had to have an income of at least £4000 per year – which was a fabulous amount in those days. The uniform was changed in 1862 and at one time the gentlemen-at-arms were mounted and had elegant costumes to match their mounts. Nowadays the same unit that guards St. James's also guards Buckingham Palace and the Tower.

GREEN PARK

Green Park, although the smallest of the London central parks, covering only 53 acres, has nevertheless known quite a turbulent history. Originally it was common land, marshy and wooded, where the locals could wander at will to collect berries, herbs, wild flowers and to replenish their larders with rabbits and wild duck. When Charles II came to the throne he had some of this land enclosed and it became known as Upper St. James's Park. He did not however go to the extent of landscaping the area and left it more or less as it had always been – a wild piece of common land and so it was named Green Park. It had no set pattern of flower beds as did the other parks, and the name has stuck throughout the years. Piccadilly was a rough lane called Pikadilla running through the area and it is here that Thomas Wyatt led his rebellion across the dry ditches of the Park. The outcome was that Wyatt and some of his followers ended up on the gallows and Lady Jane Grey and her husband were murdered.

After the Civil War, Cromwell, known as the Great Leveller, ordered that no revels should take place in parks or elsewhere. But he had no answer to the reactions of the citizens of London to his orders. They decided to wear the brightest colours imaginable and to parade, dressed as bright as peacocks, in all public parks. For a while Green Park was a mass of people dressed in all the hues of the rainbow in retaliation to the puritanical regime.

Queen Caroline, wife of George II, had a passion for designing parks and after planning alterations to Kensington Gardens and the Serpentine she turned her attention to Green Park, which she thought was in need of 'tidying up'. She first planned a wide pathway which she called 'Queen's Walk' and then had a pavilion erected which she called her library. Near by was an ice house – the mount of which could still be seen opposite 119 Piccadilly in the mid twenties. A Temple of Peace was built in the Park as part of the celebrations to mark the end of the War of Succession. It was planned to hold a firework display and the fireworks were stored in the Temple. On the opening day the Temple was burnt down and the fireworks exploded, resulting in many injuries. A young girl was severely burnt and a drunken cobbler fell into the central marsh and was drowned. The Temple of Peace had cost £90,000 to build and was destroyed before it was ever used.

George II held a spectacular parade of Dragoons in Green Park during his reign. He was in a bad temper for one reason or another and insisted that all the Dragoons should turn out – whether alive, sick or dead. Thus the sick were represented by their horses with riding boots in the stirrups pointing forward and the dead were represented by the boots pointing backwards.

The Park was a favourite place for duels in the eighteenth century and they were usually fought over a woman. The most romantic that I have come across occurred between two gentlemen, called Vittorio Alfieri and Viscount Ligonier. Ligonier's wife was Alfieri's mistress and the husband became so jealous that he challenged the lover to a duel. He called on Alfieri when he was going to the opera and as they were both wearing evening suits and carrying swords they decided to fight it out in the meadow next to St. James's Park – Green Park. Although Alfieri had suffered a broken clavicle only two days previously he insisted on going on with the duel. Ligonier wounded his opponent and strode away. After Alfieri had been attended to by his second, he decided to go on to the opera for the last act. When the show was over he was taken to the house of a friend and who should be there but his mistress, who was only too happy to dress his wounds. In the divorce proceedings that followed it was learnt that the wife had been having a much more passionate affair with her groom. Both husband and lover concluded that women were not worth bothering about and they became good friends.

During the nineteenth century the craze for ballooning began and Green Park became the home ground for balloon ascents. Cartoonists of the day were quick to take up the new sport and make fun of it. At one time this new idea of air transport included ascending in a balloon carriage, astride a horse! One such man and his steed stayed up for an hour and a half. Is this a record, I wonder?

Three times in 1840 attempted assassinations of Queen Victoria took place on Constitution Hill which forms one of the boundaries of the Park. And in 1930 an attempt was made to take the life of Edward, Prince of Wales in roughly the same place.

During victory celebrations after the last war the crowd in the Park let their hair down and made bonfires out of park benches and railings. They also tossed naked girls in blankets – a thing which shocked some members of the public – especially as the venue was so near Buckingham Palace!

The celebration of the emancipation of slavery was held by troops in Green Park at the beginning of the twentieth century.

A contingent of soldiers in full dress uniform marched from Victoria to Hyde Park and thence to Green Park, headed by a negro boy richly dressed in satins embroidered with gold. The street children, pale, starved and ragged, ran along the pavements to keep up with the splendid and costly display. Such was the irony of the spread of wealth in those days.

HYDE PARK

The word hyde is the Saxon term for a portion of land and also has strong links with the Greek word hudor which means water. So it is more than likely that the original 'hyde' described a watery or marshy piece of land. In the Domesday Book the Manor of Hyde is recorded as part of the Estate of Eia. There were sheep tracks which stretched to the Manors of Neyte (Pimlico) and Eabury (Chelsea). In the tenth century the property was bequeathed to the monks of Westminster, by one Geoffrey de Madeville in return for Masses to be said for him before and after his death. He was known as the Anglo-Saxon Master of Horse and his steeds were kept on this land. It was wild countryside in those days and inhabited by wolves which, being a constant menace to the traveller, were hunted down by the Saxon lords led by Geoffrey de Madeville. The lower, southern, part of the land was marshy and consisted of eleven pools, commonly called 'drips'. The upper, northern, slopes were wooded and known as 'folds' and the monks set to work to cut down some of the trees and make a causeway over the pools, draining the land as best they could. The Serpentine now lies where the pools once were and the stumps of trees felled by the monks can still be seen by the aqua diver. The drained land was used for arable farming and soon fields were yielding barley, wheat and purple clover. The honey produced on the Hyde had a special flavour and was a great favourite with royalty. Up to the Dissolution the Manor of Hyde brought in an annual income of £14. When Henry VIII took over the land and property he used it for hunting and tournaments. The woods were already conveniently stocked with deer and buck – especially around the stream called the Eye Burn. Elizabeth too used the area for tournaments and horse racing –

but it was not open to the public until 1637, just before the Civil War. On an urn on the east side of the lake is an inscription that indicates that a conduit was set up on the spot by Edward the Confessor to supply water to Westminster Abbey. Henry did not interfere with this and his daughter Elizabeth issued a charter authorizing the continued supply of water to the Abbey in 1560.

After the Civil War Cromwell used the Park to review his troops – sweet revenge for the times when Charles I did the same. After the Park had been opened to the public it became a great social centre where the rich and élite met to drive around and show off themselves and their possessions. A place known as the Ring was set up where horse-drawn carriages drove round and round. Not to be outdone Cromwell himself used the Ring but met with an unfortunate accident there one day. While driving a coach and six he was thrown and dragged in the mud for about a quarter of a mile before he could release his foot which had been caught in the cross bar. To top it all, his pistol exploded in his pocket during the incident. This was too good for the Royalists to miss and according to Neville Braybrook in his book *London Green* these lines appeared on a broadsheet the next day:

> Every day and hour has shown the power
> And now he has shown as his art.
> His first reproach was a fall from a coach,
> And his next will be from a cart.

Under the Puritans the Park, like all the others, became a morbid and depressing place; no revels or entertainments were allowed and a toll of a shilling for a coach and sixpence for a horse was charged at the entrances. But by May 1654 the populace had had enough of these restrictions and a huge contingent of gallants, beautiful women, fiddlers and the like descended on the Park and no one attempted to stop them. It was rumoured that even Cromwell was in their midst.

Hurling, the forerunner of rugby, was a favourite game to be played in the Park at this time. The players were divided into two teams and the object of the game was to get the ball into a goal – the goals being two or three miles apart. The ball was often coloured in gold or silver to represent the sun or the moon, and was passed from one team member to another. When in possession of the ball a tackle was made by the opposition and this seemed to be the essence of the game as there were often eight or nine wrestling matches going on at the same time!

When the monarchy was restored Hyde Park and the Ring became more popular than ever with the dandies of the Court, royalty, and ladies parading in their finery. Pepys records many good days spent watching the parades. Stalls selling refreshments, including syllabub, sprang up and in Queen Anne's time there was a small but élite market serving the aristocracy. Remnants of the Ring can be seen today as vehicles circle the circumference of the Park. Years ago a foreigner remarked that Hyde Park was indeed a strange mixture for not only did royalty and the upper classes visit it, but not far away sheep, cattle and pigs grazed, cared for by the yokels, and often intermingled with the coaches.

The asthmatic William III moved to Kensington Palace with his wife, Queen Mary, not long after they had been crowned at Whitehall, in the hope that the purer air would benefit his health. In those days footpads and thieves were numerous in the parks and it was dangerous to go out alone at night. William had 300 lanterns put up in Hyde Park to show the way after dark. His route from Whitehall was soon dubbed La Route du Roi – the royal way – and it became known by the locals as Rotten Row, a name that has survived. It is now used as a track for horse riders.

Charles Withers designed the Serpentine at the wishes of Queen Caroline, and its shape, although built in a curve, does not live up to its name. The lake covers 40 acres and is supplied by the river Westbourne. It was dredged and cleaned during the mid nineteenth century when hundreds of skeletons of babies and young children were found. The lake was obviously a favourite spot to dispose of unwanted illegitimates. During the cleansing operation the sewerage which had hitherto drained into the lake was diverted into different channels. Fishing in the lake was allowed in those days for those who purchased a licence, and while the cleaning was being carried out the fish were caught, put into water tanks and transported to the Round Pond in Kensington Gardens. There is no fishing allowed in the Serpentine today.

Queen Caroline wanted to enclose all the London Parks and make them the private property of royalty once again. She summoned the Prime Minister, Sir Robert Walpole, and inquired how much the undertaking would cost. His reply, so we are led to believe, was, 'Three Crowns, Ma'am – England's, Scotland's and Ireland's.' Caroline had to be content with fencing off a part of Hyde Park which then became private land for those who lived in Kensington Palace and known as Kensington Gardens.

The well preserved bridge over the Serpentine was designed by Sir George Rennie who, with his brother, built London Bridge which was opened by William IV in 1832. The Serpentine bridge was built in 1826 and still serves the public.

The northern landmark of Hyde Park is Marble Arch, designed by John Nash and built in 1821 out of solid marble from Servezza. It was originally intended as a grand entrance to Buckingham Palace, but became the cause of much embarrassment when it was found that it was just a few inches too small to allow the State coach to pass through. It was then moved to the northern boundary of Hyde Park in 1851 and served as an entrance until 1908 when its use there was abandoned due to concentrated heavy traffic in that part of London. So Marble Arch remains on an island with gates firmly shut, a beloved white elephant which is now just part of the London scene. Near the Arch is a small plaque which marks the spot where the gallows of Tyburn once stood. Quite a number of common criminals could be hanged on the Tyburn tree at the same time in days gone by. They were brought in tumbrels from Newgate prison along Oxford Street, which was named Tyburn Street in those days. The spectacle of the hangings was regarded as good entertainment by the locals and on special occasions platforms were built for viewing and tickets sold for the pleasure of witnessing these gruesome scenes. The highwayman Jack Sheppard gave good value for money at his hanging by picking the chaplain's pocket of a corkscrew and dying with it in his hand. The last peer to be hanged here was Earl Ferrers wearing his wedding clothes! He insisted on being executed with a silken cord as was the privilege of gentry. The executions at Tyburn ceased in 1783 but were still carried out in public outside Newgate prison. Later, the death penalty was enacted in private in a more civilized manner. A man named George Selwyn boasted that he had never missed an execution at Tyburn in 40 years. He witnessed the last and one wonders what he did for entertainment after that!

When it was decided not to use the Tyburn tree as a gallows the people of Hyde felt that they had lost a focal point and meeting place. Old habits die hard and the northern part of the Park continued to be used for public meetings when there seemed a grievance to air. In 1855 a group of shopkeepers gathered to protest against the Sunday trading bill which had recently been passed by Parliament. Small traders relied on Sunday trading for a good percentage of their profit and the public were also enraged by the inconvenience caused by the Act. A request to hold a seminar was refused by the then Commissioner of Police, Sir Richard Mayne. A month or so later a carpenter decided to call a meeting, without asking permission, which passed off quietly without any interference from the police. He then decided to call another a month later but this time there were riots and the police were called in to maintain order. The site near Marble Arch was becoming well known as a public place of oratory, similar to St. Paul's Cross many centuries before. Rallies became organized, some in connection with home affairs and others with events abroad such as the efforts of Garibaldi in Italy. By now a society known as the Reform League had been formed and the committee approached the Commissioner for permission to hold another mass rally. This was refused as other rallies had resulted in bloodshed. Nevertheless, nothing daunted, the band of reformers marched to the Park only to find the gates barred by the police who had been tipped off beforehand. Furiously, railings were torn up and the marchers entered the Park by force and proceeded to demonstrate loudly under a tree which from then on became known as the Reformers' tree. The police tried to stop the demonstration but there followed a bloody battle from which they were forced to retire. After consultations with the Commissioner of Works it was arranged that a venue be officially assigned for public meetings, roughly a hundred yards from the tree under which the battle had taken place. This came to be known as Orators' or Speakers' Corner and the permission was granted in 1872. Bonar Thompson, a speaker for many years, wrote a book about his experiences. Thompson would only accept voluntary contributions and then always outside the Park gates, but other speakers were well paid by influential people to promote ideas and sometimes stir up trouble amongst the listening audience. Neville Braybrook, in his book *London Green*, relates that a man named Harry Diamond was a speaker in Hyde Park for five years prior to 1958. He gave this advice to hecklers: 'Get near enough to the speaker to shout him down – and far enough away so that he can't hit you!' In the early nineteen fifties the evangelist Billy Graham preached in the Park, and so too did another man, Prince Monolulu, remembered by many as a very colourful character, dressed in rich robes with gorgeous plumage upon his head, who was a speaker for a long period during the first half of the last century.

The Great Exhibition, the first international trade fair held in Britain, was staged in Hyde Park, and opened on 1 May 1851, under the patronage of Prince Albert, Consort to Queen Victoria. The great Crystal Palace was built for the Exhibition in the Park and was in itself a marvellous piece of architecture built almost entirely of glass. There were over three thousand people in the Park to witness the opening and representatives of most countries in the world were invited to attend. The scientific discoveries of four continents were on display. There was a glass fountain, palm trees of all kinds and exotic flowers and shrubs. The Exhibition lasted six months and a profit of over £165,000 was made. It was decided that the money should be used to build a museum in South Kensington – the Natural History Museum. This too was a project sponsored by Prince Albert. The glass palace was dismantled after the Exhibition and re-erected at Sydenham but unfortunately was accidentally burnt down in 1936.

Prince Albert died ten years after the opening of the Exhibition, in 1861 and his memorial statue, a very grand affair, was built on the east side of Kensington Gardens looking south at the Albert Hall and the museums at South Kensington. He holds an Exhibition catalogue in his hands, not a Bible as many people are led to believe. Work on the memorial was started in 1864 and took twelve years to complete. During that time workmen engaged on the project had many succulent meals served up to them on trestle tables made from scaffolding planks. Beef, mutton, plum pudding and cheese were supplied as well as ale, or ginger beer for the abstainers. The Queen herself organized this fare, and insisted that Grace was said before every meal. These banquets were greatly appreciated by the workmen, many of whom had never tasted such good food before. The statue was designed by Sir Gilbert Scott and is very impressive, with a canopy over the figure of Albert to protect him from the dirt and grime of London.

The dogs' cemetery, founded by the Duke of Richmond in 1880 for one of his wife's pets, is situated at the north-west flank of the Park. Prior to the First World War dogs, cats and birds were buried here and some of the epitaphs are endearing. A quote from Shakespeare reads 'After life's fitful slumber, he sleeps well'. The dead animals came from wealthy homes and the upkeep and price of a memorial stone was high. Lack of space prevents animals being buried here in modern times.

KENSINGTON PALACE AND GARDENS

Kensington Palace, originally the country home of the Earl of Nottingham, may be described as a rather homely building, designed partly by Wren and partly by Kent. It became the London dwelling of William and Mary after their accession to the throne. Mary died from smallpox in 1694 and William was killed in a riding accident in 1702. There is a statue of William outside the south front of the Palace. Mary's sister Anne succeeded to the throne and the Palace then became her London residence. She was a great lover of gardens, consequently becoming known as the Great Flora, and designed the Orangery and a fascinating sunken garden complete with fountains and small streams. In fact each monarch who lived here had the buildings altered to suit his or her individual taste.

George II and his Queen Caroline preferred this royal dwelling to St. James's Palace and lived here most of their time in London. The Queen fenced in the gardens and then planted a group of elm trees which were said to be the exact pattern of the massing of the Guards at the Battle of Blenheim when John Churchill, Duke of Marlborough, personally led his troops and was victorious against the French in 1704. Owing to disease the elms were cut down roughly 50 years ago and now have been replaced by limes.

Queen Victoria was born in Kensington Palace and lived there as a child and it was here that the Archbishop of Canterbury awoke the nineteen-year-old Princess early one morning to tell her that she was Queen of England. One of the first things the new queen did was to open the gardens to the public. Although this brought pleasure to thousands it also brought thieves and footpads and the down-and-outs. The shelters in the Orangery became known as 'cough holes' where homeless people, often stricken with disease, huddled against the cold and damp. Park rangers were employed in an attempt to control the vagrants and the Park was closed at sundown. Before she died, Queen Victoria ordered the opening to the public of some of the rooms in Kensington Palace and later the London Museum was housed here (except for certain periods during both world wars when it was transferred to Lancaster House) until it was moved to the Barbican. During the last war the Palace was taken over by the military and the Gardens used for drill. There was one order that every soldier had to obey and that was to duck through the hooped archway which had been built to suit the height of Queen Victoria and has always been kept that way. Today Kensington Palace is the town residence of Princess Margaret and other members of the Royal Family.

A great attraction in the Gardens is the Round Pond, a good place in which to sail boats, and watch many species of water birds. In days gone by ravens and kites scavenged the area; now it is the gulls which circle around looking for food, to remind us that London is still a port with access to the sea. Years ago the Park offered different picnic areas for rich and poor. Those with money and food brought their picnics – two meals to last all day – and were allowed to sit near St. Govor's Well where the grass was lush and green. The well, now covered, was named by Sir Benjamin Hall, of Big Ben fame, after the patron saint of Llanover. Sir Benjamin was the first Commissioner of Works, 1855–58, and was later given the title of Lord Llanover. The well marked the spot of an ancient spring, and is now a drinking fountain with a commemorative plaque to be found just east of Broad Walk. The poorer people who entered the Park were told to sit on the north side where the grass was thin and bare patches of gravel were predominant.

The gardens of the Palace are of special interest to children.

The success of Sir James Barrie's book *Peter Pan* is recalled forever by the statue of the boy who never grew up which was designed by Sir George Frampton and unveiled in 1912. Peter Pan is poised playing on his pipe – reminiscent of the god Pan. He is surrounded by fairies, animals and an adoring Wendy and this surely must be the special place for children to visit when in London. Next to the dogs' cemetery is the children's playground with swings that were originally given by Sir James Barrie. Here, too, is the Elfin Oak – a shaped wonder of wood carved by Ivor Innes from half a tree stump found in Richmond Park in 1930. It shows an owl wearing a mortar board and gown and elves and dwarfs in abundance. It has a mystical quality about it that attracts children of all ages. It was renovated in 1966 and the plaque says that the work was done by fairies but those in the know think that Spike Milligan had something to do with it.

BUCKINGHAM PALACE

Buckingham House, the predecessor of Buckingham Palace, was built on the site of a residence known as Goring House belonging to Hugh Audley. To the west was a cherry orchard and kitchen garden. Some historians think that Goring House was a place of disrepute. It was pulled down in 1703 and John Sheffield, Duke of Buckingham, purchased the land and had a house built there designed by William Winde. Winde was an exiled royalist and had been brought up in Holland, where he was greatly influenced by Dutch architecture. The house was much admired for its two clock towers and soon became a model for many Georgian houses. George III purchased the property in 1762 as a town dwelling for Queen Charlotte and they occupied it as a private, rather than a State residence.

The building of the present Palace was started in 1821 under the orders of George IV. John Nash was employed to plan a pleasing building and he designed it on the lines of Palladian architecture. When Queen Victoria ascended the throne in 1837 it became the official London residence of the monarch and has remained so ever since. Nash retained the shell of the red brick old building and much of the plan – although the facing stone

was changed to Bath stone. He designed the new building round
a three-sided court open on the east, in the front of which stood
Marble Arch. The façade of the east wing was rebuilt in Portland
stone in 1913 as part of a scheme that included the erection of
the Queen Victoria memorial beyond the forecourt of the Palace.
The Palace yard is nowadays patrolled by sentries of the Guards
division in full dress uniform. On most days the colourful
ceremony of the Changing of the Guard is performed and a
Guards' band plays. When the Queen is in residence the Royal
Standard, her personal flag, flies at the mast head. With the
exception of the Queen's Gallery and the Royal Mews the Palace
in not open to the public.

There are over 300 rooms in the Palace. The state apartments
are in the west wing and are approached by the Grand Hall and
the Grand Staircase with its marble stairway and gilded bronze
balustrading. The largest room is the Ballroom which was built
for Queen Victoria in the 1850s. It is lit by six immense chandeliers
in the form of crystal bowls. The room contains the Throne Dais
at one end and at the other an organ and musicians' gallery. State
balls, banquets and investitures are held here. The Blue Drawing
Room, which was the ballroom before the present one was built,

is said by some to be the most beautiful room in the Palace. The 'Table of the Commanders' is here and was made for Napoleon I in 1812. It is composed of green and gold Sèvres porcelain. After the defeat of Napoleon at Waterloo in 1813 the table was presented to George IV, then Prince Regent. The White Drawing room is a white and gold room with delicate yellow upholstery and curtains and a marvellous flowered carpet. The furniture includes many fine examples of English Regency and French craftmanship. The Throne Room, with a marble frieze depicting the Wars of the Roses of fifteenth century England is lit by seven cut-glass chandeliers and the thrones on the dais were used by George VI and Queen Elizabeth (the present Queen Mother) at their coronation in 1937. Those on either side were used by George V and Queen Mary in 1911. The ivory and gold Music Room, used by Victoria and Albert for musical evenings, has a domed ceiling and a half-dome over the bow; the elaborately moulded plaster work is richly gilded. The two cut-glass chandeliers are the finest in the Palace.

The Queen's private apartments are in the north wing and the east wing is mainly used as guest rooms on occasions such as State visits. When the east wing was added, George IV's oriental pavilion at Brighton was sold to contribute to the cost. Much Chinese-style furniture was available and two porcelain pagodas with mirror-glass doors stand at the end of the principal corridors of Buckingham Palace. As with all main corridors in the Palace it serves as a gallery displaying portraits and other works of art. The Balcony Room is hung with fine embroidered panels of old Chinese silk of imperial yellow, and the central window is used by the royal family to step on to the balcony on important occasions when crowds gather before the Palace, such as the Silver Jubilee in 1977 and more recently the wedding of Prince Charles and Lady Diana.

It has been a tradition for many years for private concerts to be given at the Palace to entertain the royal family and their guests. In Edwardian times and earlier, the performers usually came from Covent Garden opera house. The performers could ask for big money, perhaps £200 per performance, and Paderewski, the famous pianist, was often paid double this amount.

Edward VII would rise at five most mornings to sign documents and to attend to state matters in general. He valued his leisure time and in this way had much of the rest of the day to himself. He travelled in Europe a good deal and became known as Edward the Peacemaker. He was interested in all exhibitions held in London and did his best to open and to visit as many of them as he could. Edward treasured a quaint old desk owned by his father and inherited over forty years before he came to the throne. It was of a pedestal design and could only be opened by a gold key which he took everywhere with him. The desk contained his private and personal papers and letters which were seen by no one else. One of the rules that Victoria had imposed on her family was that no person of royal descent should dine in a public restaurant. This was most annoying and irksome for the Prince and was soon abandoned when Edward came to the throne. Although he and his Queen, Alexandra, attended many weddings the King made it a rule never to attend funerals of his friends. Christenings, on the other hand, were frequently attended by members of the royal family, who were and still are asked to be Godparents to a number of children.

The Palace gardens, covering some 45 acres, extend to Hyde Park Corner and were laid out for George IV by W. T. Aiton. They comprise a lake, lawns, paths and a large variety of flowers and trees, including the mulberry tree planted by James I. The Châlet in the grounds, a favourite play place for royal children, was renovated in Edward VII's time. In those days the king had his own special watermen dressed in splendid uniforms when on duty ready to take the king and his party on the lake or river. Nowadays the gardens provide the venue of royal garden parties at which the Queen, the Duke of Edinburgh and other members of the royal family meet some of the 22,000 or more guests of many nationalities and walks of life.

The south wing of the Palace contains the Queen's Gallery which was opened to the public in 1962 to display art treasures from the royal collection. The small chapel within is screened off from public view.

The Royal Mews or Stables on the south side of the gardens can be viewed by the public twice a week. They were designed by John Nash and completed in 1825. The Gold State Coach with panels painted by the artist from Florence, Cipriani, is the most spectacular exhibit. It is made of gilded oak and was completed in 1762 and used for the coronation of George IV in 1820 and for all coronations since. Four Tritons support the coach body, eight palm trees form the framework and the nine Cipriani panels depict scenes from the parables. On the roof are three cherubs representing the essence of England, Scotland and Ireland. The harness is made of red morocco and the whole coach weighs almost 4 tons. Many other coaches and carriages can be seen including a miniature barouche presented to the children of Victoria in 1846 and used by successive royal children since. The Irish Coach which was built in 1852 by the Lord Mayor of Dublin, M. Hutton, was bought by Queen Victoria when she visited Dublin. She only used it twice; both occasions were the opening of Parliament, in 1887 and again in 1897. Later sovereigns have driven in the Coach to open Parliament, and it is also used at royal weddings and funerals. The wooden body was originally painted maroon but many varnishings have given it a black appearance. The coach is drawn by four or six horses. Queen Victoria's State Sledge is on display together with other royal sleighs. The Mews houses one of the finest collections of State harnesses and saddlery to be seen in the world today. The famous horses, such as the Windsor Greys and the Cleveland Bay carriage horses, can be viewed and the royal cars can also be seen here.

REGENT'S PARK

This Park, probably the most gracious of all the London Parks, is the most recent. It was however one of the royal hunting grounds in the Middle Ages, and a mound was built to keep the animals in and the poachers out. Lodges were also built in those early days for the gamekeepers who were paid 4d per day to apprehend thieves and poachers. Before the Civil War Charles I had 1,000 trees cut down in this area to provide timber for the navy. The Park was designed by John Nash in 1812 for the Prince Regent, after whom it was named, and was planned as being the culmination of Regent's Street, where the Regent lived, Portland Place and Regent's Crescent. The Prince Regent originally planned to build a palace in the Park but this did not materialize. The

Park covers approximately 400 acres and is roughly circular in shape. Regent's Canal, about which there is more later, was built in the Park in 1820 and connects the Grand Junction Canal at Paddington with the Thames at Wapping.

The zoo is, of course, the main attraction in the Park and was founded by the Zoological Society in 1829 – by private donors. At first it was just a private collection of animals, some having come from the menagerie in the Tower on the orders of the Duke of Wellington, and others coming from St. James's Park. It proved such an attraction that it was soon opened for public viewing on certain days during the summer months. The wide variety of animals was amazing right from the beginning. Every animal had its cage and keeper who was dressed in uniform as they are today. The cages and conditions were not so conducive to the well-being of the animals as they are in modern times, but nevertheless Regent's Park zoo became world famous and even from its inception had considerable success in the breeding of some species.

In 1836 a chimpanzee was brought to the Park which was the first to be seen in these lands. He did not last long however, because of the cold climate, but attracted thousands of people during his short life. They laughed at his antics and poets and wits of the day had plenty of material to write about. One, Theodore Hook, wrote in *Blackwood's magazine* of the time when four prominent men in the Cabinet, namely Lord Melbourne, Lord John Russell, Lord Palmerston and Lord Glenelg, the Speaker of the House, went to the zoo to see Tommy the chimpanzee. As a Tory supporter Hook wrote and published the following:

> Lord John came up the other day,
> Attended by a lady gay.
> 'Oh dear!' he cried, 'How like Lord T.!
> I can't bear to look at this chimpanzee.'
> The lady said with a tender smile,
> For all his sorrows to beguile,
> 'Oh, never mind, Lord John: to me
> You are not in the least like a chimpanzee!'
>
> Glenelg mooned up to see the brute,
> Of distant climes and rarest fruit,

And said to the keeper, 'Stir him up for me:
He seems but an indolent chimpanzee.'
Says the keeper, 'My Lord, his is a snug berth –
He never does nothing whatever on earth:
But his brother Bob, who is over the sea,
Is a much more sprightly chimpanzee.'

The Speaker next, to make him stare,
Proceeded, dressed as he is in the Chair;
When Tommy saw him, such a scream raised he
As had never been heard from a chimpanzee.
'What's the matter, Mr. Keeper?' the Speaker cried,
'Why, really, Mr. Speaker' the man replied,
'I hope no offence, but I think that he
Takes you for the late Mrs. Chimpanzee.'

The animals adapted themselves to caged conditions amazingly well. One old bear used to amuse the crowds by slipping his paw beneath one of the bars of his cage and rattling it which produced a loud tinkling noise and for this he usually received buns as a reward. The Indian rhinoceros, Jim, was the longest living inmate in the early days – he died in 1908 and had been at the zoo since 1864. The elephant and the rhinoceros were allowed in the same pen and became good friends. When the elephant took a bath with the rhino, he delighted the crowds by scrubbing the rhino's back for him. On the other hand alligators that turned nasty towards one another were muzzled with ropes. The giraffe house, which at one time housed as many as five of the animals, attracted much attention. On the whole people had never seen wild animals before and the tall giraffe was so unlike anything they had ever imagined that for many years it was thought by the community that they came from a different planet. Another attraction was an orang-utan, a quiet affectionate specimen who would hug and kiss her keeper, put on the clothes provided for her and drink a cup of tea with such human-like movements that the crowd could not believe their eyes. The keeper sat at the table and seemingly conversed with the animal in low tones. This surely was the forerunner of the chimpanzees' tea party which has been a popular event in modern times.

Queen Victoria presented the zoo with rare birds and in 1875 an extensive addition to the gardens was made by purchasing land on the north side of the canal which is crossed by a bridge, thus allowing an additional entrance to be opened for public use. In 1876 the Prince of Wales returned from India with a collection of animals for the zoo, including tiger cubs, goats, sheep, dwarf oxen and dwarf elephants. The new arrivals were housed temporarily in sheds in the extended part of the gardens. Nowadays a bird sanctuary, designed and opened by Lord Snowdon, occupies much of the land over the canal and is enclosed so that the individual species are maintained.

In Edwardian times the Zoological Society consisted of over 3,000 members. Sunday visits were free to those belonging to the Society and a liberal number of tickets was issued for them and their friends. Monday was half-price day for the public, when tickets were reduced to 1s 6d for adults. The zoo employed over a hundred people and today it employs over a thousand.

In modern times the Park is surrounded by a carriage way named the Outer Circle which is connected with the Inner Circle by two roads. The Inner Circle was originally a sawdust track used for horse riding. Within the Inner Circle is a beautiful part of the Park, known as Queen Mary's Garden as it was devoted to the growing of roses, her favourite flower, which became a spot very dear to her. The Garden was taken over by the Royal Botanic Society in 1932 and replanned. It now includes a small lake and an island rock garden devoted to the growing of alpines and miniature perenials. The boating lake in the Park covers 22 acres and is a popular attraction. On the north side is an open air theatre and many performances are given here in the summer including Shakespeare's plays – the most usual being *A Midsummer-Night's Dream*.

5

Money, Merchants and Mayors

The Romans minted the first coins in this land. The early ones were in the shape of rings and many have been found in the London area. For many centuries silver was the most popular metal and was mined in Devon, Cornwall and Wales from early times. In 1296 it is recorded that Edward I received 704 lbs of silver from Devonshire alone, and silver was mined in the West Country until the reign of George I.

The first silver penny was minted in the reign of Ina, king of the West Saxons, between 679 and 726 and was revived later during the reign of King Alfred. The penny was in fact a measure of weight and the term pennyweight is still used in colloquial terms to this day. The signs for pounds – £ or l for sterling and lb for weight – are derived from the same source – the Latin word *libra*. Our coinage, up to 1971, was measured in £.s.d., the s. standing for *solidi* meaning solid silver and the d. for *denarius*, which was an old Roman coin. The word pound also comes from the Latin, *pondo*. From early times there were two systems of weight: troy weight, used for gold, silver and gems and avoirdupois weight used for ordinary goods. A grain was a measure of weight also and in troy weight there were 24 grains to a pennyweight, 20 pennyweights to 1 ounce and 12 ounces to 1 pound, or lb. Therefore, from Saxon times up to 1971, there were 240 pennies in £1 sterling. In avoirdupois weight 16 ozs equalled 1 lb and this too remained constant until the metric system took over.

King John first introduced the term sterling to this country. He asked German money advisers to come over to England to help regulate the silver coinage which up to then had been very unreliable. The Germans were called Easterlings having originally come from a commercial confederacy formed on the eastern shores of the Baltic in the eighth century. Pennant, a writer in Elizabethan times, describes the Easterlings as 'our masters in the art of commerce'. They settled in an alley near St. Paul's called Old Change and were known as the Hanseatics, forming the Hanseatic League. The term hanse is synonymous with gild or guild and it is round about this time that the first guilds were formed in London – influenced by the Easterlings who had such organizations back in Germany. In fact King John in his charter to Dunwich says 'We grant them a Hanse' – meaning a charter to form a guild. To induce the Easterlings to stay in London they were allowed to import and export goods to and from London, paying only one per cent tax.

Up to Edward I's reign all coins had been minted square but according to an old legend coins would be minted round when the Prince of Wales was crowned king of England in Westminster Abbey. After the defeat of Llywelyn in Wales his severed head was brought to Westminster Abbey on the orders of Edward and crowned with willow and flower garlands. Then the first round silver halfpennies and farthings were minted. Later, in 1346, during Edward III's reign, the first gold coins were made and they were called farthing nobles or ferthings. In this reign too, small gold coins from Florence made their appearance on the English scene and were called Florins and had the same weight and value as six silver shillings. It was not long before baser metals were used to eke out the gold and silver coins in common use, and copper coins that we know in the twentieth century were first minted in the shape of farthings and halfpennies in the reign of Charles I. He was very short of cash and seized all the money in the Mint – which incidentally belonged to the merchants of London – and this, coupled with other acts of folly, brought about the Civil War. The figure of Britannia, prominent on coins that we know today, was modelled on a lady called Frances Stuart, who afterwards became the Duchess of Richmond.

Other sources of gold bullion were ready made. In 1842 China paid Britain two million dollars ransom money in gold and silver. It was packed in chests and escorted by the 32nd Regiment and passed over London Bridge on its way to the Bank after being unloaded from her Majesty's ship 'Conway'. It was melted down and used as currency. Many a pirate ship in the past was raided by our navy for its cargo of gold and silver to replenish the English mint. The first official mint was established in the Tower by William the Conqueror. Queen Elizabeth I was advised by her counsellors to recall all old currency and have it melted down to provide newly minted coins. The melted basic metal gave off such pungent fumes that men employed in the work became ill. They were advised by a doctor to drink river water out of a skull to alleviate their distress. They duly crossed London Bridge, so we are told, and having obtained skulls that were spiked on the gates, scooped up some of the river water and drank. The remedy was not successful and most of the men died.

In 1811 a new mint was opened on Tower Hill. Previous to this all coins had been fashioned by hand but the new premises had elaborate machinery – for those days – to produce coins *en masse*. This mint could receive as much as £50,000 of gold bullion one morning and return it the next morning in the shape of coins. The money then had to undergo the trial of the Pix, meaning testing the weight to ascertain that the correct amount of metal was incorporated into each coin. The Goldsmiths' company and others were responsible for this trial and they made up the Privy Council which had to be present at the weighing. The use of gold in currency was withdrawn in 1914 but gold is kept in the form of ingots at the Bank of England as reserve money for the country and government. The words mint and money come from the Latin *moneta*.

The Jews, who first lived on our shores in mid Saxon times, were encouraged to settle in London by William I who had a great respect for their business acumen and the way they handled money. He employed them to sort out and make profitable the London markets. It was not long before the English merchants sided against them, for the Jews began to monopolize trade in the City. Jews were harassed and their property attacked but future monarchs did not interfere, as they were usually in debt to the money-lenders or relied on their patronage to pay for the expensive whims of the royal way of life. The Jews were given no rights of citizenship by the City and were therefore exempt from the common law. Instead, they were the property of the king who could 'do what he thought fit with them'. Their bonds were kept at Westminster Palace in the room known as the Star Chamber – from the Hebrew *starrs* meaning bonds. Although the Seminites lived in one place in London, known as Old Jewry, this did not stop their persecution. Many of them were hung without trial on fictitious charges, one being that they were responsible for the murder of young children during sacrificial rites. King John at first took the side of the Jews and allowed them to hold their own courts and choose their own Rabbis. They were useful to him as money-lenders but when the King was found never to honour his debts, the Jews refused to increase his overdraft. John then changed his tune and pleased the Londoners by having the money-lenders imprisoned to suffer torture and death. This encouraged the mob to release its fury anew, and the Jews were persecuted mercilessly. They took refuge in the Tower and, in 1290, at their own request were expelled from London. It is said that a contingent of Jews sailed down the Thames on their way to find other lands in which to settle but their ship was deliberately scuttled by the captain and many hundreds were drowned.

During the Middle Ages Cheapside was used as the window dressing for London and it was important that the citizens put on a good show to impress foreign merchants alighting at the London docks and passing through Cheap to the City. Cheap is derived from the Saxon *Ceap* which means market, and the goldsmiths and silversmiths, the rich mercers and furriers had their shops here and the glittering displays of wealth caught the eye of visitors as they were meant to do. As soon as the Jews left, the Lombards, merchants dealing with gold and silver, moved in. (The name Lombard is derived from a place called Lange Borde in the Lower Elbe district of Italy.) They had been waiting on the sidelines as it were to grasp the first opportunity to come to the City which meant good investments and thereafter wealth and prosperity. The Lombards settled in a street which came to be known as Lombard Street and because of their valuable wares they had special strong vaults built. Shortly afterwards, people began to ask whether they could deposit their own private treasures in the vaults for a small fee. The merchants gave receipts for these wares and this is how cheques and the idea of paper money first began. As time went on citizens asked the Lombards to settle their debts for them out of the valuables housed in the vaults. The money-changers had their stalls in the street and benches or counters were erected where the exchange of goods and money could easily be carried out. The Italian word for bench is *banca* and this is where the word bank stems from. The wording on our bank notes is intriguing – 'For the Govr and Comp^a of the Bank of England' – the way Company is spelt is a survival from those times when the Lombards in their own language were classed as 'compagnias'.

It was not long before the Lombards also were in trouble with the citizens of London – for the same reasons as the Jews. Although they established a banking system in the City they were not popular with the other traders. The story goes that animosity came to a head when a Lombard seduced the wife of an English merchant and persuaded her to bring the family plate with her when she left home. The merchants demanded a court hearing but the result of this was unjust to say the least as the Lombard was acquitted and the husband was arrested because he had not paid for his wife's keep when she was living with the Lombard! Francis de Bard was the wife-stealer and a week or so later was the guest of Henry VIII at Greenwich Palace. He was heard to joke in public about the embarrassment of the husband in the case and was given a public warning by merchants of the City who were also at the gathering. The consequence of this scene was that 28 City apprentices joined forces and attacked the Lombards, the French and other foreigners in the City. Newgate was stormed and people who had been imprisoned for attacking foreigners were released. Henry retired to Hampton Court and kept well out of the way because his affairs were so tied up with the money lenders that he dared not interfere. For a while the whole City was in an uproar but at last, with the help of the armed forces, order was restored. The rioters were brought through the streets, roped together and thirteen were hung, drawn and quartered after being dragged on hurdles to the gallows which had been set up in various places in Cheapside. Henry then stepped in and pardoned 400 more.

THE BANK OF ENGLAND

In 1694 a Scotsman by the name of William Paterson had the idea of setting up an institution which he called the Bank of England to protect the State's and individuals' money from the thieving hands of the Crown. The House of Commons agreed to the project and it was set up by Royal Charter. The first subscribers numbered about 1,300 and deposited a total of £1,200,000. The interest rate charged to the Government was 15 per cent – a high rate because security was so bad. The Bank of England was on trial for ten years but became a national institution after lasting for nearly three hundred years. Since about 1797 the Bank, popularized by the poet Sheridan as 'An elderly lady in the City of great credit and understanding', has affectionately been known as 'The Old Lady of Threadneedle Street'. The word Threadneedle may have been derived from the name Three-needles Street.

Bank notes were issued by the Bank from the mid eighteenth century and the first forged notes were found in 1758. The person responsible, a Staffordshire draper, was executed. The comparative ease with which notes could be forged was not stopped for a good many years. The forgers were hard to trace because the Bank had no means of finding out which notes were forged except by an intricate test done by a machine which was almost inaccessible to the clerks of the Bank – only a few officials knew how to work the machine at all! People who were convicted of forgery were punished by the death penalty and those who were found to be in the possession of forged notes met the same fate even though they were innocent of any crime.

A famous case of defrauding the Bank was that of the chief cashier, a Mr. Aslett, who in 1803 reissued Exchequer bills robbing the Bank of £320,000. Another case, in 1824, concerned a Mr. Fauntleroy, the acting partner of the Berner's Street Bank, who forged powers of attorney by which he sold large sums of money belonging to creditors out of the funds of the Bank and continued to pay the dividends until he was found out. The total loss in this instance was £360,000.

There was a run on the Bank in February 1797 when an article in the *Gazette Extraordinary* reported that there had been an invasion by French troops from a frigate anchored off the Welsh coast. Fears of a French takeover ran high and people clamoured and fought to get to the counters and withdraw their money. George III was on holiday at Windsor at the time and was urgently requested to return to the City to attend a meeting to discuss the crisis. It was the first time that a monarch had come to town to attend to business on a Sunday. After the discussion it was decided not to issue any more money in real currency or cash; instead tokens were to be minted called Spanish dollars, with the impress of the London mint, valued at 4s. 6d. each, and these were available from March onwards. Also the Bank issued its first official £1 and £2 notes, thus keeping the gold bullion from going abroad and being melted down for foreign currency.

In 1810 the famous Bullion Committee declared for the first time that gold and bank paper were equivalent in value – obviously they did not have inflation in those days! From then onwards the Bank manufactured its own paper but even so the forgeries went on. In the mid nineteenth century a quantity of paper was stolen and it was some time before the miscreants were tracked down, during which period the Bank lost thousands of pounds. In Edwardian times if a note was handed in at the Bank and loose change was given in exchange, a corner of the note was torn off and it was then stored and never used again. After three years of storage these notes were burnt. On one occasion a lady asked for change of a £100 note which she held in her hand. She was told by the cashier to go to a counter with bars across where such large sums were handled. She must have been short sighted because, instead of doing this, she stepped across to an ornamental fireplace and thinking that there was a clerk behind the bars, put her note up the flue and the draught blew it up the chimney! Eventually, after much ado and excitement, the flue was pulled down and her note returned to her – it had got stuck in a crack.

The Bank of England houses its own private museum consisting of articles which were found in excavations or used by the Bank during its long history. There is a variety of human shoes to be seen and something called a hippo sandal, an old iron-shod horse-shoe, which was fastened around the horse's foot instead of being nailed to the hoof. In fact centuries ago horses wore shoes as humans did. A vast collection of tally sticks, a way of recording, can be seen. Notches on a piece of wood made up the tally stick which was used well into the nineteenth century. Receipts for loans were kept this way and there is the original tally stick which recorded the £1,200,000 loaned to the Bank in 1697. There is an armoury on the premises for the defence of the Bank and I am sure the latest techniques employed against robbery are in operation to live up to the saying 'As safe as the Bank of England'. Up to 1908 the largest cheque on record was one for over £11 million made out by the Chinese government to Japan. The Bank issued a £1 million cheque at this time. From an early date the chief cashier had his signature on every note as he still does today.

The Bank was built in the parish of St. Christopher-le-Stocks (next to the Stock Market) though the church and tower of that name were pulled down for security reasons. The Bank is a parish in itself, when entering its grounds through the Threadneedle Street doorway there is a garden court with trees and a fountain, all that is left of the churchyard of the old church. The Bank has been provided with a guard every night since the No Popery riots of 1780 when it was threatened by the mob. Soldiers from Wellington Barracks march every evening to the Bank and leave the next morning. For many years the bank guards were the only state troops allowed in the precincts of the City. Tradition has it that in times gone by the captain and men enjoyed a good supper and the captain had the privilege of a choice bottle of port.

The Bank of England is the only bank to be nationalized and is the bank used by the government to pay out national debts and receive credits. All the other banks, including the big four, National Westminster, Barclays, Midland and Lloyds, have accounts at the Bank and so does the government. It is also the only English Bank allowed to issue bank notes, although there are several in Scotland that do so. The Bank stands on an island site of roughly three acres and has no windows and only one entrance open to the public. The present building dates from between the two world wars of the last century and an extention added after the last war makes the building vast and impregnable.

From early times people who worked at the Bank wore special attire. Their gay colours are attributed to a long forgotten dignitary who had a passion for flowers and so designed the uniforms to remind him of flower colours. Thus a beadle, when he took off his crimson and black cape, which he was allowed to do once the temperature reached 70°F, revealed a uniform of puce and scarlet. The Bank Messengers' official uniform was a puce, swallow-tailed coat and scarlet waistcoat.

THE ROYAL EXCHANGE

The Royal Exchange was the first of the stock exchanges in London and was the brain child of Sir Thomas Gresham, a wealthy merchant who lived at the time of Elizabeth I. He came from an established Norfolk family and, being brilliant at economics, was appointed by the Crown to visit the Netherlands to arrange loans from wealthy merchants living in Antwerp and elsewhere in the Low Countries. At Antwerp there had been built earlier that century a place of assembly for merchants to do business, called a Byrsa or Burse, the name Burse coming from the medieval Latin for a purse or place of wealth. It was long thought that London should have such a meeting place and Gresham resolved to build and finance it out of his own resources.

A store room, two gardens and thirty-eight houses were cleared away to make room for the new building and leading merchants had a say in the design. It consisted of a wide place of assembly surrounded by pillars and an upstairs gallery consisting of Pawns – small rooms which represented the most important shops and traders in the City. The first stone was laid in 1566 and the building was finished and opened by Queen Elizabeth in 1571. Gresham's crest, a grasshopper 11 ft high, was erected on the highest part of the building. Stow reports that on opening day Elizabeth travelled from her house in the Strand – Somerset House lately belonging to the Earl of Somerset – entered the City through Temple Bar, accepting the sword of allegiance as she did so, and carried on through Fleet Street and Cheap to Sir Thomas Gresham's house in Bishopgate Street, where she dined. Then she went to the Burse through Cornhill and inspected every part of the building especially the Pawn which, being richly furnished with the best wares in the City, she found most fascinating. Then she ordered the heralds to sound the trumpets and officially opened the building, calling it 'The Royal Exchange' and laying down that it should never be called anything else. It is said that Gresham was so overcome and delighted with the occasion that he had a pearl worth £1,500 ground down to powder and put in a glass of wine with which he toasted the Queen. This was termed a carouse – an act, of ancient origin, to toast a greatly honoured person. The poet Thomas Heywood wrote these lines:

> Here fifteen hundred pounds at one clap goes,
> Instead of sugar, Gresham drinks the pearl
> Unto his Queen and mistress; Pledge it, Lords!

The building was burnt down in the Great Fire and rebuilt with a chime of bells which played tunes, including 'Life let us cherish', 'God save the king' and 'There's nae luck aboot the hoose'. In 1838 the building once again caught fire and was burnt to the ground while the bells rang out 'There's nae luck aboot the hoose' as their swan song, before crashing through the roof of the entrance arch. Firemen went to the top of the building to try and save some money and valuables. They threw out bags of cash into the street below where it was instantly seized by onlookers and never seen again. Only two bags of gold worth £200 and the Great Seal were saved.

A new Royal Exchange – the third since Gresham's original, was opened by Queen Victoria in 1844. Corinthian columns are the most striking feature of this building, which also houses many statues including one of Gresham, one of Queen Elizabeth and one of Queen Victoria – and the grasshopper, still the original 11 ft long, holds a position of prominence. It is interesting to remember that the term pawn came from the Pawn in the original Exchange. When merchants and traders went bankrupt their goods in the Pawns were seized by the money-lenders and put into pawnshops. Today on an outside wall of the building the figures of two men, who each in his way contributed quite a bit to the history of the City, can be seen. One is Sir Richard Whittington, four times Lord Mayor, and the other is Hugh Myddleton, the man who channelled water to London from Hertfordshire during the Elizabethan era.

THE STOCK EXCHANGE

In the time of William and Mary the Royal Exchange became too full of trivial business and sightseers for any proper transactions to be carried on, so the merchants removed the venue to Change Alley, where the Easterlings used to meet centuries before, adjacent to the Bank of England. They used coffee-houses in which to discuss business and this is where the Stock Market really began. The necessity of having an official meeting place soon became apparent and at first rooms on the corner of Threadneedle Street were rented. Later a place was built in Capel Court. In the seventeenth century a man name Edward Lloyd had a coffee-house in Tower Street. From there he moved to the corner of Lombard Street where he thought he could do more business, and people concerned with shipping began to patronize the premises and there discuss the business of the day. Edward Lloyd took advantage of this and employed scouts to scour the dock area and bring back news regarding ships at sea and the arrival and departure times. He next published a newspaper to make his findings known. The House of Lords for some reason took a dislike to it and had it suppressed. However, nothing daunted, Lloyd continued to publish shipping journals and the news was read out to the coffee-house clientele by the head waiter. The Marine Insurance group, which had been set up earlier in the Royal Exchange by the Lombards, joined forces with Lloyd's coffee-house and thus the world-wide marine insurance known as Lloyd's officially came into being. The premises were moved into the Royal Exchange and the enterprise went from strength to strength, weathering the American War of Independence which nearly ruined it. In 1871 Lloyd's was incorporated by Act of Parliament.

Nowadays you can get almost anything insured at Lloyd's – it does not have to be shipping. During the last war Lloyd's continued business from a bomb shelter 60 feet beneath the building in Fenchurch Street. Up to the middle of the present century, 5,000 people were employed by Lloyd's and during the war the bomb shelter housed them all.

The Lutine Bell is rung when there is special news to impart – good or bad. It is in the underwriters' room and belonged to a frigate named *La Lutine* which was captured by the British in 1799. It sank in the North Sea and its value was put at £140,000. As the papers had been lost a special Act of Parliament gave Lloyd's the right to investigate the wreck and salvage what they could. Eventually £40,000 worth of valuables were recovered. A cannon from the wreck was presented to the Corporation of London which was returned to Lloyd's when their new building opened in Leadenhall Street.

Up to the nineteenth century the merchants and bankers of the City lived over their places of work – there was no other place for them to live in London at that time. Westminster housed court and government officials and Bloomsbury, Mayfair and Marylebone were fashionable areas for the wealthy aristocracy. There was a great deal of snobbery felt at this time and the tradesmen of the City, albeit they were bankers and stockbrokers, were not welcomed in fashionable circles. As London expanded the men in the City began to drift away from their places of work and set up comfortable homes in the suburbs. This move was greatly helped by the improved transport system, especially the underground railway. The drift continued and in present times the City is an empty shell at night, except for restaurant owners and caretakers who in their way play host to late-night sightseers.

MERCHANTS AND MAYORS

Although there must have been groups of tradesmen working together perhaps before Roman times, there are no records of the City Companies prior to the Norman Conquest. The Weavers claim to be the oldest registered company, bearing the date of 1164 but the Mercers or wool merchants were the leading and most powerful guild in the early days. Apart from the Weavers there were nine other leading Companies, these being the Mercers, with a charter granted in 1303, the Grocers in 1345, the Fishmongers in 1384, the Goldsmiths and Skinners in 1327, the Bakers in 1307, the Saddlers in 1280, the Carpenters in 1349, and the Parish Clerks in 1232. There were and still are roughly seventy more, some of which have taken precedence over the original ten.

Even before the Great Fire, each guild had its guild- or gild-hall and the term came from the Saxon *gild-hallas* where wares were exposed for sale under cover in most market towns. The town hall of the City of London, namely the Guildhall, was built in 1411 by Thomas Knowles, Lord Mayor and alderman at the time. Previously there were two guild-halls of inferior design, the first being built in 1189 in Aldermanbury. Knowles's Guildhall, has been burnt down and restored many times, the last being after the Blitz in the last war. Today the Guildhall houses the banners of the twelve leading Companies. These are: Mercers, Grocers, Drapers, Fishmongers, Goldsmiths, Skinners, Merchant Taylors, Haberdashers, Slaters, Ironmongers, Vintners and Clothworkers.

The merchant guilds sprang up after the Norman Conquest and were greatly influenced by the Hanseatics. Soon they were providing religious entertainment for the poor and uneducated. Church services were either in Latin or French at that time and the layman had no idea of what was in the Bible or indeed what the services were all about. The merchants began to enact scenes from the Bible in English and these of course proved very popular with the man in the street. Later they took advantage of these gatherings to advertise their wares and crafts. Soon the idea of biblical plays and advertisement of wares combined became a regular practice and processions using decorated floats were often to be seen in the City. There developed within the guilds a code of practice that raised the standard of finished goods, and ensured that the public received good value for money and were not cheated in any way. As trade increased more and more crafts applied for charters to form guilds. Members paid a fee which was used to help fellow members when they were sick or became too old to work. When a guild had been formed it meant that only members belonging to that guild could practise that particular trade in that area. Outsiders had to pay a fee before being allowed to sell goods in a 'chartered town'. The guilds had their own courts and if a member was found guilty of shoddy workmanship or providing short measure then he was either fined, put in the stocks or sent to prison. Hardened offenders were expelled for life from the guild and thereafter found it very difficult to earn a living.

To ensure the continuity of the trade or craft and its high

standards, apprentices were taken on and trained for seven years. They were also trained to become good citizens, for many of them were destined to become future Lord Mayors. After the initial period of training the apprentices became journeymen, after the French word, *journée*, meaning a day's work. The journeyman often had to produce a fine piece of workmanship, known as a masterpiece, and then work three more years before he was accepted as a master craftsman in his own right and allowed to join a guild. In the fifteenth and sixteenth centuries journeymen formed a guild of their own to try and persuade their masters to give them increased wages, shorter working hours and better living conditions. Surely this must have been the first trade union!

The Mansion House, which is now the official residence of the Lord Mayor, was first built in the mid eighteenth century. Previous to this the Mayors had to live in their own houses and hold meetings at the Guildhall. The Mansion House was designed by George Dance senior, and the ground floor rooms are laid out as State rooms which include a 90-ft long Egyptian Hall. The private rooms of the Lord Mayor are on the top floor. Sir Crisp Gascoigne was the first Lord Mayor to reside in the Mansion House.

Before becoming king, Prince John realized that he would benefit by being on good terms with the richest men in the land and he therefore requested the merchants of London to appoint a leader with whom he could confer. This spokesman was to report annually to Westminster Palace to hold discussions with the king. This was the beginning of the tradition of Mayors and organized processions such as the Lord Mayor's Show.

London's first Lord Mayor, then titled only 'Mayor', was Henry Fitz-Ailwin in 1191 and he had his residence near the London Stone – left by the Romans as a milestone from which to measure distances from London. There is a legend that whoever struck the stone with his sword should command the City. Certainly the ruffian Jack Cade posing as Lord Mortimer did this when he thought he had won London for himself in 1450.

An incident that was supposed to lead up to the signing of the Magna Carta solidified the position of the Mayor and his supporters in the City. John soon became unpopular with the money men after he was crowned king by taking their wealth without honouring his debts. The owner of Baynard's Castle was Lord Robert FitzWalter who had a beautiful daughter known throughout London as 'Matilda the Fair'. John wanted her, not as his wife, but as one of his mistresses. Finding his suit rejected he threatened to use force to abduct the maiden. The barons supported FitzWalter and rallied forces around the castle which proudly flew the City flag in defiance. John said he would drop the matter and not bother the lady again. The barons took the King at his word and withdrew their forces, but when the way was clear John stormed the castle, destroying it, and taking Matilda prisoner. She resisted all his amorous advances and in revenge John had her poisoned. The citizens were so enraged at the incident that they banded together and forced John to honour the rights of the common man by signing the charter at Runnymede.

In the early days the chief magistrate was no more than a provost but was given the title of Mayor or Major-in-chief. Major is a Latin word which in loose terms means a person in charge of a large household or gathering. The title of Lord was not added until a later date when the Manor of Fensbury, or Finsbury, anciently called Vynesbury, on the Cripplegate and Moorgate boundaries, was annexed to the City boundary. The Mayor then became Lord of the Manor of Finsbury. Hence over the years the two titles were intertwined and the Mayor became known as Lord Mayor. As a mark of favour, Edward III, in 1355, bestowed upon the Lord Mayor of London the privilege of having gold and silver maces carried before him. At the same time mayors in other towns were only allowed maces made from copper. With the first appointment of the Mayor, the Court of Common Council was formed. The City was divided into twenty-four wards and a record of this has been found, dated 1285. Some wards were hereditary, being privately owned, and aldermen were appointed to preside over the rest. The term alderman does not seem to have been used in London before the Normans although it was well known in the shires. The Saxons used the appellation of ealderman, alderman or elderman and one was chosen, because he was 'older' and had experience of life, to see that law and order were kept. The title of Earl also stems from this. Directly under the alderman were the Sheriffs and this body of men is the oldest of all, being mentioned over 1300 years ago. The word

HYDE PARK

Above: *Marble Arch*
Below: *Rennie's Bridge over the Serpentine*
Photographs: Robert Harrowven

A STOCKES TO STAYE SURE AND SAFELY
DETAYNE LAZY, LEWD LEUTERERS
THAT LAWES DO OFFEND

OXFORD OXFORD CIRCUS STREET

Oxford Market (TYBURN ROAD)

Pantheon Theatre

HANOVER SQUARE

GT. MARLBOROUGH ST.

BERWICK ST.

WARDOUR STREET

DEAN STREET

SOHO SQ

BROOK STREET

DAVIE'S STREET

GROSVENOR ST

GROSVE NOR STREET

NEW BOND STR.

CONDUIT ST.

SAVILLE ROW

The game of Pall Mall

GOLDEN SQUARE

SHAFTE

Picc Ha

MOUNT STR.

FAIR LEMONS
AND
ORANGES

BERKELEY SQUARE

BRUTON ST.

OLD BOND STR.

PICCADILLY CIRCUS

St. James's Market

HAYMARKE

REGENT STREET

CHARLES STR.

ROYAL INSTITUTION

BERKELEY STREET

Burlington House

ROYAL ACADEMY

PICCADILLY

ST. JAMES'S FAIR

DEVONSHIRE HOUSE

BERKELEY HOUSE

Egyptian Hall

White's Chocolate House

JERMYN ST.

ST. JAMES'S SQUARE

Norfolk House

CHESTERFIELD HOUSE

ZON ST.

CURZON

Brook's

Boodle's

ST. JAMES'S STR.

KING ST.

Almack's

PALL MALL

Carlton House

SHEPHERDS MARKET

(PORTUGAL STREET)

St. James's Hospital

LANCASTER HOUSE

ST. JAMES'S PALACE

CLARENCE HOUSE

MARLBOROUGH HOUSE

ST. JAMES'S PARK

GREEN PARK

LOOKING FROM CONSTITUTION HILL TO
THE WEST, SOUTH AND EAST, THE EYE
RESTED UPON FIELDS AND MEADOWS
INTERSPERSED WITH VILLAGES

THE MALL

CONSTITUTION HILL

GROSVENOR PLACE

MULBERRY GARDEN

BUCKINGHAM PALACE

HOUSE 1702
PALACE 1836

CHARLES I WALKED ACROSS THE
GUARDED BY FOOT SOLDIERY, TO T
SCENE OF HIS EXECUTION AT W
HIS SON JAMES II WALKED
THE PARK FROM ST. JAME
HE HAD SLEPT, TO WHITE
THE MORNING OF HIS CORO

BIRD CAGE WALK

Queen Anne's Gate

WELLINGTON BARRACKS

LONDON TRANSPORT H.Q

TOT

ROYAL MEWS

A PRINCELY PALACE ON THAT
SPACE DOES RISE
WHERE SUDLEY'S NOBLE MUSE
FOUND MULBERRIES

ROMAN
A.D. 43 - 410

ANGLO-SAXON
A.D 411 - 1066

NORMAN
A.D 1066 - 1154

MEDIAEVAL
A.D 1154 - 148

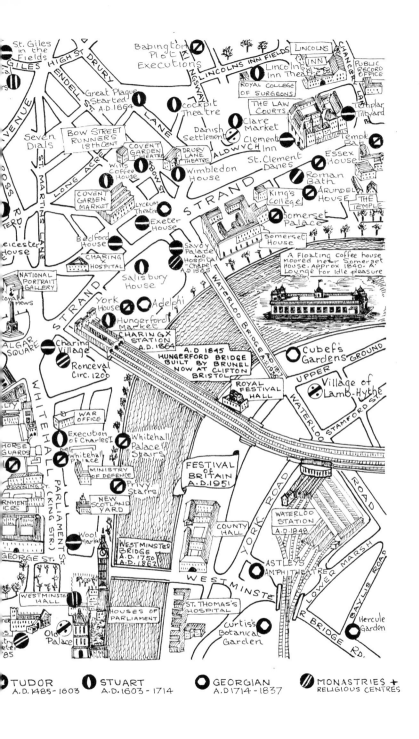

St. Giles in the Fields

GILES

HIGH ST.

DRURY

Babington Plot Executions

LINCOLNS INN FIELDS

LINCOLNS INN

CHANCERY

PUBLIC RECORD OFFICE

Lincolns Inn Theatre

ROYAL COLLEGE OF SURGEONS

THE LAW COURTS

Templar Tiltyard

Great Plague Started A.D.1664

Cockpit Theatre

Clare Market

Danish Settlement

Temple Bar

Seven Dials

BOW STREET RUNNERS 18th CENT

COVENT GARDEN THEATRE

DRURY LANE THEATRE

ALDWYCH

Clements Inn

St. Clement Danes

Essex House

THE TEMPLE

Wills Coffee House

Wimbledon House

STRAND

Roman Bath

COVENT GARDEN MARKET

LYCEUM Theatre

King's College

ARUNDEL HOUSE

Leicester House

Bedford House

Exeter House

Savoy Palace and Hospital Chapel A.D.1505

Somerset Palace

Somerset House

A Floating coffee house moored here. Somerset House. Approx 1640. A Lounge for Idle pleasure

NATIONAL PORTRAIT GALLERY

Royal Mews

STRAND

Salisbury House

York House

Adelphi

Hungerford Market

CHARING X HOSPITAL

CHARING X STATION A.D.1864

A.D.1845 HUNGERFORD BRIDGE BUILT BY BRUNEL NOW AT CLIFTON BRISTOL

Cubef's Gardens

UPPER GROUND

TRAFALGAR SQUARE

Charing Village

Ronceval Circ. 1200

ROYAL FESTIVAL HALL

Village of Lamb-Hythe

WHITEHALL

WAR OFFICE

WATERLOO

STAMFORD S

HORSE GUARDS

Execution of Charles I

Whitehall Palace Stairs

FESTIVAL of BRITAIN A.D.1951

YORK ROAD

WATERLOO ROAD

Whitehall Palace

DOWNING ST.

MINISTRY OF DEFENCE

Privy Stairs

NEW SCOTLAND YARD

WATERLOO STATION A.D.1848

GOVERNMENT OFFICES

PARLIAMENT St. (KING STR.)

Wool Market

COUNTY HALL

LOWER MARSH

GEORGE ST.

WESTMINSTER BRIDGE A.D.1750 A.D.1862

ASTLEY'S AMPHITHEATRE

BAYLIS ROAD

WESTMINSTER HALL

HOUSES OF PARLIAMENT

WESTMINSTER

St. Thomas's Hospital

R. BRIDGE RD.

Old Palace

Curtis's Botanical Garden

Hercule Garden

85

TUDOR
A.D.1485-1603

STUART
A.D.1603-1714

GEORGIAN
A.D.1714-1837

MONASTRIES +
RELIGIOUS CENTRES

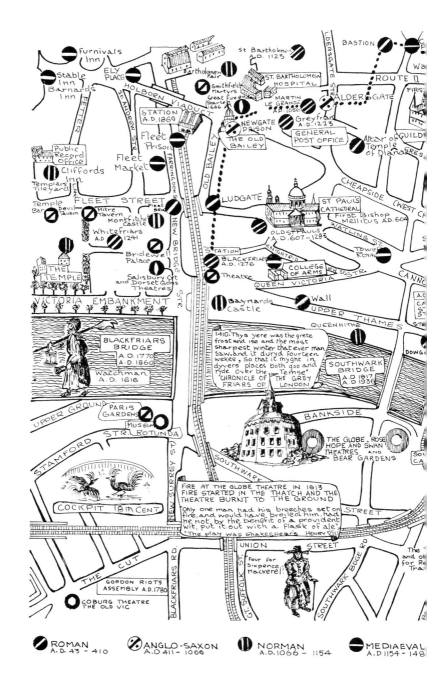

Furnivals Inn

St Bartholomews
A.D. 1123

BASTION

Stable Inn
Barnards Inn

ELY PLACE

Bartholomew Fair

ST. BARTHOLOMEW HOSPITAL

ROUTE II

HOLBORN VIADUCT

Smithfield Martyrs
Great Fire 1666

MARTIN LE GRANDE
A.D. 1056

ALDERGATE

FIRST

FETTER ST. ANDREW ST.

STATION A.D. 1860

Fleet Prison

NEWGATE PRISON

Greyfriars
A.D. 1223

GENERAL POST OFFICE

Altar of Temple of Diana

GUILD
GRES

Public Record Office

Fleet Market

THE OLD BAILEY

Cliffords Inn

Templars Tileyard

Temple Bar
Devil Tavern

FLEET STREET

Fleet Bridge

LUDGATE

OLD ST PAULS
A.D. 607-1283

CHEAPSIDE WEST CH

ST PAULS CATHEDRAL
First Bishop
Mellitus A.D. 604

WATLING ST.

Mitre Tavern
Montfitchit Castle

Whitefriars A.D. 1241

OLD BAILEY

NEW BRIDGE

Bridewell Palace

STATION
BLACKFRIARS A.D. 1276

KNIGHTO'D

Tower Royal

THE TEMPLE

Salisbury Crt and Dorset Gdns Theatres

Theatre

COLLEGE OF ARMS

EARL ST.

CANNO

QUEEN VICTORIA STR.

VICTORIA EMBANKMENT

Baynards Castle

Wall

UPPER THAMES

A.D
CA
ST

BLACKFRIARS BRIDGE
A.D. 1770
A.D. 1860

Watchman A.D. 1616

QUEENHITHE

1410. Thys yere was the grete frost and ise and the most sharpest winter that ever man saw, and it duryd fourteen wekes, so that it myght in dyvers places both goo and ryde over the Temse. "CHRONICLE OF THE GREY FRIARS OF LONDON"

SOUTHWARK BRIDGE
A.D. 1817
A.D. 1936

DOWG

UPPER GROUND

PARIS GARDENS

BANKSIDE

So
CA

STAMFORD STR. ROTUNDA

MUSEU

THE GLOBE, ROSE HOPE AND SWAN THEATRES AND BEAR GARDENS

SOUTHWARK

COCKPIT 18TH CENT.

FIRE AT THE GLOBE THEATRE IN 1613 FIRE STARTED IN THE THATCH AND THE THEATRE BURNT TO THE GROUND

Only one man had his breeches set on fire, and would have broiled him, had he not, by the benefit of a provident wit, put it out with a flask of ale. The play was Shakespear's HENRY VIII

STREET

UNION STREET

The and ol for Ri Tra

THE CUT

GORDON RIOTS ASSEMBLY A.D. 1780

NEW SURREY ST.

BLACKFRIARS RD.

GT. SUFFOLK ST.

"Four for sixpence Mackerel!"

SOUTHWARK BDGE RD.

COBURG THEATRE THE OLD VIC

ROMAN
A.D. 43 - 410

ANGLO-SAXON
A.D. 411 - 1066

NORMAN
A.D. 1066 - 1154

MEDIAEVAL
A.D. 1154 - 148

ST. MARY OF
BETHLEHEM
A.D.1246
MOORGATE
POSTERN
LIVERPOOL
ST. STATION
A.D.1875

COMMERCIAL

LONDON WALL
Bishopsgate

First City
Charter A.D.1086

AN APPLE
SELLER
WHENCE THE NAME
COSTARD
MONGER
A.D.1841

Augustinian
Friars
A.D.1253

Bastion

OLD BROAD ST.

MIDDLESEX STR.

HOUNDSDITCH

BISHOPSGATE STR.

Crosby
Hall
St Helen's
A.D.1212

Petticoat
Lane

STOCK
EXCHANGE

OF
LAND

HIGH ST. WHITECHAPEL

MANSELL STR.

LEMAN ST.

SEDAN CHAIR

Y
ROYAL
EXCHANGE

CORNHILL
coffee
house

LEADEN HALL STREET
ALDGATE

Lloyd's
LEADENHALL
MARKET

MANSION
House
LOMBARD ST.

BASILICA
AND
FORUM

HOLY
TRINITY
A.D. 1109

Wall

Order of
St. Clare
A.D. 1293

GRACECHURCH ST.

MINORIES

LONDON
STONE
WICK ST.)
reputed
man
milestone
Roman
element

FENCHURCH STREET

BOAR'S HEAD
TAVERN

Holy Cross
Friars
A.D. 1298

FENCHURCH
ST. STATION
A.D. 1836

EASTCHEAP
THE MONUMENT

GREAT FIRE
STARTED
A.D. 1666

PORT OF
LONDON
AUTHORITY

TRINITY
HOUSE

Wall

ROYAL MINT STREET

ROYAL
MINT

EET

OLS
1513

GT. TOWER STR.

TOWER
GREEN
SCAFFOLD

LOWER THAMES STREET

ROMAN
BATHHOUSE

EAST SMITHFIELD

N
GE
31

BILLINGSGATE
MARKET

CUSTOM
HOUSE

TOWER
OF LONDON

ST. KATHERINES
HOSPITAL
A.D. 1148

t Mary
very
1106

Roman &
Anglo Saxon
Bridge

ST. KATHERINES
DOCKS
A.D. 1828

DUKE STR.

Thames
Barge

TOWER
BRIDGE
A.D. 1894

Roman
suburb A.D.1836

LONDON
BRIDGE
STATION

HILL

ST. THOMAS
HOSPITAL

TOOLEY

GUY'S
HOSPITAL

TOWER BRIDGE R.

PROCESS OF
COINING
18TH CENTURY

NOW FIELDS

ade's
A.D. 1450

STREET

TUDOR
A.D. 1485-1603

STUART
A.D. 1603-1714

GEORGIAN
A.D. 1714-1837

MONASTRIES +
RELIGIOUS CENTRES

The Guildhall

The Guildhall
Photographs: Courtesy of the Guildhall Archive

Gog and Magog

THE GUILDHALL

Today the Guildhall is home to the Corporation of London, the City's local authority. Because it represents 800 years of civic government it has served as a model for many cities and towns across the country. Its ancient walls are steeped in history, and although the Great Hall was badly damaged in two disastrous fires (the last being in the Blitz of 1940), needless to say it was soon restored and completed to the designs of Sir Giles Gilbert Scott in 1954. In 1973 the west end of the Guildhall Yard was remodelled and the crypt dating back to the thirteenth century was restored.

The Great Hall measures 152' by 49'6". The main 'minstrels' gallery occupies the length of the west wall and Gog and Magog can be seen at each corner. Legend has it that they are linked with the founding of London. The previous statues were destroyed in 1940 and the present ones are carved in limewood by David Evans and stand 9'3" in height. Magog's shield shows a phoenix – the symbol of renewal after fire.

Many monuments can be seen including a seated bronze statue of Sir Winston Churchill. A tablet on the north wall tells us that the trials of High Treason took place within the Guildhall of Lady Jane Grey and Archbishop Cranmer.

The windows bear the names of all the Lord Mayors and their time of office and the banners of the twelve great livery companies hang proudly along the south wall.

The elections of the Lord Mayors and Sheriffs take place within the Great Hall and according to tradition it is the venue for sumptious banquets to mark national events. To celebrate the defeat of Napoleon in 1814 a lavish display included guests such as the Prince Regent, the Czar of Russia and the King of Prussia.

Hyde Park

Above: *Sunshine and Showers*
Below: *Speakers' Corner*
Photographs: Bryony Dean

sheriff has its roots in the word shire.

Today the square mile of the City is ruled over by the Court of Common Council of the Corporation of London which is elected by voters in the area. The Council is usually made up of liverymen and aldermen representing the guilds of the City. Sheriffs are elected to serve for one year; to be elected as Lord Mayor, a term of one year at least as sheriff has to be served. The Lord Mayor is selected by liverymen meeting on Michaelmas Day at the Guildhall. The liverymen are members of the City guilds and are entitled to wear livery according to the grading of the company, in fact the whole company is dressed in full regalia for this event.

Edward III saw that the merchants of London were becoming even more rich and powerful so he gave them special powers to increase their domain, the most important being that they were allowed to buy land outside the City. He saw, too, that it would be beneficial to himself if he became a member of a guild and so joined the richest, the Merchant Taylors, lately the Linen Armourers, and this guild was the first to boast a monarch in its midst. Richard II, four dukes, ten earls, ten barons and five bishops all followed suit, and throughout the years most of the leading Companies have had royalty included in their membership. They alone have had the privilege of entertaining foreign royalty, and of course members of our own royal families, throughout the centuries. These companies have provided the Lord Mayors and Councillors of London from the beginning.

During Edward III's reign another guild was making itself felt by its monetary power – the Grocers. They threatened to ruin other establishments by being wholesalers – the word grocer comes from the old French *grossier*, meaning a dealer in large quantities. The Grocers bought up large amounts of produce and sold them to the public at a cheaper price than other smaller companies could afford. To break this monopoly a law was passed saying that one guild could sell only a limited variety of goods. The Grocers were in fact formed from a more ancient guild of Pepperers. There was a law which lasted many centuries that a licence had to be obtained to sell pepper and it had to be displayed over the doorways of shops, rather like a modern shop has to show a licence to sell liquor.

The Goldsmiths became very rich and when the idea of hall-marks was introduced to measure the amount of gold and silver in one article, they were appointed in charge. In 1300 a law was passed ordering that no gold or silver article was to be sold until it had been tested by the 'Gardiens of the Craft' i.e. the Goldsmiths, and when passed, stamped with the sign of the leopard's head, the London stamp which is still in use today. From that time forward the company has been known as the Worshipful Company of Goldsmiths and has taken on the testing of precious metals in London, in Goldsmith's Hall – hence the term hallmark. Other signs such as a fish or a key, were introduced on the articles showing the maker of the product and these signs were often displayed outside gold- and silversmiths.

Quarrels developed, naturally, between the companies, the most bitter perhaps being between the wet and dried fishmongers. A price could not be decided on as the wet fishmongers could sell their fish only in season whilst the dried, or store, fishmongers were able to sell their wares all the year round and so became much more wealthy. In Elizabethan times the bakers came to blows in Cheapside as they could not agree to make white and brown bread under one company. For years therefore there were two guilds – one making white bread for the upper classes and the other brown for the poorer folk. Later, when the class snobbery over the colour of the bread had receded a little, the guilds joined forces and made both kinds of bread under one company.

Years ago many of the companies owned elaborate salters, usually a magnificent piece of plate containing a very important commodity. The Mercers, for instance, owned a splendid example which can still be viewed. In the Middle Ages when a banquet was being held a division was drawn between the upper and lower part of the table. The salter was placed fairly centrally and to be seated above the salt was a mark of honour but if the host wanted to mortify some of his guests he placed them below the salt, giving rise to the expression 'worth his salt'.

It is the Freemasons, formerly the Stone Masons, that still hold a position of power and esteem in the world today. Out of the mysteries practised by the stonemasons when executing their craft at guild meetings, a club was formed which extended and developed these secrets and in the ensuing centuries the idea became universal. During the eighteenth and nineteenth centuries secret societies flourished and the Masons became known as the Freemasons, and allowed others unconnected with the craft to join the exclusive club. The only criteria seemed to be dedication to the cause and a plentiful supply of money. In 1863 a Freemasons' Hall was erected in London – although the Stonemasons already had a well preserved building. The special handshake, the signs and the inauguration ceremonies were incorporated into the new venture and have united men the world over to help each other in times of trouble, albeit sometimes against the law of the land.

The livery companies wore different coloured ceremonial robes: the Mercers wore dark red, trimmed with fur, the Drapers were in blue and yellow and the Haberdashers in fur-trimmed dark blue and so on. This old jingle bears this out and dates from the Middle Ages:

> Hinkety, Dinkety, Poppety Pet,
> The merchants of London they wear scarlet,
> Fur at the collar and gold at the hem,
> Merrily march the merchant men.

Swan upping on the river Thames is a custom of ancient origin. Kings treated the swan as a royal bird so that the monarch only, and no subject, could own or keep them. Gradually, however, the privilege was extended to subjects who were granted a particular Swan Mark applied usually to the beak of the birds by way of identification of ownership. The monarch had begun to grant the favour of a Royalty of Swans as early as the latter part of the fifteenth century. It is possible that the Dyers' Company has been the possessor of a Royalty on the river Thames since those early days. The Vintners' Company also has a grant of swans on the Thames. They are still preserved on the river by Her Majesty The Queen and by these two companies. The work of Swan upping takes a week. The stretch of the river that is covered is between London Bridge and Henley on Thames. In 1979 this was changed to cover the stretch from Walton to Whitchurch. Each year in July the men of the Queen and of the Dyers' and Vintners' Companies go up the river to take up, inspect and mark the cygnets. The birds belonging to the Crown are left unmarked but those belonging to the Vintners are given two nicks in their beaks and those of the Dyers one nick. This explains why some public houses are called *The Swan with the two Necks* (nicks).

The Vintners' Hall is one place where the gathering is called to raise five cheers instead of the usual three. This goes back to Edward III's reign when the Vintners proudly entertained five kings – called the Feast of the Five Kings. They were Edward III, King David of Scotland, King John of France, King Waldemar of Denmark and King Amadeus of Cyprus.

On the Second Saturday in November the Lord Mayor's Show takes place. The procession starts from Guildhall, proceeds past St. Paul's into Fleet Street and on to the Law Courts, where the new Lord Mayor is presented to the Lord Chief Justice who represents the monarch. The Show then winds its way to the Mansion House, where a grand banquet is served in the evening. The coach, built in 1757, weighs 4 tons and is pulled by six matched brewers' horses. It was painted by Cipriani and is carved and gilded. It is over 10 ft high and can only be stopped by a wheel brake at the back which is operated by a footman walking behind. The coachman is dressed so ornately in scarlet uniform trimmed with gold and lace, a tricorn hat similar to the Lord Mayor's, that he is often taken for that gentleman! The coach is guarded by soldiers from the Honourable Artillery Company of Pikemen and Musketeers which was formed by Henry VIII. It is a privilege to serve in this Company and many famous people have done so, including Milton, Pepys and Wren. Cromwell issued the soldiers' drill book in 1635 and it is to these instructions that the H.A.C. still perform. They are dressed in a Cromwell-style uniform of breast- and back-plates, stockings, knee breeches and tunics. A Roundhead helmet with a swirling feather completes the costume. The uniform weighs about 25 lbs per man and the regiment is the oldest in Britain and perhaps the world.

Lord Mayors come and go but coach drivers go on for ever, or so it seems. Early in the last century one driver drove 27 Lord Mayors without a break. A story goes that one Lord Mayor wished to change his driver but the man pleaded with him to reconsider his decision. His master said he could keep his job if he could drive from the Mansion House to Buckingham Palace without passing through a street. The coach went by Cheapside,

Poultry, St. Paul's Churchyard, Ludgate Hill, Creed Lane, Carter Lane, Broadway, Water Lane, the Victoria Embankment, Northumberland Avenue, Trafalgar Square and the Mall and the driver kept his job.

Up to 1454 it was the custom of Lord Mayors on inauguration day to ride through the streets to Westminster to be enrolled by the monarch. John Norman, having been chosen Lord Mayor, introduced a new method of transport. He had a splendid barge built at his own expense and was rowed from Cheapside up the Thames to Westminster. He was followed by many City Companies in their own sumptuously adorned barges; the whole carnival procession provided a striking spectacle which the populace enjoyed. The watermen were delighted as it benefited them in many ways. Not only did they row the boats but many of them were boat builders and probably built the ceremonial barges. They composed a song of praise to the new Lord Mayor, the first line of which is: 'Row thy boat Norman, row to thy leman'. This water-journey custom was kept up for almost two hundred years and is of course where the term 'float' comes from used in carnivals to this very day.

By tradition the City of London is an independent state, bowing to no one, not even the monarch. Many Lord Mayors in the past went to the Tower and thence to the execution block for disobeying the orders of the Crown. The election of the Lord Mayor and Common Council has been compared on a smaller scale with the election of Parliament at Westminster, the Lord Mayor being on a par with the ruling monarch or Prime Minister, the Aldermen with the Lords and the Councillors with the Commons. The officials in the City are treated with respect by their opposite numbers in the House of Commons. For instance, when a monarch dies the Lord Mayor of London is one of the first people to be told and he authorizes the ringing of the mourning bell at St. Paul's. The Corporation of London is the only body of men with the right to present petitions at the Bar in the House of Commons. In days gone by the City had three mottoes. Today it is the third one that is used: *Domine dirige nos* – O Lord direct us.

There is not enough space to recount all the stories connected with Lord Mayors throughout the centuries. Many of them served as apprentices and came from lowly stock. William de Sevenoke, for example, Mayor in 1418, was a foundling. There are however two stories which cannot be ignored, and the first concerns Wat Tyler and William Walworth, Lord Mayor in 1381. Richard II ascended the throne in 1377 when he was only 11 years old. In the second years of his reign a law was passed taxing all people of 15 years old according to their status, called a poll tax. Tradesmen were taxed with their wives and children at 4d. per head, the Lord Mayor was rated as an earl at £4, and the barons at £2. Government agents were employed to collect the money and complaints about the treatment of decent citizens were manifold. The women suffered, especially those of lower ranks as the tax men had to prove the age of the female and consequently this was often the excuse for brutal assault and rape. The excitement of the people over this practice came to a head when a man named Walter Hilliard, by profession a tyler, known afterwards as Wat Tyler, became so angry at the treatment his daughter had received that he beat up the offending collector causing his death. Tyler lived in Kent, and to save himself from prosecution he persuaded the populace to rise in his defence and march on London to protest about the heavy yoke of taxation and the way it was extracted. First he went to Maidstone to release a priest named John Ball who had been excommunicated for his doctrine that all men should be equal. Ball made famous the motto: 'When Adam delv'd and Eve span, Who was then the gentleman?'

The army grew to 100,000 strong and camped on Blackheath. They heard that the King had refused their demands to be freed of the tax, so they then marched on London, vowing to kill all royalty and nobility in the two cities, London and Westminster. Tyler camped at Smithfield and requested that Richard should meet him there. This the young King did and when Tyler saw Richard riding to meet him surrounded by his guard he rode forward until he touched the croupier of the king's horse, whom he rudely accosted. The King immediately ordered Wat Tyler's arrest and Lord Mayor Walworth as magistrate with jurisdiction in that area was told to carry out the command. He drew his dagger and struck Tyler a severe blow on the head which caused him to fall from his horse. His body was immediately seized and thrown into the nearby St. Bartholomew's Hospital, and there the rebel died. His followers were so angry at this that they bent their bows intending to annihilate the King and his troops but at this moment Richard, with great courage and presence of mind for a fifteen-year-old, rode forward and addressed the crowd. He cried, 'What, my friends! Will you kill your King? Be not troubled for the loss of your leader, I will be your captain and grant what you desire.' This action and promise from the young monarch temporarily subdued the rebels but in the meantime the Mayor and aldermen had been assembling a thousand armed citizens in the side lanes and sent them in to surround the rebels, who when they saw they were trapped, threw down their arms and pleaded for mercy. The Lord Mayor and various aldermen who had taken part were knighted and given generous pensions, and Sir William Walworth's memory has been perpetuated in the name of the village where he was born.

The question as to whether the dagger present in the coat of arms of the City is the one which Walworth used to kill Tyler has been the subject of controversy for centuries. But it appears that the year before a new coat of arms incorporating Westminster had been introduced. The ancient seal of office, as it used to be called, was enlarged and renewed and bore the images of St. Peter and St. Paul as well as the shield of arms of the City, supported by two lions, and two niches containing the images of the apostles and the Virgin Mary. So the cross and sword on the shield are in fact taken as representations of St. Paul and not the dagger of Walworth because they were in place before the event.

There is a statue of Walworth, who was a member of the Fishmongers' Guild, in Fishmongers' Hall which depicts him killing Tyler with a dagger. The wording underneath reads:

> Brave Walworth, Knight, Lord Mayor, you slew,
> Rebellious Tyler in his alarmes,
> The King therefore did give in lieu
> The dagger to the City's arms.

In spite of the fact that it has now been proved that the dagger on the City coat of arms was there before the incident – the inscription still stands!

I have refrained from mentioning the most famous Lord Mayor of all until last in this chapter. So much has already been written about him that I thought I had nothing new to add. But I was wrong, for when delving into an ancient book on London entitled *The Great Metropolis* I found something about Sir Richard Whittington, four times Lord Mayor of London, which I hope is not generally known. He was born of lowly stock in Gloucestershire and as a boy came to London to seek his fortune. He arrived in London in 1368 and being destitute applied to Clerkenwell Priory for help. The Grand Prior at that time was Sir John Pavely and he took the boy in. Whittington proved a lively and intelligent servant and being literate was soon given minor clerical work in the Priory. He did not remain there long, but his work and testimonials put him on the first rung of the ladder to success. He probably served an apprenticeship to the Mercers' guild as later, with his business acumen, he became a wealthy Mercer and married Alice Fitzwaryn, the daughter of a Dorset knight. He was elected Lord Mayor of London in 1397, 1398, 1406 and 1419. Over the centuries the pantomime story of Dick Whittington and his cat has become a national tradition, and historians have tried to find the link between Sir Richard.Whittington and a cat without success. They have assumed that the cat that presumably played such an important part in the life of Whittington was of the animal variety. Many theories have been put forward – too many to mention here – but not one holds the slightest credibility that Whittington favoured cats at all. But he did make his fortune by one – and this is the story:

In 1306 an ordinance was issued by the king prohibiting the burning of coal in the City of London because it produced foul and polluted air which was dangerous to the health of the inhabitants. Coal was used in breweries, by dyers and in other factories in those days as well as in private dwellings. The penalties for burning coal were severe and at least one person was executed for infringing the law. However, over the period of Whittington's power in London it is reported that coal was imported in great quantities even though the Act had not been repealed. To celebrate Henry V's victory at Agincourt Whittington held a banquet for the King at the Guildhall and it is said that during the celebrations he tore up bonds for the £60,000 which he had lent the King to finance the battle, and cast them into the fire. One good turn deserves another and the King turned a blind eye to the import

ARMS OF THE
CITY OF LONDON

DOMINE DIRIGE NOS

of coal by Whittington, even authorizing that Whittington had the monopoly in this field. Such favours of the Crown towards individuals were common in those days – even though the law of the land was abused. And our most famous Lord Mayor took advantage of the favour and increased his money supply by means of a cat – a small coastal vessel specially designed on the Norwegian type of ship, with a narrow stern, projecting quarters and a deep waist. In fact Whittington was soon importing coals from Newcastle in a ship which he had christened a cat because of its stealth and quickness through the water. The word cat comes from the Icelandic *kati* and small coal-carrying vessels in modern times are still called cats in some quarters. The pantomime story and its ingredients are all here. The king, the cat, the ship and the fortune, but somehow the basic facts have been misinterpreted throughout the years. Ballads were composed after the death of Whittington and this is where the pantomime story began. This explanation of Whittington's cat has been taken from a comedy by Foote entitled *Nabob* in which one character, Sir Matthew Mite, offers the explanation of Whittington's fortune and the coal-carrying cat.

However Sir Richard Whittington came by his immense fortune, it is well known that he spent his money wisely and helped the poor and needy in the City. When he died in 1423 he left money to rebuild Newgate prison, to restore the Guildhall, to replenish libraries and to rebuild St. Bartholomew's hospital.

6

Markets, Streets and Street People

As we have seen in the opening chapter, Billingsgate must be accepted as the oldest London market, probably dating back to pre-Roman times. But up to the fifteenth century it was of secondary importance as a fish market. Queenhithe on the other side of the Bridge enjoyed the patronage of early monarchs and their queens, and so ships were ordered to bring fish through the Bridge to be unloaded on the Queenhithe wharves. This arrangement did not suit the fishermen as the hazards of 'shooting the Bridge' were great, especially with the precious cargo. So gradually Queenhithe lost favour and Billingsgate was destined to become the largest fish market in the world – prior to the introduction of the railways. The streets known as Old Fish Street and Old Fish Hill which are not situated near Billingsgate are reminders of the lanes which once led to Queenhithe market. By the mid fifteenth century Billingsgate had become a large and thriving market and the Fishmongers' guild had become nearly as wealthy as the Grocers', Goldsmiths' and Wool Merchants'. In Edward I's time certain regulations were laid down concerning the sale of fish. It was forbidden to sell fresh fish later than two days after it was caught and fish was not to be watered more than twice daily on the stalls, though street vendors were allowed to water it more often. Buyers for the king and barons, called purveyors, had first choice of any fish for sale. The prices were fixed: 3d. per dozen for best soles, 6d. each for best turbot, mackerel were 1d. each, pickled herrings 1d. per score, fresh oysters 2d. per gallon and best eels 2d. per quarter of a hundred. It has been stated in the previous chapter that quarrels often broke out between the fresh- and store-fish vendors and the differences were settled by the Mayor and his Council; the outcome depended upon which guild the Mayor represented at the time. The store, or stock fishmongers who could sell salted fish throughout the year were the wealthiest, as an old couplet reminds us:

Spend herring first, save salt fish last,
For salt fish is good when Lent is past.

Ling was the fish most commonly used for stock.

When the news of Edward I's victory over the Scots was received in 1298 the Fishmongers made a triumphant and solemn show through the City with several pageants and more than a thousand horsemen.

Many churches were patronized by the Fishmongers although they do not seem to have built one of their own. St. Michael's in Crooked Lane was the favourite for the stock or salt fish-sellers and St. Peter's Cornhill for the wet or fresh fish-vendors.

Up to Elizabethan times fish was caught and sold from the river Thames but after this the river became too polluted for fish to survive. It is interesting to note that up to a hundred years ago many people living away from the sea or a river in Britain had never tasted fish as there was no quick way of transporting it. In the nineteenth century and probably before, fish caught out to sea could be kept in a frozen state in huge blocks of ice for up to 6 days and this was of course the beginning of refrigeration. At the turn of the last century boxes of fish covered with crushed ice were carried into the market by porters wearing a kind of flat iron cap on their heads on which they balanced heavy weights.

With the advent of the railway network the fishmonger out of London found it more practical to buy straight from fishing ports such as Hull, Grimsby and Fishguard and so Billingsgate lost much of its trade during the last century.

In its heyday, the morning trade at Billingsgate began about 5 o'clock when prices were fixed by Dutch auction. The trains and lorries were loaded first, then the shopkeepers had their choice and what was left went to the barrow boys. The market was then washed down and was closed by about ten o'clock.

Leadenhall market, near Billingsgate, sold poultry but had no stalls, only shops under cover. In Edwardian times swans and singing birds could be purchased here as well as the normal poultry.

Smithfield was originally called Smoothfield and was sited outside the precincts of the Tower as an extension of the Bartholomew fairground.It became one of the world's most famous meat markets. In early days this piece of 'smooth ground' was a popular venue for tournaments and jousts and its size was such that large audiences could appreciate the entertainment. From the sixteenth century it was also a place of executions; the first recorded was a man named John Rose, a cook who was supposed to have poisoned the broth in the household of Bishop Fisher and killed two people. He was boiled to death, a fate specially reserved for poisoning it seems. Catholic and Protestant martyrs were burnt at the stake here in Henry VIII's and Mary's time. Most of the 227 religious executions took place in Mary's reign. Before Tyburn, a gibbet was hung on the elms on Smithfield marshes and it was here, on St. Bartholomew's Eve in 1381 when the crowds were arriving to attend the fair, that the body of Wat Tyler was taken from the hospital where he died and hung on the elms.

A horse market had been at Smithfield since Saxon times and when St. Bartholomew's Fair was established the animal market was incorporated in it. In 1615 the venue was paved and sewers laid to take away the water used in cleaning the area. The market was fenced in and on certain days certain types of animals were sold. Thus, on Mondays and Wednesdays cattle and sheep were sold and, on other days, horses and hay. The authorities charged 1d. for each animal entering the market. Cruelty to animals was rife but gradually farmers began to realize that well cared for and healthy stock was a good investment and brought in more money and so the condition of the animals improved over the years. The meat market had been at Newgate for centuries but in 1852 this market was closed and the live animal market moved to Islington, which was still a village in those days. Smithfield became the principal meat market of London and the hygenic buildings and conditions were one of its main attractions.

One of the most famous of all London fairs must surely be St. Bartholomew's and it has a long and explicit history. Rahere, the jester to Henry I, became bored with Court life and with the King's permission went on a pilgrimage to Rome. There he unfortunately caught malaria and became very ill. When he was

Islington Green, 1830

in a high fever he dreamt that he was carried far above the world by a wondrous, dragon-like beast and suspended by its claws over the depths of a fiery furnace – hell in other words. He called out for help and St. Bartholomew came to his rescue by catching him as the beast let go and flew away. The story goes on to say that St. Bartholomew brought Rahere safely back to earth and told him to return to his native land when he had recovered his health and dedicate the rest of his life to building a priory and hospital just outside the City walls.

In pre-Christian times Romans who needed healing went to the Temple of Aesculapius to pray to the gods for restored health.

When Christianity came to Rome the building was still used to pray for the sick in hope of a miracle of healing. The place was dedicated to St. Bartholomew and this is where the connection with the saint comes in. A man named Bartholomew is mentioned in the New Testament in Mark, Matthew, Luke and Acts. Bartholomew is an Aramaic patronymic meaning son (bar) of Tolmai. He may have had another personal name and it is thought by some that it could have been Nathanael. Another tale tells how Bartholomew was a Christian missionary in Ethiopia or Armenia in the second century and that he was martyred for his faith by King Astyages and was later canonized by the pope. His relics, so we are told, are to be found in the Roman Catholic Church of St. Bartholomew on an island in the Tiber. His feast is celebrated in the Latin Church on 24 August and in the Greek Church on 11 June.

Rahere recovered quickly and on arrival in London went straight to Henry and told him of his revelations. The King was very impressed and gave permission for Rahere to use some of the land on Smithfield for the ensuing project. At this time the meadow was marshy. By pretending to be half-witted, Rahere cunningly encouraged people to throw pieces of masonry, stones and other rubbish on to the soggy land, which soon gave it a sound foundation. The ordinary folk regarded it as a kind of game and joined in with good humour. The ground was consecrated by Richard Belmeis, Bishop of London, and the monastery was opened in 1123, with Rahere as its first Prior. There were as expected many valuable relics to be seen in the Priory and pilgrims travelled from all over Europe to see them and to hear at first hand the tale of Rehere's dream while in Rome. It is said, too, that miracles of healing took place in the shrine of St. Bartholomew; the blind being made to see and the lame walk.

After twelve years the King granted a charter to hold a fair annually to raise funds for the running of the Priory and hospital and it was incorporated with the horse market held at Smithfield. The fair was held on 23, 24 and 25 August and was at first essentially a trading fair, dealing with live animals and cloth. Rahere succeeded in closing all shops and markets on the fair days so that the people would purchase only the goods sold on his territory.

A small chapel was opened to serve the hospital and both church and chapel can be seen today, being called St. Bartholomew the Great and St. Bartholomew the Less. In the Great the tomb of Rahere can be seen and an effigy of him created long after his death.

As with other early fairs St. Bartholomew's was subject to the Court of Pied Poudre (the court of dusty feet) from a French idea to appoint officials to see that law and order was kept during fair days and that the public were given good value for money. When the Dissolution came about the Priory was bought by Sir Richard Rich who gained the rights of the fair. He passed on the responsibility to the Lord Mayor and Aldermen of the City, who opened it each year. It then became an amusement fair with tents for wrestling, plays and unusual sights such as human freaks. 'Bartholomew fair babies', overdressed dolls, were on sale and 'fairings', gingerbread in all shapes and sizes such as drums, trumpets and other toys, wrapped in gilt paper. Live rabbits were often let loose on fair days and boys ran to catch them – for what they caught they kept and this provided much amusement for the visitors.

Charles II, who enjoyed fairs, increased the length of the fair from three to fourteen days. Theatres in London closed for this time and the actors came to perform their plays at Smithfield. Ben Jonson wrote a celebrated comedy entitled *Bartholomew Fair*. In addition to the professional actors there was a multitude of what we might call circus people who worked for themselves, usually in families, performing for the pleasure of the crowds such feats as tight-rope walking, dancing, conjuring and light skits on the classics such as a version of the Siege of Troy and other Greek myths, the adventures of Robin Hood, Jack Sheppard the highwayman, and so on. The plays were performed on raised platforms and food and drink were sold in stalls underneath. Animals, too, were taught to perform and often played musical instruments such as the drums. Freaks included a woman with three breasts, a monster with one head and two bodies, a live child of three months with three legs, and a woman from Essex who stood over 7 feet tall. Pig-faced babies could also be seen and also learned pigs who so we are told, could tell fortunes by the cards. There was a mummified mermaid with a monkey's head and body and a fish's tail in a glass case, and a negro boy with a mottled black and white skin.

Up to Queen Victoria's time royalty enjoyed visiting and patronizing the fair, but during the early part of the nineteenth century the gathering, like so many others, became bawdy and rough and was closed down in 1855 at the wish of the Queen. So the fair which had run for seven and a half centuries was officially finished. But it was revived recently by the hospital to raise funds and there is more about this in the next chapter.

St. Bartholomew's Close and Cloth Fair are two names of lanes which remind us of the old fair by its original site. The drapers and mercers attending the gathering used to meet in an ancient tavern called the Hand and Shears.

Covent Garden was, until a few years ago, the biggest market in London and derived its name from the Convent Garden cultivated by the monks of Westminster to provide fruit and vegetables for the Abbey in 1222. Before the Dissolution, as happened in many pleasant walled and well kept gardens in the vicinity, people took to using it as a meeting place to enjoy a convivial hour and buy what produce the monks had to spare. After the Act of Supremacy all was changed and the produce of Covent Garden previously provided by the monks was not now forthcoming. But old habits die hard and people still drifted to the spot to talk and perhaps exchange goods. The tradition of the market did not die out and it was not long before people were setting up stalls and selling country produce as the monks had done before them, even though there were only a few permanent thatched cottages on the site at the time. The Garden, with a field called Seven Acres or Long Acre, was given by Edward VI to Sir John Russell, 1st Earl of Bedford first and during the next hundred years or so some fine buildings were erected, including Covent Garden's own parish church of St. Paul – 'the handsomest barn in England'. Inigo Jones planned the first fashionable square in London and built it in the style of Palladian architecture originating in Italy. The houses were grand but their titled occupants were constantly irritated by the habit of common folk wandering into their private land and holding fruit and vegetable markets. Charles II made it worse by authorizing a charter to hold a market here in 1671. Gay, in his *Trivia*, gives this picture of the place:

> Where Covent-Garden's famous temple stands,
> That boasts the work of Jones' immortal hands,
> Columns with palin magnificence appear,
> And graceful porches lead along the square.
> Here oft my course I bend, when lo! from far
> I spy the furies of the football war;
> The 'prentice quits his shop to join the crew –
> Increasing crowds the flying game pursue.
> Oh! whither shall I run? the throng draws nigh;
> The ball now skims the street, now soars on high;
> The dextrous glazier strong returns the bound,
> And jingling sashes on the penthouse sound.

By this we can see that the game of football was enjoyed in the square by the young bloods of the day and the grand houses and nobility meant nothing to the folk who had always regarded the area as common land. There was a herb market in Clement's Inn Fields and the Stocks and Honey Lane markets in the City provided the citizens with all they needed. However, with the opening of Westminster Bridge in the mid eighteenth century the whole set-up changed. The new influx of travellers crossing the bridge each day and the increased population in the area brought a good deal of trade and the fruit and vegetable market expanded and flourished. The other markets dwindled and died out but Covent Garden became well established, receiving fresh goods from the countryside over the new bridge. Taverns and coffee houses sprang up in the square and there was also a puppet theatre, which the crowds called Powell's theatre, where Punch and Judy reigned supreme. A man named Rich worked the puppets with such dexterity that Garrick said of him 'He gave the power of speech to every limb'. Theatre Royal, Drury Lane opened in 1663, and the Covent Garden Theatre, now the Royal Opera House, was established overlooking the Piazza in 1732.

Gradually the business side of the market and its accompanying rowdy element drove out the nobility, who left their properties to be taken over by the taverners, and sought more exclusive squares in London in which to live.

In 1828 the old sheds were pulled down and new buildings

were erected under the direction of the Duke of Bedford. They were respectable and airy and served the market for nearly another 150 years. The first British gardener to grow cabbages, cauliflowers, turnips, carrots and peas settled in Surry in 1650 and began to supply the population with these vegetables which hitherto had only been grown on the Continent and were unknown to the ordinary citizen. Middlesex provided fruit and from that time onwards more and more market gardens were set up near London to supply Covent Garden. Onions came from Deptford, cabbages from Battersea, asparagus from Mortlake and Deptford, celery from Chelsea, and peas from Charlton – in fact every suburb grew its own special produce to supply the market. Potted plants made their début here: daisy roots being the first to be sold, it is believed. Fruit was sold by auction in one of the halls, especially the more expensive kinds such as bananas and pineapples. In Victorian times women were employed to sit in the market and shell peas. Also in this era the flower ladies came early in the mornings to collect their wares and be off to the pitches assigned to them. The market grew to be the largest in the world and in these days, owing to modern transport and technology, out-of-season produce can be sent to the four corners of the earth at a moment's notice. The market has now moved to new premises in Nine Elms and the Covent Garden site has become a busy commercial centre. The Covent Garden Opera House, of which we shall hear more later, still overlooks the old site.

The Frost fairs played an important role in the social life of the City prior to the building of Rennie's London Bridge in 1832. Practically every winter centuries ago, the Thames froze to such a degree that people could cross over it on foot and more often than not a coach pulled by six horses could be driven across with the utmost safety. With this wide expanse of common ground available with no rent to be paid it was not long before some enterprising trader set up stalls and sold his wares upon the ice. The water above the bridge was deep and calm and this is where most of the Frost fairs were held. In 1281–2 the river froze, so we are told, and carts crossed it with ease, but when the thaw set in many of the starlings of the bridge were damaged. In 1144–5 the water froze below the bridge as far as Gravesend and the merchandise, usually transported by boats upriver, was brought up by carts on the ice. Stow reports that in 1564 on New Year's Eve many games were played on the ice below Westminster, including football, but on the third day a quick thaw set in causing much flooding and many people were drowned in their houses. In 1608 a great Frost fair was held in London – one of the first to be organized on a grand scale. There were dancing, games, archery and football. Booths were set up and all kinds of refreshments were on sale including hot chestnuts baked over braziers on the ice. There is a rare tract describing this Fair, with a woodcut showing the stalls with London Bridge in the distance. It is entitled 'Cold Doings in London, except it be at the Lottery' and is mentioned by Gough in his *British Topography*. From Elizabethan times people skated on the ice with skate blades made from animal bones.

In Charles II's time whole oxen were roasted on the ice and banquets were held in tents put up for the occasion. Printing presses were a new attraction and many were set up at Frost fairs and people queued to have their name, the date and place printed on a card to take home as a memento of the occasion. Charles visited one of these booths with his family in January 1684 and had these words printed on a card:

Charles, King,
James, Duke,
Katherine, Queen,
Mary, Duchess,
Anne, Princess,
George, Prince,
Hans in Gelder.

James, Duke of York, was Charles's brother, later to become James II. Katherine was the wife of Charles. Mary and Anne were the daughters of James. George, Prince of Denmark, was Anne's husband. Hans in Gelder was included by Charles probably with his tongue in his cheek and represents Anne's unborn child. Hans in Gelder literally means 'Jack in the Cellar'. Anne had 17 children and survived them all.

The printer was G. Croom who later published this verse entitled 'Thamasis's Advice to the Painter from her frigid zone':

To the Print-house go,

Where Men in the Art of Printing soon do know;
Where for a Teaster, you may have your name
Printed, hereafter for to show the same;
And sure in former Ages, ne'er was found,
A Press to print, where men so oft were drowned.

A line of tents across the ice from Temple Stairs was temporarily named Temple Street in February 1684.

The last Fair to be held on the ice was in 1814, and the weight must have been tremendous; there were bookstalls, swings, dancing in a barge, all kinds of meats cooked on fires on the ice, skittles and the usual booths for eating and freak displays. The printing presses were there, greatly improved models to those first displayed in the Stuart era. On 5 February the ice cracked suddenly and all booths and equipment floated away and sank – the traders losing everything they had. By curious coincidence the last card to be printed was for a lady known as Madame Tabitha Thaw!

The chronicler FitzStephen who wrote in the twelfth century recorded that the bazaar system, one place being known for one particular kind of commodity, existed in London in those days. The names of the older streets in the City such as Bread Street and Milk Street, Cornhill, Fish Street and Hill, Poultry, the Vintry, Honey Lane and so on reflect the wares sold there, probably going back to Saxon and even Roman times. FitzStephen says: 'The followers of the several trades, the vendors of various commodities and the labourers of every kind are daily to be found in their proper and distinct places, according to their employments.' He also mentions that on the river bank in those days were wine and eating shops and some of the liquor was sold to customers from the moored ships – people took their own containers on board and bought it duty free.

Eilert Ekwall in his enlightening book entitled *Street Names of the City of London* mentions the following places and their original trades:

Do Little Lane – now Knightrider Court – meant, as the name says, a place where people were lazy and did nothing for a living.

Cannon Steeet was named after the chandlers or candlemakers who lived and worked there. Pepys knew it as Canning Street and its old English name was Candelwyrtha, meaning Candle-wright.

There were four lanes named Love Lane and this usually denoted a street where harlots lived, or it may have been descriptive of a harmless pastime – namely a place where lovers walked – such as Lover's Lane which is common today.

Friday Street near Billingsgate was so called because it commemorated the meatless day, Good Friday, the day of Christ's death. This started a custom of eating fish on Fridays and Friday Street sold fish.

Stew Lane was a place south from Upper Thames Street where hot baths could be obtained.

Fowle Lane, now merged in Cross Lane near the Tower, meant as might be expected a place which was dirty and unclean, as was Stinking Lane now King Edward Street near Aldersgate – a place where butchers lived, and their meat often went bad. It is interesting to note that Pudding Lane was not a place where puddings were made. In fact the word pudding in olden times meant offal, which was often rat infested. These parcels of waste were called puddings and were wrapped up and transported down Pudding Lane to be tipped into the river, near Lower Thames Street in Eastcheap. Rattones Lane meant the same thing.

Seething Lane was a place where corn had been threshed and was full of chaff or bran, first recorded near Tower Street in 1258. Cow Lane, now King Street, was where cows were kept and milked and Honey Lane was the place where bees were kept, the honey providing the only sweetener in early times.

Lad Lane was a place where ladles were made and Shoe Lane was named after the piece of land next to it shaped like a shoe, and was not a place where shoes were made.

Birchin Lane was the place where barbers cut hair, derived from the English word Beardceofere. Billiter Street was a place where bells were cast and the word is a corruption of Belzettarse or Belsetters Lane. Fetter Lane was known as a place where cheats and people shamming illness lived. Haggen Lane was so named because ugly old women lived there!

Public toilets were often mentioned in early records and the name Sherbourne may indicate that a toilet was once here, derived from Shiteburgh.

Spittle Lane or Spital Lane is derived from hospital, of which there were many attached to monasteries before the Dissolution. In Chancery Lane a house was chosen by the reigning monarch which he thought safe enough in which to deposit valuable papers and rolls. In time this became the seat of Chancery and now the Public Record Office stands on the site.

Duke Street was originally called Duck Street and, of course, housed ducks.

Turnagain Lane was a blind alley west of Snow Hill and was known in 1293 and 1413.

Ivy Lane, Paternoster Row and Newgate Street were thoroughfares where ivy grew prolifically. By the side of St. Paul's the makers of rosaries and scripture writers lived and the names such as Ave Maria Lane, and Amen Court reflect this. Later St. Paul's churchyard became famous for its printing and publishing works.

Piccadilly was named after Piccadilly House – the home of a manufacturer of shirt frills which he called 'Pickadills' – but Gerard, in his famous *Herbal* published in 1596 mentions a dry bank in an area called Pickadilla where the plant named the wild buglosse could be found growing. As dilly is an old country name for wild flower, the name was probably applied by the locals to a place, near Green Park, where wild flowers could be picked – long before the shirt manufacturer came on the scene.

Many more of the street names remind us of conduits and rivers which once served the community with 'sweet water' such as Conduit Street, and Holbourne (Old Bourne) and there is more about this in the section dealing with the water supply.

A lane had only to be wide enough for two men to roll a barrel and this is remembered in Fye Foot Lane – one only five feet wide in early times – now merged with Queen Victoria Street. Henry I stipulated that a street could not be named as such unless it was paved and was wide enough for sixteen knights to ride abreast.

In Tudor times houses with bay windows were introduced and people started to use these windows to display their wares and this was the beginning of the closed-in shop that we know today. Each shop or tavern had a sign board outside because most people were illiterate and could only recognize pictures or emblems. Some banks have retained their original signs to this day: the black horse for Lloyds, the black eagle for Barclays and the cat and fiddle for the Royal Bank of Scotland. Until recently there was a sign in Fish Street which was originally on the Old London Bridge and indicated rope or net makers. It showed a boat called a Peter-boat, after St. Peter, and two men rowing, one holding a net. The emblems were the work of the College of Heraldry and each design had to be different.

In the records of Knightsbridge Chapel is to be found the record of the marriage of Robert Hand to Mary Gwin, Nell Gwyn's sister, on 13 January 1667. It is known that their mother lived near Neate House in Pimlico, not far away. Chelsea buns were produced roughly thirty years later in the 'Old Original Chelsea Bun-house' in Jews' Row, and the business was owned by a baker named Richard Hand, who baked buns with currants in them, topped with sugar which became a great favourite with Londoners. It is probable that this man was the nephew of Nell Gwyn. The bakery and shop was a one-storied building with a verandah projecting over the footpath. It was often visited by royalty – George II and Queen Caroline and George III and Queen Charlotte were great Chelsea bun fans. Queen Charlotte presented Mrs. Hand with a silver half-gallon mug with five guineas in it. On Good Fridays up to 5,000 people queued up to buy buns and the Chelsea variety outshone the hot cross variety at this time. Trade from Ranelagh, a nearby mansion with extensive grounds, patronised by the nobility, was extensive.

Up to the middle of the last century there were many shops of ancient origin to be seen still trading in London. The oldest tea trader in the City was Davison and Newman and Co. Ltd., and the story goes that they supplied the tea for the famous Boston tea party. The shop was in Creechurch Lane off Leadenhall Street near Aldgate Pump, and the sign was dated 1650 and showed three lumps of sugar and a crown. We are a nation of shopkeepers as Napoleon rightly said and nowhere in the world are shops dated as they are or were in London up to recent times. It is with pride that they display proof of centuries of continuous trading and those that have had the advantage of supplying royalty have a coat of arms signifying this honour. The Soho tradesmen, with their ageless shops, were mostly descended from an old Huguenot family. The legend that the streets of London were paved with gold may have originated from the fact that these tradesmen had a wealth of gold, silver and precious metals which they made up into every knick-knack imaginable. They gave the area a sense of grandeur and splendour; their shining windows reflected the lamplight on to the wet roads in the damp London weather, and seemingly turned the very pavements to gold. Later this part became known for select eating-houses for the more unconventional clientele.

One of the most interesting shops in Cheapside was Bennet's clock shop, which thrived until the twentieth century. This shop was of unique design incorporating eight clock faces which told the time in different parts of the world. It had two bell alcoves – one housing Gog and Magog. On the roof was a ball six ft in diameter which dropped down its pole with a resounding boom precisely on every hour. The shop was demolished in 1929 and Henry Ford bought the figures Gog and Magog and installed them in the Edison Institute at Greenfield, Michigan.

The large bazaar shops, many under one roof and usually glazed, came into being around 1845. (One is mentioned specifically in the section dealing with Bow Street Runners.) In 1909 a large departmental store opened by Gordon Selfridge in Oxford Street was a great step forward in the development of trade to the general public. People flocked to see this wondrous shop where one was allowed to wander round freely without being pressed to buy. Baird gave his first public display of television in this shop and many other attractions were organized to lure the people in, as they are today. Selfridges put Oxford Street on the map as one of the busiest shopping centres in the West End. Park Lane, St. James's Street and Bond Street have some of the most exclusive shops in London, serving royalty and monied people from all over the world. Mayfair, once the site of a disreputable fair which was closed in George III's reign, turned over a new leaf and became a very fashionable area indeed. Fortnum and Mason claim to be the oldest store in London and have a neatly recorded history to prove it. Not many shops have kept records and Fortnum and Mason are to be congratulated for their diligence.

But enough of the successful, the people with property and money and a chance to survive and become prosperous. London's streets had another story to tell – the story of the poor. For if we have a Third World today, then in Victorian times we had a Third London. A London that nobody seemed to care about. Only a few, like Mayhew and Dickens, tried through their writings to draw public attention to the plight of the sick, starving and dying masses. Roughly two-thirds of the population of the capital were living a hand-to-mouth existence at this time. Babies and very young children were often left unattended all day whilst their parents were out looking for work to earn a few coppers for food and rent. Young children were often drugged by a substance called Godfrey's cordial, a mixture of treacle and opium, or were given gin, to put them to sleep and dull the pangs of hunger. Both these remedies often resulted in addled brains and ultimate death at an early age. If a child survived until the age of five or over then it was sent out either to beg or become a small-time vendor, selling watercress or matches or some such trivia. Some became crossing sweepers, buying a broom for 2½d. and working in the West End where the richer people lived. Boys often served as apprentices to chimney sweeps and nobody cared if they got stuck in a flue or choked to death – they were expendable. Charles Kingsley in his *Water Babies* vividly portrays these conditions.

Many parents were too ill to work and had to 'lie up' in decrepit hovels, hoping that their children would earn a few pence to keep them alive. The Rookeries were notorious tumbledown shacks bought up by hardened landlords and let for a few pence to the poorest of the poor. They were uninhabitable by our standards, had no water, no sewerage arrangements and were liable to collapse and often did, killing or maiming the luckless tenants. Lice, vermin, filth and disease were the companions of the people who lived in the Rookeries.

Mudlarking was considered the lowest and most degrading occupation of all, and it was often left to the children to wade into the water of the Thames to search for and salvage anything of value from the river. Pieces of coal dropped from coal carriers, bones, nails or pieces of iron would be sifted out of the mud and put aside to be sold later to the costers or people in houses near by. The poor little mudlarks depended on the flotsam and jetsam of the river to keep them alive. When the end of the day came they would trudge back to their shacks and sleep in mud-soaked rags until it was time to start all over again. Clothes were a problem – old-clothes shops known as 'fripperies', dating back to

Fleet Ditch, 1841. Back of Field Lane

Elizabethan times sold trousers and coats for roughly 2d. or 3d., caps and mufflers for 1d., but shoes were much dearer so the very poor went barefooted.

A group of men known in those days as 'shore men' gained a living by working down the sewers. They worked in gangs, never on their own, as the sewers were infested with fierce rats, some as big as cats, which would attack and kill a man working alone. They were more skilled than the mudlarks and certainly earned themselves a better standard of living. For there was money in the sewers, literally – coins were often dropped accidentally down drains and sinks as were other articles, especially silver spoons and jewellery. Keys and many other items found their way underground and became lodged in cracks in the brickwork. In those days the sewers emptied their contents into the river by open ended pipes and this is where the shore men gained entrance underground. This was dangerous work, for not only were the rats a menace, but if there was a heavy rainfall the underground pipes became full and overflowed into the streets, thus sending the sewage back to the people as it were. The shore men were in danger of being drowned when this occurred. Later, the sewer exits were blocked so that the water could only flow outwards; the shore men could not gain entrance and many lost their livelihood. They had character names like Lanky Bill, One-eyed George, Short-armed Jack and so on, and also had many stories to tell about their adventures down the sewers. One such tale concerned a sow who, it was said, wandered down an open sewer and got lost underground. She had a litter and fed herself and the piglets on garbage and offal. The breed multiplied and became a wild herd of hogs inhabiting the sewers under Hampstead Heath. They were known as the Hampstead monsters. Inhabitants in the area swore that they heard grunts and squeals coming from underground although they were never seen by anyone but the shore men. After the closing of the river pipes, many shore men went to work for the councils, cleaning out the sludge which accumulated on the walls of the brick tunnels, and also of course they still carried out their search for valuables.

Coster-Monger's Barrow

The produce found in the sewers and river was often sold in the streets, and street vending, dating from pre-Roman times, gathered impetus during the last century. The outstanding group of street vendors in Victorian times was the costermongers. The name of coster came originally from 'custard', a kind of apple introduced during the Roman occupation. The coster was usually a cheerful individual who had a barrow and a loud cry and comic patter to attract the customers. The shop keepers saw to it that as costers did not pay rent or rates they were not given a licence to sell their produce on one particular pitch. Therefore they were not allowed by the police to rest their barrows for a minute, even when making a sale, and were compelled to push the carts through the streets all day long until they were sold out or had to retire through exhaustion. The police became the enemy of the costers who did everything they could to annoy the officers of the law, including developing two kinds of slang to baffle the listeners.

One was to talk backwards – 'look at the policeman' became 'cool the namesclop' — and the other was rhyming slang, the origins of which I have gone into in detail in my book *Origins of Rhymes, Songs and Sayings.*

When not selling their wares costers would spend leisure time in taverns, holding lively singsongs, spending their money, and organizing dancing in the street to which their womenfolk were invited. They were loyal to each other and if one went sick or was sent to prison the others would rally round and help his family. Gradually this aid became more organized. Groups were formed within the parish and a leader elected. They would collect money for their own from their own: farthings, halfpennies — whatever could be spared went into the 'distress fund'. The costers were a proud race and would rather go to prison than ask for help from the 'Big House' as they called the workhouse. They collected for the East End hospitals for, unlike the people in charge of parish relief, the doctors and staff there were 'on the side' of the poor and always did their very best for them. But hospitals depended on charity and so the costers did their very best to collect funds in every way they could. Clubs were set up to raise money; some were temperance societies but the costers usually met in public houses. These societies dressed up at the weekends and paraded the streets collecting money – one such club was termed the Jolliboys and according to Pearl Binder in her fascinating book *The Pearlies*, Fred Tinsley was a Jolliboy before becoming the first Pearly King of Southwark. Strangely enough it was not a coster that first sewed pearl buttons on to his clothes but a road sweeper. Henry Croft was less than five feet tall but what he lacked in inches he made up for in vitality. An orphan himself, he devoted his life to helping the poor and soon joined the costers of Pancras where he lived joining in the dressing-up parades and carnivals. There is a legend which relates that around 1880 a boat carrying a cargo of pearl buttons foundered in the Thames and jettisoned its cargo. The poor of London, so we are told, waded in the water and collected the thousands of pearl buttons. Henry Croft had the idea of sewing buttons on to his old worn suit, copying a music-hall star of the day who had sewn brass buttons on to his costume for decoration. He not only covered his suit in 'smother' fashion, so that not one thread of material was showing, but he also covered his old worn-out top hat, shoes and stick. He made his appearance at a carnival and was an immediate success. Soon every coster who could afford it was sewing pearlies on his clothes. As many as 60,000 buttons were needed for a 'smother' costume, which weighed up to $\frac{3}{4}$ cwt. Henry Croft was elected Pearly King of Somerstown and one of his pearly jackets bore the message 'World King of the Pearlies'. Soon every district in the East End had its own Pearly royalty and the early Pearly families passed on the traditions to the next generation. Although Henry Croft had twelve children none of his family, regrettably, carried on the Pearly line and his name was not perpetuated after his death. It is estimated that he collected over £5,000 during his lifetime, all in small change, and when he died in 1930 the costers gave him the best 'send off' that they could muster. Four hundred Pearlies dressed in splendid costumes followed his coffin with decorated donkey carts and it formed one of the most spectacular of all London funerals. He is buried in Finchley cemetery with his family and there is a monument of him over the grave dressed in his Pearly outfit, complete with top hat and walking-stick. Incidentally one of his Pearly suits was found in an attic in 1974 by a member of his family and this inspired the Pearly Exhibition held at Selfridges the same year.

As the 'smother' outfit was heavy and expensive it was replaced generally by patterns and mottoes in pearl buttons sewn on to clothes, usually indicating which part of London the coster represented. The shimmer of pearl buttons fascinated the costers – they were the emblem of Cockney royalty as precious to them as the Crown Jewels were to the royalty of England.

Today the cult of the Pearlies is declining. The welfare state has stepped in and taken away the burden of the poor to a large extent. There are still some cockney royalty that carries on the traditions and they are in great demand to open fêtes and exhibitions, especially overseas where interest in the Pearlies is still high. Long may they reign!

Soon the wheeled barrow as used by the costers was developed to serve the community in many ways and licences were obtainable to vend in the streets. Enterprising salesmen thought up all sorts of ways to earn money. Thus the cat-meat man was a regular roundsman, selling pieces of horse meat on skewers like kebabs.

Handcart for Cat's Meat, 1903

If the lady of the house was away she would leave a note for the cat-meat man to put a stick of meat through the letter-box to feed the cat shut up in the house. The cat-meat barrow was followed from street to street by dozens of cats and dogs, many of them starving, hoping that a morsel would be dropped from the cart. Among others there was a knife grinder, a tinker, a stall that sold cups of tea (financed by the temperance society!) and even a photographer who walked the streets with his camera perched on his barrow. Advertising, too, started this way, with barrows displaying advertising boards. Later, hot foods such as chestnuts, pies and hot potatoes came on the scene.

Tea Stall to discourage drunkeness, 1885

Knife Grinder's Handcart, 1877

The oldest street vendors of all, the people selling from trays such trivia as matches, buttons, watercress, laces, cottons and studs, could be described as the human pavement fringe. The vendors who had spirit and enterprise chose their pitches in the West End, where the monied people lived, and fared rather better than the ones who were too exhausted or ill to move far from their dwellings.

The old lady of Charing Cross sat selling newspapers in London all her life. Her mother had brought her there as a baby and she sat on her mother's knee until she was old enough to carry on the business. She sat in a decrepit chair in the midst of London's traffic until she was well advanced in years and when she finally retired the lamp-post under which she used to sit was pulled down and a cross put in the pavement to depict a water main. Passers-by who knew and loved her said the cross was her monument.

Another lady, with genteel manners, good looking even in old age, used to sell pipe cleaners and collar studs in Fleet Street. She was wise and gave counsel to anyone who asked for it. The other vendors in the area respected her and she was called the Queen of Fleet Street.

A woman called Mary of Dockland was a hunchback, not smart or even very clean, but she possessed the kindest heart imaginable, devoting her life to the service of sailors. They used her address in Canton Street as a place for their letters and documents to be sent. Mary was more trustworthy than any naval establishment.

She stuck the letters in the frame of her mirror and they stayed there until the sailor owners came to collect them.

The real beggars, those who were deformed, blind or had been wounded in wars, had to rely on friends to take them to and from their pitches each day. They also had to rely on the generosity of passers-by who would contribute a coin and receive nothing in return. Animals, especially dogs, played a large part in extracting money from the public for their beggar masters, and even as early as Edwardian times it is known that dogs were used to guide their blind masters along the streets. There was a brigade of begging dogs organized by the Boer War wounded that collected money for this cause – there was no other relief given at this time. A dog named Tim collected money for the widows and orphans of the Great Western Railway outside Paddington station for many years. Royalty favoured this dog and many gold coins were given. It is recorded that he collected over £1,000 for the fund. Another, named London Jack, a dog who had done many brave deeds for mankind, was remembered outside Waterloo station and substantial sums of money were collected in the box under its effigy. Later a live dog took over the pitch to collect money for the Orphanage Fund.

Photographer's Handcart 1877

Pavement artists or skeevers were many in Victorian times and after, and they were allowed a pitch on which to draw by the police. Again the West End was favoured and many of the artists were very talented and did in fact supply a picture gallery for the streets. Ladies, too, indulged in this occupation and in Edward VII's reign a small boy used to draw with chalks on the pavement whilst his mother went round soliciting alms. It is said that one day the King stopped and gave a gold sovereign to the boy. Today, skeevers can still be seen in some parts of London.

Street musicians were common during this period, many of whom were blind. Trumpets, violins, and organs were played – the last perhaps being the most prolific, with a monkey, often badly treated, sitting on top. The German band was well known during Victoria's reign and usually gave good quality renderings of the popular songs and tunes of the day.

The distress of the poor in London in Victorian times was great indeed, but towards the end of the century various individuals had set up centres to lessen some of the suffering for, as Tennyson said,

> Is it well, that while we range with
> Science, glorying in the time,
> City children soak and blanken
> Soul and sense in city slime?

The newly formed police force helped to alleviate the situation by picking up ragged children from the streets and taking them to one of the recently opened shelters such as those set up by Dr. Barnardo or Thomas Coram. As early as 1739 a Royal Charter was granted to Coram, a master of a trading vessel, to receive illegitimate children into a hospital provided for this purpose. At first a house in Hatton Garden was commissioned but it could only take twenty when more than a hundred children a day were offered for acceptance. This resulted in a riot by the mothers, many of whom were prostitutes. Henceforth women balloted for a place for their child by drawing balls out of a bag. The present hospital, named the Foundling Hospital, was built by Jacobson in Brunswick Square and, in 1745, 600 children were moved there, and the government provided an income of £10,000 per year. A basket was hung outside so that unwanted babies could be deposited after the bell had been rung to give warning. The consequence of this practice was lamentable – prostitution greatly increased as women did not worry if they knew their babies would be taken care of. It also resulted in a high percentage of sickly babies, many of whom died. Hogarth, Ramsay, Reynolds, Gainsborough and many other artists became interested and supported the work of the hospital as did Handel, who presented an organ and an original manuscript of the *Messiah*. Coram is buried in the vaults of the building. Today, though no children live in, about thirty live in foster homes.

Much has been written of how, towards the end of the nineteenth century, Dr. Barnardo set up homes for waifs and strays in London, as well as schools where children could learn a trade and at the same time be fed, housed and cared for. By 1908 more than 50,000 children had passed through the hands of Dr. Barnardo and his teachers and many were sent to the Commonwealth – Canada taking a large proportion – to work on the land. When the children grew up many of them helped the organization that had given them a start in life. Dr. Barnardo built many homes in London all with 'the ever open door'. One was situated near Bow Church and called simply the 'Tinies House'. In Stockwell Orphanage a small boy named Bray was dying in 1888. He gave all he owned, 4s. 6d., to the foundation for bricks to build the newest wing – a house for girls. It was then built, and 'Bray's bricks' have been famous ever since.

Shelters and doss houses were provided by the Salvation Army and other relief organizations. Penny sit-ups were common in Victorian times, which was certainly better than sleeping rough on the embankment or under a bridge. People were allowed to sleep on a bench under cover for the night for the price of a penny. Other houses provided clothes-lines where down-and-outs paid a penny or tuppence to sleep standing up with their head and arms hanging over the rope. This is where the expressions 'I could sleep on a clothes-line' and 'to drop off' come from. This method of passing the night was also termed 'a tuppenny hangover'. A man, nicknamed the 'valet', cut the rope at 5 a.m. and the sleepers had a rude awakening. The phrase 'it's a case of knowing the ropes' is derived from an experienced dosser knowing the doss-houses which provided the best 'rope facilities' for the money.

With the coming of State education in 1871 the lives and hardships of the poor of London were brought to the notice of the authorities in no mean way. Teachers learnt first-hand of the sufferings of poor families and the squalor in which they were forced to live. Committees and councils were set up by the government to help the distressed and although the rates went up, naturally, the living conditions of the slum people gradually began to improve. There were more charities, more hospitals, more crèches and free kitchens. Public baths became available and more recreational facilities were provided, including free public libraries, and people were encouraged to learn to read.

I have mentioned some of the shops of the rich but have not said anything about the shops, especially the food shops, serving the poor during the Industrial Revolution and after. Poor people queued 'round the back' of big West End food shops to buy broken food, pieces of meat, misshapen loaves, trimmings of fish and stale biscuits and cakes at greatly reduced prices. In the East End the 'farthing shops' supplied the needs of the destitute. All goods were sold loose and the buyer brought his own container. The smallest amount sold was a farthingworth – thus a farthingworth of milk could be bought and taken away in a strong paper bag shaped like a cone. A small chunk of bread could be bought for the same amount, also a pickled onion. These shops stayed open for very long hours and all day Sunday – and the shopkeepers never had a day off.

STORIES OF FLEET STREET
AND THE INNS OF COURT

Fleet Street and the Inns of Court as we know them today had a communal beginning. In the thirteenth century a large stretch of land in Holborn belonged to the monastery of Blackfriars, but towards the end of the century most of it was sold to Henry de Lacy, later to become the Earl of Lincoln. The gardens produced expensive fruit and vegetables which served the aristocracy of the time, and were watered by the river Fleet. This was a small but rapidly flowing stream rising in Hampstead and gathering other streams which became a wide and useful waterway before it

Fleet Ditch, 1749

reached the Thames. In the Middle Ages the Fleet was deep
enough to take large ships inland as far as Camden Town. It was
crossed by four bridges, Oldbourne and Fleet being the best
known. Many Saxon and Roman relics, including ring coins, have
been found in the river mud and seem to prove that the Fleet
was used probably before Christ. During the eighteenth and nineteenth centuries the area deteriorated into near slums and the
river Fleet was polluted beyond measure. Over the years it was
gradually filled in and now serves as a sewer under Farringdon
Street. The old Stocks market was removed to the site of the Fleet
and the area that had been a market was used to build the first
Mansion House.

Fleet Street extends from the junction of Farringdon Street and
New Bridge Street to the site of the now-removed Temple Bar.
This was and still is the boundary of the City, the Strand on the
other side belonging to the City of Westminster. It is one of the
most known and celebrated thoroughfares in the City and for
many centuries has been famous for its exhibitions and processions; its printers, stationers and booksellers; its early coffee-

houses, taverns and banking houses. The shops were just rude shacks in early times and the vendors cried: 'What d'ye lack, gentles? What d'ye lack?' The Street was encumbered with posts upon which performances at theatres were advertised – hence the term posting bills or posters. Although it was the home of the lower classes, used by the apprentices for playing football, and was also the haunt of rogues and thieves, the monarchy had a soft spot for this part of the City. Queen Elizabeth I used to take pleasure in riding through it and giving alms to the poor as did other monarchs.

The Street has its stories to tell, some bloody and others pathetic. In James I's reign, after the discovery of the Gunpowder Plot, feelings against the Catholics, and Spain in particular, were running high. The Spanish ambassador was mobbed by a band of apprentices and the King ordered them to be whipped through the streets from Aldgate to Temple Bar. As the soldiers were carrying out this punishment other apprentices banded together, attacked the soldiers with clubs and rescued their fellow workers. James wisely ignored this action as he knew that if he had claimed retribution he would have had to fight over a thousand apprentices. Thus a very bloody battle was averted. After the accession to the throne of James I from Scotland the influx of Scotsmen was inevitable. They found Fleet Street to their liking, as did the Irish who came over to London to work as navvies after the Great Fire later in the century. These clans came to settle in Fleet Street and open taverns and eating houses. They made good hosts and the journalists found plenty of material to write about while listening to the blarney of the Irish and the tales told by the Scots. In 1715 political feelings came to a head in Fleet Street when the Jacobites, supported by the Tories, pressed hard for the son of James II to be crowned king, but he was a Catholic and unacceptable by English law. The Whigs upheld George of Hanover, a German with links with the royal line, and he was crowned King of England even though he could speak no English. Riots broke out and the Whigs took over certain taverns in Fleet Street in which to hold meetings. These places became known as 'mug houses'. The derisory term 'mug' for an ugly face is derived from the fact that the face of Lord Shaftesbury adorned the drinking vessels in the Whig taverns at the time. The Tories also took over certain meeting houses in the Street and many battles developed. The Tories supporting the Jacobites wore white roses, rue, thyme or rosemary in their hats and carried oak branches decorated with green ribbons. According to Claud Golding in his book *London – the City* the Tories had rallying cries of 'High Church', 'No King George' and 'Down with Presbyterians'. The Whigs wore orange cockades in their hats and chanted in reply 'With heart and hand by George we'll stand', and the term 'By George' dates from this. On royal birthdays the Whigs lit bonfires outside the taverns occupied by the Tories and in July 1716 there ensued a fierce battle and at last the 'greens' had to retreat. They planned a counter-attack but changed their minds when they heard that the Horse Guards were assembled in Horse Guards Parade to quell further fighting. The Tories, or Jacks as they were called, attacked Whig ale-houses and a certain Mr. Read, proprietor of a mug house in Salisbury Court, was accused of murdering a man called Vaughan by shooting him in cold blood. This was a case for the courts but the jury members, being either Whig or Tory, could not agree on a verdict. At last Read was given bail and five rioters were hanged at Tyburn. This caused so much fury amongst the Tories that the mob pillaged and burnt Read's property and nobody dared to intervene.

In 1745 at the time of the second Jacobite uprising, when Bonnie Prince Charlie, already crowned King of Scotland, reached the Midlands, the position of the Jacobites in London was very strong. King George had already made arrangements for a ship to take him to the Continent should the Scottish army reach London, and the Scots had flags and posters to welcome their Scottish hero who would undoubtedly have been crowned King of England. But this was not to be and Charlie, taking the advice of his generals, turned and retreated to Scotland, to be routed by the English at the Battle of Culloden Moor.

Two stories of Fleet Street show the cruelties that apprentices had to bear whilst other folk went about their business in ignorance. One tells of two young girls taken from a foundling hospital by a certain Mrs. Brownrigg to help with work in the family. Mrs. Brownrigg had access to the hospital as she was a midwife there. The girls were treated so badly that one of them escaped and went back to the hospital but the other was not so lucky and was constantly beaten and maltreated because she was in a sickly condition and could not work well. She was frequently stripped and caned with her hands tied to a beam above her head. Her wounds became septic and she developed a high fever and was locked in a cupboard in the cellar. A baker who lived opposite heard cries and moans issuing from a grating and called the overseers of the parish to investigate. The girl was found near to death and was taken to St. Bartholomew's Hospital where after a day she died. Elizabeth Brownrigg and her son disguised themselves and escaped to Wandsworth where they were finally caught and brought to trial at the Old Bailey. Brownrigg was sentenced to death and on her way to Tyburn the fury of the mob showed itself and she was pelted with stones and would have been lynched but for the guards who wanted her to die in the manner decreed by her sentence. After the execution the body was thrown into a cart and taken to Surgeons' Hall for dissection. Her husband and son were sentenced to six months' imprisonment but never came out of prison alive.

The other story is entitled 'The Chick Lane Ghost' and concerns a mother and daughter called Metyard who ran a milliner's business in Chick Lane, just off Fleet Street. They took two young girls as apprentices from a nearby workhouse. One girl, named Anne Naylor, was unwell and could not do the work allocated to her. She was ill-treated by the Metyards and tried to run away but was caught. For punishment the Metyards tied her to the back door without food and water for four days, where she died. The mother and daughter hid the body in a box and told her companion that Anne had run away again. After about two months the stench became unbearable and in the dead of night the Metyards cut up the body and carried it in sacks to the river Fleet where they intended to deposit it. They were interrupted and had to leave the sacks on the bank where they were found by a warder. Although the body was examined, no charges were made at this time. Later the mother took to beating her own daughter and when a lodger came to live with them, a man named Rooker, he saw her plight and persuaded her to go and live with him elsewhere as his mistress. This infuriated Mother Metyard and everywhere the couple went she followed and caused trouble. The daughter began to make mysterious references to 'The Chick Lane

Ghost' and eventually told Rooker the whole story. Mother and daughter were sent to trial and were hanged at Tyburn – both blaming each other to the last.

As mentioned, the Street was famous since early times for its taverns and good food shops. The Cock Tavern was well known in Samuel Pepys's time as a meeting house for journalists. Pepys records in his diary that he spent many convivial evenings there in the company of a certain Mrs. Knap – an actress hated by Mrs. Pepys who, we are told, took a pair of red-hot tongs and threatened to tweak her husband's nose with them if he digressed again! After the introduction of sausages to Britain in the nineteenth century a celebrated restaurant called the 'Sausage Shop' was opened and such people as Kier Hardy, Hilaire Belloc, G. K. Chesterton, Edgar Wallace and Viscount Northcliffe patronized it. The Cheshire Cheese was an ancient eating house and as its name suggests it specialized in cheeses – but not only cheeses, in puddings also. Meat puddings were cooked here during the winter and the first cut of this famous dish was made in October and became a notable event – celebrities being called in to do the honours. These have included in recent years Jack Dempsey the boxer, Dean Inge of St. Paul's, Stanley Baldwin, Conan Doyle, and various titled people. The pudding took nearly twenty hours to cook and weighed between fifty and eighty pounds. When it was boiling the aroma could be smelt as far away as the Stock Exchange when the wind was in the right direction. The ingredients included beef steak, kidneys, mushrooms, oysters and spices.

Printers settled in Fleet Street from early times and we know that an apprentice of Caxton named William de Worde set up the first hand screw printing press here in the fifteenth century. A surviving imprint, *Demandes Joyous*, with the following declaration endorses this:

> Emprynted at London in Fletestre
> at the signe of the Swane by
> me Wynkyne de Worde
> In the yere of our
> Lord A M
> ccccc
> and xi

Newberry of St. Paul's Churchyard printed a pamphlet called *News out of Holland* in 1619 and it was followed by various papers giving news of other European countries. The first weekly newspaper printing news of London seems to have been one called *Certain News of the Present Week* and was edited by Nathaniel Butter in 1622. Many literary gentlemen such as Dr. Johnson, Charles Lamb and Oliver Goldsmith have lived in Fleet Street. They met in taverns to discuss the affairs of the day and here the seeds of journalism were sown. In the mid eighteenth century a room in a house in Shoe Lane just off Fleet Street became the debating venue for 'Cogers', a democratic club for tradesmen, lawyers, mechanics and so on. A man given the title of 'My Grand' was appointed chairman and was usually an important representative of a newspaper. He led the arguments, listened to opinions and supposedly wrote and published features for his paper. This was the beginning of the 'Street' as we know it today – the newspaper centre of Great Britain and perhaps the world. And, more importantly, as 'My Grand' had freedom of the Press so the tradition has continued and hopefully will never change. *The Times* was the first solid newspaper to be published in London and was revered by all right from the start. In the mid nineteenth century it occupied the site of a shop owned by Alderman Waitman, no. 103, Fleet Street. *The Daily News* was edited by Charles Dickens and first published in January 1846, but he soon handed over the post to others as he could not find time to enter into the world of journalism, as well as being an author of many books. Most of the newspapers were published in Fleet Street because this being the most convenient place between the Houses of Parliament, Whitehall and the Law Courts, they were centrally situated as far as news of the day went and Ben Jonson called the area 'the staple of news'. Up to the mid twentieth century the *Daily Mail*, the *Sunday Express* and *Evening Standard* were produced in Shoe Lane. The Daily Mail operated from Northcliffe House which bears the name of the gentleman who once frequented the Fleet Street taverns early in the last century.

The Temple had its origins in the Crusades when the Knights of the Templars built a Temple in London similar to the one built in Jerusalem to commemorate the victory of the Christians over the Saracens. People were proud of the Crusade soldiers and impressed by their bravery and soon a large monastery gave them patronage. As time went on both the monastery and the Templars alike became rich and greedy and the aims of the Crusades were forgotten. The Church quarrelled with the Knights and the Abbot finally convinced the Pope that the soldiers were opposed to Christianity and worshipped idols. This resulted in the Pope denouncing the Order and the whole concept was broken up. In the fourteenth century much of the land that had belonged to the Templars became the property of another order of knights – namely the Order of Knights Hospitalliers who sold the Temple to the lawyers.

In the seventeenth century, when the venue at Westminster became too noisy for them, the lawyers moved in bulk to the Law Courts and have been there since that time. Many of the servants of the knights stayed on and served the lawyers retaining their old name of panniers. Other customs were kept such as the lawyers dining in pairs and the judges of the Common Pleas adhering to the title of Knight. The four Inns of Court developed over the years. The area was always famous for its gardens, even before the lawyers moved in. The vegetables produced in the garden of the mansion of the Earl of Lincoln, before it became an Inn of Court were, in the days of Edward I, a luxury only the élite could afford. Onions, beans and leeks were grown, also pear trees and vines, and roses were prolific. In 1663 the garden was enlarged and Pepys mentions this in his diary with the utmost satisfaction. The garden wall in Chancery Lane is said to have been partly built by Ben Jonson and this is remembered in rhyme:

> Gray's Inn for Walks,
> Lincoln's Inn for a Wall
> Inner Temple for a Garden
> And Middle Temple for a Hall.

It is said that Shakespeare produced his plays in the Halls and Gardens of the Inns and this may be so, as his patron, the Earl of Southampton, was a member of Lincoln's Inn. All the Courts have magnificent Halls and beautiful and well laid-out gardens where sundials can be seen with such inscriptions as 'Shadows we are and like shadows we depart' and 'Time and tide wait for no man'. The queerest message of all reads 'Begone about your business' and the story goes that when the mason asked his master what inscription he would like on his new sundial the man, busy at the time, replied 'Begone about your business' and the mason took it literally and carried out the order.

Gray's Inn once had an uninterrupted view over fields to Hampstead and the gardens were laid out by Sir Francis Bacon during the reign of Elizabeth I. He planned grand avenues of elm trees and hedges and he planted a Catalpa tree which was still a feature of the garden up to a few years ago. The gardens became a fashionable quarter and Pepys visited them one Sunday with his wife after church so that she could observe the fashions of the ladies and go home and make her own!

In the eighteenth century a barber by the name of Dick Danby set up his shop within the grounds of the Inns of Court and was allowed to stay there. He became a mine of information and was popular with the members of Parliament who patronized him for he passed on the gossip of the Courts for a fat fee. He also made wigs for the lawyers which were then, as they are today, part of the regalia of Court proceedings.

There is a story that an old gateman at one of the Inns had been an office boy to Charles Dickens for much of his life. He described Dickens as a man who was always untidily dressed with a black velvet coat and trousers of a large check design – shepherd's plaid to be exact. When asked if Dickens ever wished him a Merry Christmas or gave him a Christmas box the old man shook his head and replied: 'No, he never did. He was much too busy noticing people who noticed him – important people, that is.'

Charing Cross was neutral ground between the City and Westminster and is thought to this day to be the centre of London. Its original name was the Village of Cherringe and it is believed to have been one of the sites of the Eleanor Crosses, together with the one at Cheap, erected by Edward I to commemorate the resting place for his wife's body when it was brought from Nottinghamshire to Westminster Abbey after her death. The name according to some, stems from Eleanor being the 'Chère Reine' of Edward. Another explanation is that it was put up in honour of Eleanor because she was the 'chariest' queen they had known. Charing Cross was originally built of Caen stone with Dorset marble steps, and was highly decorated with paintings and gilded metal figures. In 1647 it was torn down by the mob as were most crosses at that time and since then Charing Cross has only been remembered by the fact that it is the place where streets meet and cross – namely the Strand, Whitehall and Cockspur Street. After the Cross had been desecrated a wit of the day published this droll verse:

> Undone, undone, the lawyers are –
> They wander about the towne,
> Nor can they find the way to Westminster,
> Now Charing Cross is down.
> At the end of the Strand they make a stand,
> Swearing that they are at a loss,
> And chaffing say 'That's not the way,
> They must go by Charing Cross.'

TEMPLE BAR

Temple Bar was erected to mark the boundary between the City and Westminster and divided Fleet Street from the Strand. The earliest recording of this gate is in 1293 when it was described as a simple wooden structure which could be closed. Wards without the City walls were in fact part of the City but the land beyond Temple Bar was the exception, the monarch owning most of it up to the Strand. The Temple Bar was so called as it stood near the Temple church built by the Knights Templar. The old Bar was destroyed in the Great Fire and a magnificent structure, designed by Wren, was erected during the reign of Charles II. The second oldest banking firm was established in the rooms above the archway in the name of Francis Child, and it is said that this firm handled the accounts of Nell Gwyn.

Later, the heads of Jacobite rebels appeared on the spikes of the Bar after both major rebellions had been crushed and people bought spy glasses from street vendors to look more closely at the victims.

Owing to the congestion of traffic the Bar was removed in 1878 to widen the street at this point, and for many years it languished in a yard seemingly forgotten and unwanted. Sir Henry Bruce

Meux had the Bar transported to his estate in Hertfordshire at his own expense and it can be viewed today guarding the entrance to Theobald's Park near Waltham Cross. It must be considered the most impressive entrance to any one property owned by a commoner in this land. Later the authorities decided that they would like the Bar back to erect it once again in London, but Sir Henry refused saying that the people of Hertfordshire had just as much right to have an historical monument within their midst as the citizens of London.

7

Ambulance,
Fire,
Police

The Romans were the first known group of people to set up hospitals in pagan temples for the war wounded. When Christianity was established the monasteries built out-buildings in which to care for the sick. The term hospital is derived from the places of rest, called hospices from the Latin *hopes*, meaning guest, provided by the monks for the pilgrims who visited shrines and holy places. Gradually the monks cared for more and more sick people who lived locally so the meaning of hospital changed to a place for sick people, although the word hospitable still means to entertain a guest in a generous manner. In France a hospital is often called an 'hôtel-Dieu' (house of God) because of its religious connections.

In 1477 there were five main hospitals in the City of London and all were attached to religious houses. The Spital Sermons were preached at St. Paul's and many of the City churches and were named after a priory called St Mary Spittle, spittle meaning hospital, which was founded by Walter Brune and his wife in 1197 and stood in the parish of St. Botolph in Bishopsgate. The Blue Coat boys attended these sermons from their establishment in Newgate Street until the school was moved to Horsham in 1902.

Many of the London hospitals have long and interesting histories but there is not enough space to list them all. St. Bartholomew's, as I have previously related, has special links with the poor of London and deserves pride of place as far as historical detail is concerned. Right from the beginning it became the leading institution for medicine in the country. Although the Priory itself was not lacking in funds, none was channelled to the hospital and the cannons in charge of the sick had to beg from door to door for donations to help carry on the work. Also lay men and women were employed to help with the running of the hospital and this did not please the Abbot and monks who thought everyone who worked and lived at the Priory should be sworn into the Order. Soon merchants and other rich benefactors came to the rescue and by the time of the Dissolution the hospital income was a steady £500 per year. The Priory was dissolved and the hospital committed by Henry VIII to the care of the Lord Mayor and his Councillors. By Letters Patent the King authorized that the hospital was only to be used for the poor and people had to pass a means test before being allowed admission. This was enforced until 1948 when Barts, as it is affectionately known was taken over together with most other hospitals by the Ministry of Health under the National Health Service Act of 1946. Sir Richard Gresham was responsible for obtaining the Letters Patent and the document, sealed with the Great Seal, is still in the hospital's possession.

Paid staff were first employed in 1546 and these included a man termed a renter-clerk who was responsible for collecting the rents from properties owned by the hospital and also for writing the minutes of the Governors' meetings. Although most of the hospital property was sold in 1920 to pay for rebuilding, the post of renter – now called an estate clerk – still stands, and he is the main executive officer of the Board of Governors. The post of steward was created at this time and it was his job to show patients to their wards and to take care of any valuables that they might have brought with them. He also had to buy linen and food for the hospital. Nowadays these duties are divided amongst many and the post of steward belongs to the Patients' Service Department.

After the Dissolution the poor and sick had nowhere to go and many just collapsed and died in the gutters. To alleviate the situation the hospital management appointed eight men to act as beadles covering all sections of the City. It was their task to find people lying ill in the streets and to bring them into the hospital wards to be cared for, and thus began the first ambulance service in London. The word ambulance means at a walking pace and was applied to people carrying the sick and wounded, gently and slowly to a place of safety and healing. When the Police force was formed this task became obsolete but there are still two beadles appointed to help with the smooth running of the hospital. A post of porter was created whose job was to shut and guard the doors each night to prevent thieves or down-and-outs entering illegally and molesting the patients. Today of course there are a great many porters with many varied duties. In 1546 the hospital was created the parish of St. Bartholomew the Less and its Vicar and Curate in modern times are responsible for the spiritual welfare of the patients and those that live on the premises.

First Aid Stretcher Trolley, 1885

The nursing of patients was not of a very high standard in the early days and the staff consisted of a master, eight brethren and four sisters. The sisters wore a grey habit and hood and lived under the rule of St. Augustine of Hippo. Many of the sisters had the 'privilege' of making the hospital their work and home for the rest of their lives in return for gifts of property and money. In 1546 the place became a secular institution and a matron was appointed to see that the sisters carried out their duties in an orderly manner. The tasks covered all kinds of work including cleaning the premises, washing linen, preparing food and so on but not enough time was given to caring for the patients, many of whom died. The sisters now came from the poorer districts of Southwark and Smithfield and were often drunk, rowdy and rude. In an attempt to improve the standard of nursing uniforms or liveries were introduced, the material being described as 'russet frieze' and costing 1od. per yard. The matron and officers had been dressed in blue for some years before this and later the Governors decided that all employees at the hospital should be dressed in 'watchet blue' their uniforms to be made from material which cost 6s. per yard. Today sisters at Barts and in many other hospitals wear blue dresses and the tradition stems from this. Gradually the grading of nurses developed and there emerged the helper, the nurse and the sister, all answerable to the matron who seemed to have increased powers as the years went on. The standard of care however did not improve as nurses were given too much to do and were poorly paid. Very few women therefore, were attracted to the service other than the ignorant and un-educated. Charles Dickens portrays a typical nurse at Barts of his era in his character study of Mrs. Betsy Prigg in *Martin Chuzzlewit*. The sister lived in her ward, fetching the patients' food, washing linen and spinning.

Before the Dissolution the monks used herb remedies and were experienced in healing the sick, but their knowledge and expertise was lost after the closing of the monasteries. In 1548 there were three surgeons at Barts with salaries of £18 per year. The hospital took 150 sick people and the daily allowance to feed and care for the patients was 2d. per person. The surgeons performed operations without anaesthetics and sometimes people fainted before the incision was made, which was convenient, or sometimes they were put out by a blow on the head. Hospitals were feared by the sick and for good reason because before antiseptics were introduced most people died of blood poisoning. It was not until 1865 when Lister developed the use of antiseptics at Charing Cross Hospital that operations became relatively safe. Barts has had many distinguished surgeons and doctors serving between its walls throughout the centuries. Thomas Vicary was appointed physician to Henry VIII after successfully treating his leg. He was a member of both the Barbers' and the Surgeons' Companies and was responsible for their union. The combined Companies were presented with a union charter by the King. William Harvey, who was responsible for demonstrating the circulation of the blood, served at Barts. He was physician to Charles I and accompanied him during the Civil war. Whilst he was away his lodgings in London were sacked and many of his priceless manuscripts were destroyed. Probationers and medical students had to pay for the privilege of being trained and this was the case in all teaching hospitals up to the Second World War.

The standard of nursing improved considerably when Florence Nightingale opened a school for training nurses at St. Thomas's Hospital and St. Bartholomew's soon followed suit. Of course today the standard of nursing in most of the London hospitals and other hospitals in Britain is the highest in the world. Incidentally in the early days the lucky patients who came out of the hospitals alive were told by the doctors to lead a respectable life and not to sin again – as if it was their moral conduct that had brought on the illness!

St. Thomas's Hospital was also a religious establishment to begin with and was founded by Richard Prior of Bermondsey in 1213. In 1538 all the buildings were seized by the King and left to deteriorate. Roughly a hundred years later the lands around the hospital had been bought by the City Council and a charter obtained from the Crown to reopen the hospital. Money was short and funds from the Savoy and other sources were pooled to make the project viable. Up to 1862 this hospital was situated in Southwark and had become a parish in line with Barts. When the site was required to build a railway station the lands were sold for £300,000. The task of finding a new site centrally situated was not easy but at that time the Victoria Embankment was being planned and large portions of the riverbed were to be reclaimed. Eight and a half acres of this slimy land was purchased at Lambeth and this is where St. Thomas's stands today. The foundation stone was laid by Queen Victoria in 1871 and the whole building erected with no cost spared. The frontage was 17,000 ft long and 250 ft deep. It was a teaching hospital and it was here that Florence Nightingale set up a training centre for nurses after her experiences during the Crimean War. In fact she was consulted about its design and her ideas were carried out.

It is said that the citizens of London did not take kindly to the Victoria Embankment or the reclaiming of the river, which they regarded as common property. The Mayor and Council produced a charter issued by Henry VII which stated that all river soil belonged to the City. To counteract this the government produced a tract supposedly issued by Charles II which said that all river land outside the City boundaries belonged to the Crown and the Bill to build the Embankment was passed. The brothers Adam, Court architects, were appointed to plan the site. A satirist of the day wrote the following skit:

> Four Scotchmen by the name of Adam,
> Who keep their coaches and their madam,
> Quoth John in sulky mood to Thomas,
> 'Have stolen the very river from us'.

Thomas Guy who founded Guy's Hospital early in the eighteenth century had made his fortune on the Stock Exchange by devious means but spent it in such a commendable way that he was redeemed in the eyes of all. He commenced the building of the hospital when he was 76 but died before its completion in January 1725. The rest of his estate which amounted to £220,134 was used to improve the buildings and help with the running costs. At first sixty patients were admitted but as donations grew the hospital was able to expand and at the end of the nineteenth century the annual number of patients was over 84,000. The entrance to Guy's is in St. Thomas's Street by an iron gate which opens into a square where there is a brass statue of Thomas Guy by Scheemakers. Its plinth bears the arms of Guy, Christ healing the sick and the Good Samaritan.

It is said that sisters and nurses were trained here before Florence Nightingale started her scheme. The medical students had to pay for their training as was usual in those days. The fee was 15 guineas for eighteen months and the physicians were paid a stipend of £105 per annum out of these fees – an increase on their Tudor predecessors. Dressers were employed to dress wounds and take down the particulars of the patients to hang over the bed. Dressers watched the condition of the patients and reported any changes to the nursing sister, as did the night watchers who were employed to watch the sick at night. From 1760 the schools of surgery of both St. Thomas's and Guy's were united and fees paid by the students studying surgery were put into a common fund. Medical lectures were delivered at Guy's and surgery took place at St. Thomas's. This arrangement ceased when a disagreement arose amongst the surgeons and the hospitals then went their separate ways.

The Royal Hospital Chelsea was set up in the reign of Charles II and the story that the idea was instigated by Nell Gwyn has some truth. As we have seen both her mother and sister lived in that area so it was not surprising that the King chose that part of London in which to establish the first Royal Military Hospital. Legend has it that as Nell was travelling down a crowded street in her coach she was caught in a traffic jam. A disabled man hobbled out to the coach and spoke to Nell through the window. He said that he had been severely wounded during the Civil War fighting for Charles I and because of his disability he could not get work. He entreated Nell to help him. She was very touched by his story and gave him some money and promised to do what she could. The outcome was, so we are told, that as usual Charles II agreed to help anyone who had helped his father and issued a charter to build a hospital for war wounded and pensioners. Charles gave £7,000 and Nell collected money from her friends and gave what she could afford. A tavern sprang up in Chelsea not long after the hospital had been opened called the 'Nell Gwyn' and this does appear to have some significance. Also it is said that the old soldiers toast the name of Nell Gwyn on every special occasion. In the graveyard at Chelsea there is a monument to a soldier called William Riseland who lived to the great age of 112. He was born in 1620 and died in 1732. Although there are no papers available to confirm this the long inscription on his tombstone bears the correct dates of the battles that Riseland had fought in. He was admitted to the hospital in 1713, the year the Treaty of Utrecht was signed. His portrait was painted from life when he was 110 and could be seen in the Great Hall of the hospital.

There were roughly three isolation hospitals for leprosy in London in the early days – one that I have mentioned stood on the site of St. James's Palace. Lepers lived the lives of outcasts and their hospitals were called Lazar houses after the story of Lazarus the beggar who was 'full of sores' according to the Gospel of St. Luke. Leprosy died out in this country in the Middle Ages and the hospitals were then used for general cases.

Another hospital that no longer exists is the Bethlem. It was founded as a convent in 1247 by Simon FitzMary, a merchant of London. In 1403 the first lunatics as inmates were recorded. In those days it was thought that the best treatment to restore reason was to put the patient in darkness, bound with chains or manacled, and stripped of all clothing except a sheet. Frequent floggings were also part of the treatment. Bethlem was first built near Charing Cross but was removed because the King complained of the noise and the inconvenience of having a lunatic asylum on his doorstep. The new hospital was built on Moorfields and was constructed so badly that it fell down and another was built in its place. The next building it is said was a copy of a plan of the Tuileries and this enraged Louis XIV to such a degree, it is reported, that he had an asylum built in Paris from the plan of St. James's Palace! Bethlem had two statues in its entrance hall one portraying Raving and the other Melancholy Madness, both sculptured by Cibber. Oliver Cromwell's porter, a huge man, is said to have been confined here and is thought to have been the original of one of the figures. 'Tom o' Bedlam' was the name given to patients who were allowed out of the hospital to beg in the streets – they had an iron bar soldered round one of their arms to show from whence they came.

Up to the beginning of the nineteenth century a visit to London to see the sites such as Westminster Abbey and the Tower was not complete without a visit to Bethlem. People paid a penny to see the inmates who were chained in kennel-like cells and were naked except for one sheet, and only had straw on which to sleep. The house-surgeon was often insane himself, or at best a drunkard, and the ruling committee neglected to inspect the premises for months on end. The patients were termed prisoners and one man named Norris was chained by a strong iron ring riveted around his neck, with his arms pinioned by an iron bar and his waist secured in the same way. He could only advance twelve feet away from the wall and suffered this for twelve years. He was able to read books and newspapers and converse in a reasonable manner. A drawing of this poor man was made and members of Parliament visited him. When they inquired the reason for his admission to the hospital no record could be found. The case was brought up in Parliament and in 1815 an Act was passed ensuring better treatment for the patients at Bethlem. Norris was released but died soon afterwards. In 1838 the last person to be chained to her bed was released and the matron feared for her life for she thought that the woman was violent. But she need not have worried for as soon as the patient was freed she became quiet and tranquil, nursing two dolls which she thought were her children. The hospital was also used for criminals who had tried to assassinate monarchs. James Hadfield tried to shoot George III and was confined here for thirty-nine years until he died. He had been a gallant dragoon and employed himself during the long years by writing verses on the deaths of his cats and birds, his only companions in prison. A lady named Margaret Nicholson was also imprisoned here for attempting to stab George III and spent forty-two years in solitary confinement before dying in her cell. Another named Edward Fox was sent to prison in Bethlem for attempting to assassinate Queen Victoria in 1840. Later the building was pulled down to make way for new development and people were not sorry to see it go.

The Blue Coat School was founded as a hospital for poor sick children by Edward VI just before his death and was attached to Christ's Hospital in Newgate Street. The children were dressed in warm blue habits with skirts and yellow stockings, a leather girdle and a small black cap, kept but not often worn. It was in fact the humble dress of Tudor children. At first it accommodated about 350 boys and girls but after the death of Edward it became a school for boys only. Mary I, when meeting the boys in the street one day, remarked: 'I do not like the blue boys.' This may have been because the school was financed by Protestants at that time. The boys were not treated badly if they behaved themselves but if they broke the rules the punishments were severe. For instance they were put in fetters for running away and if this happened more than once the culprits were put in dungeon-like cells in complete darkness with only one blanket, in solitary confinement. The worst offenders were flogged senseless in front of the whole school and masters and pupils alike swooned at the cruelty inflicted. The Christ's Hospital boys raised money for the school in early days by walking at funerals; they were never allowed to keep the money for themselves. There was a strange custom attached to the school that a boy should never eat 'gags', the fat of boiled meat, as it was thought ghoulish to do so. It is recorded that on more than one occasion a boy was seen to take the fat meat off his plate and hide it in his locker. Then he was observed taking a bundle out at night. His mates thought he was taking food to sell to beggars and one night they followed him to a dilapidated house near by. He was followed to a room on the first floor where it was discovered that he had been taking meat to his parents who were ill and on the point of starvation. When the school governors heard about the incident they took kindly to it and gave the boy a silver medal, and what was more important they made sure that his family never suffered again. As mentioned earlier, the school was moved to Horsham in 1902 and the boys return once a year to London to attend a service in St. Sepulchre's Church.

In 1833 it was realized that out of 20 families which had produced 159 children 90 were born deaf and dumb. Earlier, in 1792, the Deaf and Dumb Asylum, the first to be opened in England, was ready to receive patients in Fort-Place, Bermondsey. The first teacher was Joseph Watson and he held the post for thirty-seven years, financed by the clergy of Bermondsey and wealthy benefactors. The children were taught to read and write and lip read or use sign language. They were also taught a trade to support them when leaving school.

Although there were thousands of sick and dying children in London in Victorian times, and before, it was not until 1852 that a hospital caring especially for children was opened. A house in Great Ormond Street, Bloomsbury, former residence of Dr. Richard Mead, was converted into a hospital for children. At first people regarded it with suspicion and on the opening day only one child was brought for admission. Even by the end of the month there were only eight in-patients and twenty-four out-patients. For a time the new venture struggled through lack of funds but help came from the Bishop of London, Lord Shaftesbury and Lord Carlisle, not forgetting Charles Dickens who pleaded for donations both by tongue and pen. His novel *Our Mutual Friend* refers to the hospital where little Johnny was taken to be cared for by good doctors and nurses, whose sole purpose in life was to care for sick children. Queen Victoria consented to become patroness and the first report stated the objectives of the hospital as follows:

1. The medical and surgical treatment of poor children.
2. The attainment and diffusion of knowledge regarding poor children.
3. The training of nurses for children.

The hospital grew in popularity and developed, and today its fame and high standard of treatment are known world-wide.

No history of London hospitals would be complete without a mention of the St. John's Ambulance Brigade. Its history and origin is shrouded in the mists of time but a charter granted by Elizabeth, our present Queen, describes it as 'The Most Venerable Order' and no better words could be used to describe the history of this esteemed Association.

Long before the Crusades, Christian communities were establishing themselves in Jerusalem and many pilgrimages were made to the Holy Places within that land. Under the auspices of Pope Gregory a hospital and library were set up for pilgrims in the Holy City around A.D. 600. Later, a pagan ruler, El Hakim, destroyed Christian churches, hostels and other buildings and killed all Christians in the area. After his death a group of merchants of Amalfi, a small republic just south of Naples, were allowed to buy the site of the church and there set up a new community including a hospital for the Christians. The eight-pointed white cross was the badge of the Republic of Amalfi and was adopted by the Benedictine monks who served in this new hospital and this is the origin of the famous emblem of the Order of St. John in our own times.

The persecution of the Christian society in the Holy Land continued and in answer to an appeal made by the Pope in 1095 the first of the Crusades was mounted by a Christian army made up of soldiers from many lands. After a hazardous journey the Crusaders arrived at Jerusalem and took the city by siege. The hospital was run at that time by a saintly man named Gerard, who, in order to help the Crusaders gain entrance, pelted them with loaves of bread, telling the Moslems who had captured the hospital that he was throwing stones. The Crusaders were tired and hungry and many of them were wounded and the gift of the bread spurred them on, and at last the hospital was liberated and the Moslems dealt with. The hospital then welcomed the Christians and cared for the wounded and provided sanctuary with rest and food. One of the army leaders was a man called Godfrey of Bouillon, Duke of Lorraine. Being a devout Christian he was elected leader and ruler of Jerusalem and endowed Gerard's hospital with land and wealth. Other Crusaders followed his example and through their generosity Gerard was able to reorganize the Brotherhood and found a new order – that of the Hospitalliers. The monks wore long black sleeveless cloaks with the emblem of Amalfi on the breast. The new Order acquired the ancient monastery of St. John the Baptist, formerly the property of the Greek church in Jerusalem, and consequently St. John became patron saint of the Order. Soon after this the Knights Hospitalliers were formed in 1113 under the direct protection of the Pope. Gerard died in old age, happy that his life's work had been fulfilled. When the Knights Templars were formed part of the Order of Hospitalliers joined them to fight and defend Christians in the Holy Land. But unlike the Templars the Hospitalliers were first and foremost a healing band and the establishment of hospitals was their foremost aim. The fame of the Order grew and branches were set up in various countries and in the twelfth century a man named Jordan of Bricett and his wife Muriel, based in Suffolk, made a gift of two acres of land in Clerkenwell to the Hospitalliers. A great Priory was built, the gatehouse of which is still in good repair and is now known as St. John's Gate. It is the headquarters of the Order in England.

In 1312 the Templars were dissolved and the Hospitalliers were given much of their property and land. The Temple in London became the property of the Hospitalliers some time later and was then sold to the lawyers to gain funds. The Hospitalliers were dissolved by Henry VIII and all but three escaped to the Continent. The three remaining refused to recant and were executed. The Grand Master was pensioned off with £1,000 a year but died of a broken heart. The hospital and church were pulled down or blown up with gunpowder and the stone used to build Somerset House in the Strand. For a while, during the reign of Mary I, the Hospitalliers enjoyed a reprieve and the Royal Letters Patent as issued by Mary have never been revoked, even though the Order was dissolved once again when Elizabeth I came to the throne. The Order of the Knights Hospitalliers was revived in

1831 and it was hoped that Protestants would be allowed by Rome to carry on the work that had lain dormant for three centuries. This was constantly refused by the Pope and in the end the Order broke away and established an independent national body in England. Today the split has been rectified and the two religions are enveloped into the Order.

After the international conference held in Geneva in 1863 which led to the foundation of the Red Cross, the Order of St. John, which had been represented at the conference by Sir John Furley, put into practice ambulance relief services and first aid at the battle-front of the Franco-Prussian War and in 1877 the St. John's Ambulance Association was formed. In 1882 the St. John's Ophthalmic Hospital was built in Jerusalem which today is one of the world's leading eye hospitals. These developments were made possible by the patronage of the Duke of Manchester. Soon after this the monarch of the land became the Sovereign Head of the Order and a member of the royal family has always been the Grand Prior – Queen Victoria being the first.

The best ways of dealing with the problems presented by war wounded was tried out by Sir John Furley who went to the siege of Paris disguised as a coachman and as such was allowed to pass in and out of the city. He gained much useful information and experience of field work and his report endorsed the tradition of the Medieval Order, namely the importance of effective transportation of the sick and wounded whether in time of war or peace.

Around 1878 ambulances were stretchers, some with wheels, manned by two stalwart men. Later two bicycles with a litter between were tried out and then later still, horsedrawn vehicles were introduced. And then of course came the mechanized vehicle.

The formation of teaching classes and the presentation of certificates to those learning first aid were introduced by voluntary helpers all over the country. Incidentally the term 'First Aid' – a combination of 'First Treatment' and 'National Aider', meaning someone who was qualified to practice first aid – did not come into general use until 1894, and was first coined at a lecture given by an official of the Order.

Since then the St. John's Ambulance Brigade has always been to the fore in war and peace to render assistance and medical first aid wherever needed. And we as a nation are indebted to them.

As mentioned, the expertise of the monks in healing and using herb remedies was lost after the Act of Supremacy and the art of healing took a downward trend. Many protective but useless measures were taken to ward off disease, especially the dreaded plague which killed off a large proportion of the population. It was thought for instance that the colour red was a protection against the plague and so bed clothes and curtains were dyed this colour. Vinegar sprinkled on clothes, and herbs carried and constantly sniffed, were thought to be effective. Also box and yew hedges were thought to give protection to the house and this is why many of these hedges, some still surviving, were planted in Tudor and Stuart times.

In 1665 the Great Plague hit Europe and soon made its way to London and the rest of the country. Charles II and his Court moved into the country at an early stage but many people stayed in London to fall victim to the disease. It was the rats that carried the bacteria; the fleas that they harboured bit humans and transmitted the deadly infection. Swollen joints were one of the symptoms and these were lanced in an effort to let out the bad blood! It was generally thought that animals carried the disease and so all cats and dogs were killed, thus the only natural deterrent to the rats was removed.

At first provisions were left at the City gates by the butchers living outside the boundaries but in time they too became afflicted and the service stopped. Two brave men, General Monck and the Lord Mayor, were the only ones in authority who stayed throughout the terrible winter to organize the collection of the dead to be buried in unconsecrated ground outside the City. Samuel Pepys, so as not to miss anything, stayed as long as he dared and reported in his diary that people fell down dead in the streets or ran about naked as the illness sent them berserk. Others, immune to the disease, died from starvation and contaminated drinking water.

There is one amusing story about a piper, with his dog, who used to haunt the empty streets playing tunes on his pipe and going into the empty taverns to help himself to all the liquor he could stomach. One evening, being in a drunken stupor, he propped himself up against a wall with his dog beside him and along came the dead cart. He was thrown into the cart with the dead bodies, and his dog, very distressed jumped in beside him. Just as the bodies were being thrown into the pit the dog managed to arouse the piper by licking his face, so that he moved and sat up, much to the consternation of the body collectors who thought he was a ghost. He was helped out of the cart and after mumbling his thanks took his pipe from his pocket and wandered down the street, playing a tune as he went, the dog, overjoyed at his master's recovery, at his heels. The story so impressed one of the surviving benefactors of the City that he commissioned Cibber the sculptor to execute a statue of the Plague Piper.

In February 1666 it was felt safe to return to London and 'pick up the pieces'. Many thousands had died but at least the Plague had died out also, to be helped of course by the Great Fire which followed in September of the same year. After the Plague many other minor diseases, all killers in their way, came to the fore. Smallpox was the main enemy of man and it was not until a vaccine was developed to counteract it that the danger subsided. Measles, whooping cough, scarlet fever, chicken pox and so on, hitherto unknown, made an unwelcome appearance.

In Victorian times the fumigation cart used to attend the better class of houses and this service was given free by the Council to those who paid substantial rates. If there had been a case of infectious disease such as measles, in a house, the men in charge would fumigate the sick room, and toys and articles used by the patient were taken out to the cart and purified by sulphur fumes which destroyed all the germs, and then returned to the owner without fear of the infection spreading.

As dealt with in the next chapter the water supply became contaminated during the Victorian era and typhoid and cholera broke out, killing as many as 14,000 a year in London alone. When a new drainage system was introduced in 1870 the death rate dropped dramatically.

In a lane off Fleet Street, called Bolt Court, there lived at No. 3 a certain Dr. John Lettsom, a Quaker physician who on his demise left his house to the Medical Society of London. By all accounts he was a caring man and did his best for all his patients with the medical knowledge at his disposal. I am sure he did not deserve this epitaph which was inscribed on his gravestone:

If any folk applies to I
I blisters, bleeds and sweats 'em:
If after that they pleased to die,
Well, then I letsom.

Barbers acted as rough surgeons in early days mainly because they had sharp razors with which to shave people and knives with which to cut hair. They often lanced wounds and did blood letting. The patient would sit holding a pole and grinding his teeth against surgery without anaesthetic. The pole was used to keep clean bandages available and they were wrapped around it to be at hand when the blood began to flow. The bandage-wrapped pole became the barbers' emblem and the striped sign is still hung outside some barbers' shops.

A story circulated by Cockneys in 1924 was that a girl had swallowed an octopus egg and that it had hatched inside her and the creature was growing. Consequently she was dying and it was thought that the kindest way to put her out of her misery would be to smother her. Law and hospitals were ignored in this case and the people sent a petition to George V at Buckingham Palace for the permission to end the life of the suffering girl. I do not know the outcome of this, but it does show that royalty in the last century was closer, perhaps, to the East Enders than it had been in the time of their predecessors.

Other hospitals were opened in London and it is not possible to list them all, Westminster in 1719, St. George's in 1733 and the London Hospital was set up in 1740 mainly for dockers and their families. From the eighteenth century onwards there emerged two kinds of hospitals – the teaching kind such as Barts, St. Thomas's and Guy's, which were supported by public funds and charities, and the hospitals which used to be workhouses but were turned into places to care for the sick by the local councils. In time these local hospitals became so good and had so much money spent on them that they surpassed the teaching hospitals in acquiring modern equipment and machinery. After the Second World War, the National Health scheme was introduced and nearly all hospitals became state owned.

FIRE

The Romans were as efficient in fire fighting as they were in dealing with every other kind of hazard. People known as vigiles were employed to quench any fires that broke out and it is very likely that Londinium as London was called during the Roman occupation had a similar force. During the Saxon era there was no organization to fight fires and the threat to the population was great. It was not until after the Norman Conquest that fire regulations were introduced to London once more. William I passed laws prohibiting all fires after curfew both in private dwellings and places of work. This law was called *couvre-feu* and took its name from a metal object shaped like half a bell which was put over the fire at sunset to extinguish the flames. As most of the houses were thatched and used straw as floor covering open fires were a constant danger but the law did not please the citizens of London and they took little notice of it although severe penalties were imposed on those disobeying. A huge fire destroyed much of London in 1086, but when Henry I, son of the Conqueror, became king, he repealed the fire curfew and thus endeared himself to the common folk.

During ensuing years fire was a constant danger and many Lord Mayors tried to bring into force regulations to ease the situation but to no avail. In 1600 the first primitive fire fighting appliance was introduced in the form of a syringe known as 'little squirts'. Incidentally the term engine stems from the simple hand operated syringe used at this time. There was a large fire in 1633 and these syringes were used but they broke down at the crucial moment and many houses on London Bridge were destroyed.

On Sunday, 2 September 1666 the destruction of medieval London by fire began and within five days the City which Shakespeare knew, with its narrow streets and high buildings, was no more. An area of 1½ miles by ½ a mile was totally destroyed – 373 acres within the City walls and 63 acres outside, which included 87 churches and 13,000 houses. The report that only six people lost their lives may not have been accurate. According to a pamphlet issued by the London Fire Brigade entitled '*A History of London's Firefighters*' the fire began in the house and shop of Thomas Farynor, the king's baker, in Pudding Lane. His assistant woke him at 2 a.m. because the house was full of smoke. The family and servants had to make their escape over the rooftops of Pudding Lane and only one servant was left behind: she refused to make such a perilous journey and consequently perished in the flames – the first victim in fact. The sparks from the burning house fell on hay and fodder in the yard of the Star Inn in Fish Street and the flames from the burning inn set alight the Church of St. Margaret. Soon the wharves and warehouses were blazing, and many of them stored inflammable material such as tallow and oil and hemp, hay and coal were heaped on the open quays. Soon the fire was half-way across London Bridge and only stopped there because of a gap in the houses left by the former fire of 1633 – and this saved Southwark.

Samuel Pepys, as usual, was quick on the scene and hastened to Whitehall to report to the King the seriousness of the situation. Charles II, with his brother James, helped organize the fire fighting. He ordered that all houses and buildings directly in the line of the fire should be pulled down or blown up by gunpowder to try and stop the blaze. The Lord Mayor of London, named Bludworth, objected to this, saying 'Who will pay for their reconstruction?'

That Sunday evening the Boar's Head Tavern in Eastcheap, where Shakespeare and Ben Jonson had drunk, was burnt down and the fire blazed for three more days. It was sweeping towards Westminster and had reached the Temple Church when James, Duke of York, ordered the destruction of the Paper House to arrest the flames, much to the indignation of the lawyers present. But the Duke, himself a bencher of the Inner Temple, saw that it was the only way to stop the progress of the fire. A passing seaman seeing that the roof of the Inner Temple was ablaze climbed up and beat out the flames.

As the fire spread house owners took their belongings to the Thames and made their escape across the river by boats rowed by watermen. The boatmen made their fortunes during the Fire of London, although their own Livery Hall perished in the blaze. Some thought Old St. Paul's would be safe and took their belongings and stacked them in the crypt, but all were lost. The Stationers and Booksellers put their wares in the crypt but a wind whipped up the flames once more, two or three days later, and

everything was burnt. An old couplet remembers this:
> Heavens, what a pile! Whole ages perish'd there;
> And one bright blaze turn'd learning into air.

The equipment for fire fighting was almost useless at the time of the Great Fire – ladders were found to be rotten and buckets leaked. No one can say for sure how the fire started but the fact that it may have been started deliberately cannot be ruled out. Robert Hubert, a native of Paris and a watchmaker, known to be mentally disturbed, confessed to the deed and was hanged for the crime. It was not until three years afterwards that it was proved that he could not have been responsible as he was in Holland when the fire started and did not return to London until three days afterwards. Another explanation is that a plot by anti-Royalists to take the Tower and set fire to the City was discovered on 26 April 1666. This was to have taken place on 3 September of that year. Although the conspirators were dealt with it seems more than just coincidence that the Great Fire of London started on 2 September of that year.

The plight of the people who had lost everything was pitiful. If they had no relatives to give them shelter they camped out on Moorfields and began to build themselves rude shacks or tents from the remaining rubble. Dryden aptly describes the scene in London when a fierce fire had deprived people of their loved ones, homes and possessions:

> Those who have homes, when homes they do repair,
> To a last lodging call their wandering friends,
> Their short uneasy sleeps are broke with care,
> To look how near their own destruction tends.

> Those who have none, sit round where once it was,
> And with full eyes each wonted room require;
> Haunting the yet warm ashes of the place
> As murdered men walk where they did expire.

> The most in fields like herded beasts lie down
> To dews obnoxious on the grassy floor,
> And while their babies sleep their sorrow drown,
> Sad parents watch the remnants of their store.

A plant bloomed on the ruins of London after the fire and was named the London Rocket – a small yellow flower with pointed leaves – the Sisymbrium Iris.

The task of rebuilding the City was great but was completed in seven years, except St. Paul's which took longer. The houses which had hitherto been built of wood were now reconstructed in brick and a thriving brick making industry sprang up in the East End where the bricks were made by hand – a practice which lasted over two hundred years. A panel of judges was appointed to allocate compensation for destroyed premises. This court gave such satisfaction that the citizens of London collected money to pay £60 for each judge to have his portrait painted. Up to the mid nineteenth century these portraits could be seen at the Court of Common Pleas and Queen's Bench in the Guildhall.

The rebuilding gave employment to thousands and people who had new brick houses started to insure their property against fire. The first known Fire Insurance Company was set up in 1667 by Nicholas Barbon or Barebones – one of the sons of the infamous Puritan 'Praise God Barebones'. The business was sold a year later to a company called the Fire Office. Many small insurance companies came and went during the next few years. In 1709 the Company of London Insurers was started and was called in later years 'The Sun'. This company is still in business today. In 1696 the Hand-in-Hand was established and was called, in the first place,

The Hand-in-Hand Fire Mark

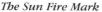

*The Commercial Union
Fire Mark*

The Sun Fire Mark

the Amicable Contributors for Insuring from Loss by Fire. This proved too much of a mouthful and the title was changed to the Hand-in-Hand. The formation of this company we are told dated from gatherings in Tom's Coffee-House where Daniel Defoe, author of *Robinson Crusoe*, was an active organizer. Each individual company had its fire mark – a metal plate of moulded lead, painted and gilded and bearing the emblem of the company and the policy number of the holder. Fire marks were attached to the outside walls of the houses insured by that company. One of the earliest can be seen in the Sun Office; it bears the policy number 838 and was issued to a house in Church Row, Fulham in 1711. Other fire marks can be seen in the Guildhall but there are not many left on walls of buildings as these disappeared as 'collectors' items' many years ago. Each company had its own group of firefighters and 'engine' and if the fire was at a house not insured by them they simply turned round and went away, leaving inmates and property to the mercy of the flames. If two or more companies arrived at the scene of the fire the result was often a fight between the brigades whilst the fire went on burning. The companies realized that suitable and reliable equipment was essential and better designed 'engines' from the Continent were introduced. Also many watermen were recruited as firemen. They were used to dangerous work and had great nerve and guts. In 1720 Strype, who had taken over Stow's work of recording the social history of London, wrote:

> There is yet another practice of great benefit and convenience used in London and that is the Insuring of houses against Fire – which any man may do for a little money for the term of

seven years and so renew again if he pleases. For which there is a certain Office kept in the City called the Fire Office in Cornhill and Fleet Street. All houses thus insured are known by a plate fixed upon them – being in resemblance of a Phoenix in a flame.

When Drury Lane Theatre was burnt down for the third time this verse was penned by James and Horace Smith in 1809:

> The engines thundered through the street,
> Fire-hood, pipe, bucket, all complete.
> And torches glared, and clattering feet
> Along the pavement flew,
> The Hand-in-Hand the race begun
> Then came the Phoenix and the Sun,
> The Exchange, where old insurers run
> The Eagle where the new.

Gradually, however, as the business of fire insurance flourished individual companies realized that it would be to their mutual benefit to join forces and form a union of insurers. Thus in 1833 the London Fire Establishment was founded and Mr James Braidwood, formerly fire chief of Edinburgh, took command. Superintendent Braidwood had eighty full-time firefighters and nineteen stations. Braidwood believed that to be really effective a fireman should get to the heart of the blaze and not depend on 'long shots' with the hose pipe, an idea still standing today. His men were called 'Jimmy Braiders' and were very popular with the locals. About this time the first steam-engines were introduced but Braidwood preferred the old manually handled ones. In 1834 a huge fire destroyed the Houses of Parliament and only Westminster Hall was saved and the insurance companies decided that the responsibility for dealing with fires destroying ancient monuments was too great and petitioned the House to provide government controlled organizations. This proved futile at the time, but after the great Tooley fire of 1861, things came to a head. Braidwood lost his life when, commanding his men fighting the blaze, a wall collapsed on him. The wharves of Southwark burnt fiercely and two thousand barrels of Russian tallow floated alight down the Thames. The rats swam in the water in their thousands and

London Bridge was so crowded with spectators that quite a few fell into the water and were drowned. The damage was estimated at £2,000,000 and it is said the fire was not extinguished for a fortnight. The fire companies threatened to close 'shop' if the government did not step in and help and this it was forced to do. The Metropolitan Fire Brigade Act was passed in 1865 supported by public money, albeit only a halfpenny in the pound. One of the world's best known fire fighting personalities was appointed as Chief Fire Officer: Captain Sir Eyre Massey Shaw. He was a personal friend of the Prince of Wales and his bravery and drive improved the Fire Brigade beyond all previous conception. His work earned him a few lines in Sir William Gilbert's opera, *Iolanthe* as sung by the Fairy Queen:

O, Captain Shaw, type of true love kept under,
Could thy Brigade with cold cascade, Quench my love, I wonder?

Shaw developed the use of steam fire engines, introduced telegraph systems, and took over the Society for the Protection of Life from Fire, thus increasing the number of street escapes organized by the firemen themselves. The Prince of Wales, later Edward VII, took a keen interest in the business of fire fighting and at Chandos Street Fire Station the Prince's fire uniform was always kept ready so that he could attend some of London's more notable fires.

When fire-carts were drawn by horses, only the warning cries of the firemen and the clattering of the wheels and the hooves of the galloping beasts told people to get out of the way. Later a bell was introduced. Horses were used to pull steam-powered engines and were not replaced by the motor-car until as late as the First World War. The last horse drawn fire-engine was dispensed with in 1921. The fire-horses on duty were roped in their stalls and already had the bits in their mouths. When the fire alarm sounded a spring was pressed by a fireman and in one action the ropes were removed, a collar was dropped on the horses' necks and the rugs snatched from their backs. The horses were then ready in the yard to be harnessed and the whole operation took less than a minute. The doors of the fire station opened automatically even as early as 1908. In this era also the fireman had his brigade dog which took part in the fire fighting and was trained to help rescue people from burning buildings.

A writer in the *Builder* in 1870 said that:

... in spite of the most powerful fire-engines in the world; in spite of an admirably organised fire brigade, the members of which are chosen for their intelligence and courage; in spite of the most adequate professional aid always at hand and much amateur assistance given from many quarters, lives are periodically lost; men, women and children are burnt to death or suffocate, unable to effect their escape from the burning timbers, amongst which firemen fall victims to bravery and self forgetfulness which distinguishes the whole body. Their deaths are registered in due course and the most satisfactory reports are drawn up, the tendency of which is generally to prove that everybody did his duty and that nobody is to blame.

Since that time many stricter fire precautions have come into being but we still witness appalling cases and this goes to prove that man's old enemy fire has yet to be conquered.

I cannot leave the section dealing with fire without a mention of the Monument, to be found in London today, commemorating the Great Fire. Although Wren was credited with the design people believe that it was Robert Hooke, the City Surveyor at the time, who was responsible for the building and decoration. Built of Portland stone it is 202 ft high and this is supposed to be the distance from whence the fire started in Pudding Lane. The fluted Doric column is 15 ft in diameter and has a pedestal of 40 ft at the top and it is generally considered to be the best single column monument in the world. On three sides of the base there is a description of the fire and on the fourth side a relief carving of London in ruins. The building of the Monument like many other buildings was paid for out of the tax on coal, and not out of the rates, which had been abolished at the time. Dr Gale the headmaster of St. Paul's school was responsible for the wording of the inscriptions. At first the column was used by the Royal Society for Astronomy but its vibration belied the accuracy needed for such work. On 15 June 1825 the Monument was illuminated by gas to commemorate the laying of the foundation stone of Rennie's London Bridge.

It has witnessed many suicides during its time. In 1750 a weaver named William Green left his watch with the door keeper and after climbing the steps on the inside, descended on the outside a good deal faster than he went up. After quite a few more deaths the authorities caged-in the top of the column in 1842.

POLICE

For centuries Britain was the only country in Europe without a professional police force. Countries on the Continent had through necessity armies to protect their frontiers. In times of international peace these soldiers were used as a police force to keep law and order within the countries concerned. The French *gendarme* for instance comes from *gens d'armes* – men of arms. England had the Channel to protect her from her neighbours and therefore no organized army was required to double up as a police force. The citizens more often than not did their own police work to protect property and family. As far back as the thirteenth century men had been appointed as 'constables' in the London area under the jurisdiction of sheriffs and justices. The word constable comes from the Latin *comes stabuli* meaning count of the stable, a high officer of State establishment. If the citizens caught a criminal he could be brought to trial if the plaintiff paid a fee! Constables, magistrates and justices were not salaried and relied on fines and bribes to make their work worth while. Robbers and murderers roamed the streets and in Charles II's reign watchmen were appointed to give protection to citizens travelling at night. These men were called 'Charlies' and were usually old and feeble and not at all able to fight or arrest a villain. Nevertheless they were Britain's first police force and the forerunners of today's London 'bobby'.

The Government evolved two methods of keeping down crime. One was to deliver severe punishments to act as a deterrent and the other was to offer rewards for thief catching. Highwaymen were worth £40 but ordinary burglars only £10. From this system a positive army of private detectives grew up. In 1729 an officer named Thomas de Veil was appointed magistrate in the West End, and ten years later when encouraging and developing the Secret Service he moved to a house in Bow Street. Although de Veil was corrupt and looked after his own pocket he had authority and his band of men respected him. When he died in 1749 his position was taken over by Henry Fielding, novelist, playwright and magistrate. Fielding formed the Bow Street Runners – a handful of trained men to act as thief catchers. They were not paid well but relied on the rewards when malefactors were caught.

Stow, the Elizabethan historian, records that as early as the fifteenth century schools to teach children to steal had been set up. The most notorious known to Stow was opened by a well-to-do merchant by the name of Wotton who had been banned from his guild for malpractice and could not find work. He bought a tavern called Smart's Key near Billingsgate and in the back room started a 'cut-purse' school. The boys learnt the art of picking pockets in the following manner: two devices were hung up, one a pocket and the other a purse. The pocket had counters in it and was hung with hawks' bells, with a small 'scaring bell' hanging over the top. He that could take the counters from the pocket without noise earned the title of a Foyster or pick-pocket. The purse had silver in it and the boy who could take the silver from the purse without vibration or noise was termed a Nypper, pick-purse or cut-purse. Other schools taught boys to become apt at petty theft such as stealing handkerchiefs. When watches came to be worn they presented a rich prize for the pick-pocket. The pilfering of shops was the next step up the ladder of crime and children soon devised ways and means of their own. A common ploy was for two boys to pretend to be asleep on the pavement outside a shop. When darkness came and the streets were deserted they would start picking at the cement underneath the shop window until a hole large enough for one of them to climb through was made. His companion would hide the hole with his body while the other rifled what he could from the store. When he had as much as he could carry he would crawl out and both miscreants would go home to count the spoils. Charles Dickens in his novel *Oliver Twist* brought to the notice of the public the schools to teach children to steal.

After Fielding's death in 1754 his half-brother, John Fielding, who was blind, took over and developed the running of the Bow Street Police Station. He established a permanent criminal record system and started organized patrols. The Bow Street Runners at that time were a fairly trustworthy band of men but after John Fielding's death the Runners became corrupt. Jonathan Wild was perhaps the most well known and had the reputation of being a zealous catcher of criminals and the knowledge that he was armed undoubtedly contributed to his success. He also managed a thriving business as a receiver of stolen goods and for this he was eventually hanged at Tyburn. Another band of Runners who brought disgrace on Bow Street made their living by rounding up innocent people and swearing that they had committed criminal offences. The citizens concerned had no defence and were immediately thrown into jail whilst their accusers collected the rewards. Eventually four Runners, Macdonald, Berry, Gahagan and Salmon, were tried before a court of twelve judges who, although they found them guilty, did not have the power, so they said, to execute them. They were committed to prison for seven years, interspersed with days in the stocks. When they were put in the pillories they faced the full fury of the crowds and were stoned to death. So rough justice was seen to be done after all.

Magistrates, as mentioned, were not paid salaries in the early days and so had to make a living out of the criminals themselves. Thus the Basket and Trading Justices came into being. It was standard practice to bring something in a basket for the judge when a criminal came up for trial. It was either game or poultry or perhaps a bottle of wine. Some judges preferred money and would let the prisoner off if he could pay a large enough fee. If he was poor and had nothing he was thrown into jail, commonly named the hole, clapped in irons and left to die unless he had friends who could petition for his release.

By the end of the eighteenth century thousands of people were making dishonest livings out of smuggling from the ships using the River Thames. Members of the Honourable West India Company took up the suggestion of an East London magistrate, Patrick Colquhoun, that a system of river patrols should be set up. With government approval they financed the project under the leadership of Colquhoun and John Harriot, working from an office based at Wapping. These Marine Police were the forerunners of today's Thames Division whose headquarters is still at Wapping. The 'Wet Bobs' as they came to be known were and are hard, tough men, and in the early days were recruited from the watermen or navy. Their gear included 'toe bags' – waterproof sacks which kept them warm and dry up to the waist. The practice of smuggling was greatly reduced, especially of snuff. One haul captured by the police looked like a cargo of oil cakes for cattle but turned out to be compressed cakes of snuff.

Even though patrols had been set up in the previous century by the Bow Street Runners the situation in London after the Napoleonic Wars was desperate. Citizens were not safe day or night on the streets of London. Robert Peel was appointed Secretary for Ireland, a post which he held from 1812 to 1818. Within that time he set up a regular Irish Constabulary the members of which were called Peelers after their founder. Peel was determined to introduce a similar system to London and he was also keen to revise the English criminal law, especially those parts dealing with capital offences. At that time there were over 200 offences, many of them trivial, for which the punishment was hanging.

At last, when Peel became Home Secretary, the Metropolitan Police Bill was passed in 1829 and at the end of the year the Force officially came into being. The first 1,000 officers were grouped into six divisions and were controlled from a central office situated at No. 4 Whitehall Place which backed on to a courtyard known as Scotland Yard because Scottish kings used to stay there centuries ago. Although the official address of the newly formed police force was in Whitehall Place, behind the new headquarters, in Scotland Yard, was another building to which the public were usually referred. This was the Commissioner's Headquarters and most people and the Press began to refer to the police headquarters as Scotland Yard. In time the unofficial name became the official one and even today the main entrance to the present building is known as 'the Back Hall'.

Many of the original officers appointed were dismissed within a year for being drunk or corrupt. To lead the force Peel appointed two Commissioners, then termed justices, in the shape of Sir Charles Rowan who had served under the Duke of Wellington and Richard Mayne, son of an Irish judge, and a barrister in his own right. Together Rowan and Mayne evolved the principles on which they wished the new Force to base its work. Over a century and a half later these guidelines, known as the 'Primary Object', are still respected by every Metropolitan Police Officer:

> The primary object of an efficient Police is the prevention of crime; the next that of detection and punishment of offenders' if crime is committed. To these ends all efforts of Police must be directed. The protection of life and property, the preservation of public tranquility, and the absence of crime will alone prove whether those efforts have been successful, and whether the objects for which the Police were appointed have been attained.

In spite of these ideals the new Police Force experienced much prejudice and dislike especially amongst the East Enders. The costers regarded them as enemies and did what they could to bring disgrace on the new regime. The uniform of the Police was at first top hat and tails and this alone made them look ridiculous. Soon a helmet replaced the hat, for practical as well as protective reasons, and a tunic replaced the coat tails. Truncheons were issued and to this day, except in special circumstances, this constitutes the arms of an ordinary 'copper'. At an early stage too, they were issued with watches and whistles, much to the amusement of the populace. Soon musical hall artistes were singing songs about the Police and poking fun at the new regime. Songs that have entered the traditional stream are 'If you want to know the time ask a policeman', 'P.C. 49' and many others.

During Queen Victoria's reign the public attitude to the Police began to improve. When legislation was introduced to relieve the suffering of the poor it fell on the Police to see that these social reforms were carried out. Thus they were in close contact with the poor, sick and needy and under orders to help where necessary. This in time endeared them to the people and it was realized that catching criminals was not their only concern. The Police in fact became the principal social and emergency services to the community.

An amusing story stems from the first published *Police Gazette*, not under the jurisdiction of the Commissioner who knew nothing about it at the time. A man named Cleave produced the *Police Gazette* without the appropriate authority from the police and when he was found out he was arrested and the offending paper burnt. Whilst in prison Cleave thought up a plan to thwart the law and continue to produce his paper. When he was released he put his plan into operation. A humble undertaker had rooms next to the premises owned by Cleave and he agreed to supply a number of cheaply made coffins. These were duly filled with new editions of the *Police Gazette* and taken from the undertaker in carts to be delivered to houses where curtains had been conveniently drawn seemingly in respect of a departed loved one. The coffins, one to each house, were emptied and the papers made up into bundles and dispatched to the nearest railway station. Under cover of darkness the coffins were returned to the undertaker. This ruse worked successfully for some time until people in the neighbourhood became alarmed to see so many coffins being issued from the undertaker and thought there must be an epidemic of some kind. The priest and some of the wardens of the parish called on the undertaker and inquired the reason, and he broke down and confessed the whole subterfuge. Cleave was again sentenced to prison and his production of the *Police Gazette* ceased to exist.

The Special Constable Act of 1831 provided that special constables could be appointed where two or more county or borough justices had reason to think that an emergency was about to flare up. In London the Act was not applied until 1848 when during the Chartists riots 17,000 persons applied to become special constables. The Specials have always played an important role and really came into their own during the two world wars. They achieved immortality in Marie Lloyd's 'Cock Linnet Song' when she sang the lines 'You can't trust the Specials like the old time coppers, when you can't find your way home.'

The Bow Street Runners were not disbanded until 1839 and continued in the interim to help the new Police in detective work and catching criminals. One of the incidents which a Runner had to deal with was the case of Chunee the Mad Elephant, in March 1826. In the Strand at that time there was a large bazaar and haberdashery store called the Exeter Exchange. Over this was a menagerie kept by a Mr. Cross. At the entrance to the zoo a large man dressed in Beefeater's costume handed out bills to the passersby and called loudly for them to visit the animals for an admission fee of 1s. There was an assortment consisting of birds of paradise, a laughing hyena, a boa constrictor, an orang utan, ostriches and of course Chunee the elephant. On this particular day the elephant became enraged and broke the bars of his cage – oak logs, three feet in girth. The proprietor, fearing that the elephant and the other animals would escape and cause havoc, sent a Runner to Somerset House for help. A sergeant and two soldiers arrived on the scene to shoot the elephant. It took half an hour to kill him and it is said that as many as 150 bullets were lodged in his body before he died, his head resting on his tusks. The firing of the guns and the groans of the elephant attracted a large crowd and as soon as the animal was dead the public was allowed in to view the corpse, at the usual price. The menagerie stayed open until midnight and Mr. Cross had never done such a good trade in one day.

Anatomists were interested in the body but although it was offered to the College of Surgeons the offer was declined as there was not enough room to house it. By Sunday the stench was great and Mr. Cross was ordered by the authorities to have the corpse removed at all costs. The dissection of the animal took place on the premises under the direction of Joshua Brookes. Pulleys and pillars were erected in the menagerie to aid the work. Chunee was a famous elephant and was valued at £1,000. He was brought from Bombay when he was five, and was generally considered very docile except in the rutting season. He had lived for seventeen years at the Exeter Exchange.

When the Bow Street Runners were disbanded it was felt that there was need for a detective department in the Police Force and so a section to deal with this kind of work was opened at Scotland Yard in 1842, with Nicholas Pearce, a former Bow Street Runner, in charge. This move was instigated by two attempts on the life of Queen Victoria. At first there were two inspectors and six sergeants. In 1878 this department was enlarged and became known as the Criminal Investigation Department, or C.I.D. Towards the end of the nineteenth century a number of riots and scenes of unrest occurred where the Police found difficulty in keeping order. During this period the Fenian Society, whose aim was independence for Ireland, was responsible for a series of explosions in London. To combat this the Special Irish Branch was formed in 1883, which later became known as the Special Branch. As time went on the Special Branch was made responsible for the supervision of aliens and activities that could be detrimental to public safety and State security.

At the end of the nineteenth century there were more than 13,000 men in the Force and the time had come to move to larger premises. A site on the Embankment was chosen because the original plans to build an opera house there had fallen through. The lower floors of this building were faced with 2,500 tons of granite which had ironically been quarried by convicts from Dartmoor prison. Carrying on the old tradition the new building was named New Scotland Yard. In 1967 the venue was changed again and New Scotland Yard is housed today in a modern building in Broadway, close to the Home Office. It is from here that the Commissioner and Receiver run the world's largest Police Force.

In 1901 a satisfactory system of classifying fingerprints was introduced which facilitated the tracking down of criminals. In 1910 radio-telegraphy was used for the first time to track down a criminal, Dr. H. H. Crippen who, after poisoning his wife, was on a ship bound for Canada. In 1920 two motor vehicles were acquired and promptly named the Flying Squad. After the Great War women were introduced to the Force and the importance of dogs in Police work was making itself felt. In fact many depots kept dogs which became more than mascots by helping track down criminals without any special training.

The conditions of the prisons in the early days were horrific. Many of the London gaols were placed above the gates of the City. Newgate, built in 1197, for example, was notorious and its buildings stretched along Newgate Street. Fleet prison was also one of the worst examples. Warders, such as Bambridge and Huggins, were cruel, depraved men who took pleasure in the torture and death of the prisoners, especially of those who had no money and no hope. John Howard and other prison reformers brought the plight of the prisoners to the notice of the public and to Parliament and gradually things started to improve.

Prison life had its lighter side. Inns were numerous inside and outside the prison gates and people from outside were allowed to enter at will and mix and drink with the prisoners. A prisoner who could produce twenty pennies was allowed out for the day. In the courtyard tennis, skittles, fives were played and card games were extremely popular. Betting and drunkenness were rife. Many illicit weddings were carried out, amongst which Fleet weddings were notorious. Defrocked parsons were glad of the fee and obligingly altered the date on the wedding certificate to suit the bride. These weddings were not registered in church and only the certificate proved marriage. Many parsons had nicknames and one, Dr. Gaynham, was called the 'Bishop of Hell' and appeared in court many times for performing illicit wedding ceremonies. He admitted that he had married over 2,000 couples but could not remember all their faces!

Unmanned warships were used as floating prisons – conveniently anchored in mid stream where the public could not hear the cries and groans of the prisoners. The criminals were manacled together with rusty chains – and as many as 500 convicts were herded together on these ships. Dickens drew notice to the convict ships in his novel *Great Expectations.*

Gradually conditions began to improve and new prisons were built – Wormwood Scrubs being built entirely by convicts. First, nine men were employed, living in temporary accommodation, who built a place to house fifty. Then fifty prisoners built a prison for a hundred, who then completed the ultimate project in 1890.

Most of the old London prisons were either pulled down or were burnt down by the mob. This was the fate of Newgate, although a few buildings were left standing when the Central Criminal Court, commonly known as the Old Bailey, was opened at the beginning of the last century. The old rooms of Newgate prison were thrown open to the public at this time and people enjoyed running down the steps and exploring the cells, galleries and court rooms. The seats and benches were sold for firewood and relics such as the old dock were haggled over. The dock was eventually sold for £10. Lord George Gordon's cell fetched £5 and the grating used by Jack Sheppard, the highwayman, went for £7.10s.

8

Water, Light,
Tunnels and Transport

When the Romans moved out of Britain their expertise in supplying the populace with water and disposing of sewage vanished also. The pagan Saxons reduced the basic needs of the people to primitive levels once again. Cess pits were dug but these, with the rivers, became open sewers. Supplies of 'sweet water', meaning pure drinking water, became scarce until conduits were set up within the City to supply the inhabitants with water from the many pools and small rivers in the area. It was King John who authorized a reservoir to be built at St. Mary-le-bone (a corruption of St. Mary's-lez-Bourne, St. Mary's by the Brook). It was on high ground and springs fed the stream at that point and a lead pipe took water from the reservoir underground to Cheapside via the Strand and Fleet Street. Once a year the Lord Mayor and his Corporation inspected the site and enjoyed a banquet in a building adjacent to it which came to be known as the Lord Mayor's Banqueting House. There were no pumps in those days and water could only reach its destination by running downhill. In return for royal patronage the King was allowed to run an underground water pipe to supply his stables and falconry which were situated near what is now Trafalgar Square. In that era there was a well at Aldgate called St. Michael's Well and the water was said to have healing properties. Later a pump was built and the well enclosed. The Aldgate pump was ornate and had a bronze spout in the shape of a dog's head. At the beginning of the fifteenth century conduits were established at Billingsgate, Paul's Wharf, St. Giles and Cripplegate. Some were of pleasing design like the one at Cheapside and others were covered and looked like small huts such as the one at Bayswater. Most of the conduits were destroyed in the Victorian age.

Conduit in West Cheap

Although lead was used for pipes in early days, it was discovered to be easily broken, removed or stolen and was soon replaced by wood. The new underground pipes were made out of hollowed out tree trunks, tapered at one end so that one fitted into another, the joint being fixed by means of an iron hoop. When water was passed through, it swelled the wood and made the joint tight.

During Elizabethan times the population of London had increased to half a million and the problem of an adequate water supply became acute. In 1581 a Dutchman living in the town, by the name of Peter Maurice, was granted the right to erect a water-wheel under the first arch of London Bridge to provide power for machinery to pump water through underground pipes to the City conduits. The force of water rushing through the starlings of the Bridge had already been put to good use to drive mills to grind corn. The Dutchman demonstrated his invention by sending a jet of water over the tower of St. Magnus the Martyr – about 70 ft high. The Mayor and Councillors were so impressed that they ordered the pumping of water into the City to begin immediately. The water carriers on the other hand saw the new project as a threat to their livelihood and tried to stop the development but to no avail. The new pumps could make water flow along level ground and even uphill! A similar plan was put into practice at Broken Wharf near St. Paul's by a man called Bevis Bulmer. The two enterprises combined to bring about the London Bridge Waterworks. It had capital of £150,000 divided into three hundred shares of £500 each. The Works were burnt down in the Great Fire but rebuilt soon afterwards. The business was so successful that the grandson of Peter Maurice was able to sell the right in 1701 to Richard Soames for £38,000. When Rennie's Bridge was constructed in 1832 the old waterworks were discarded, but the present day Metropolitan Water Board recognizes the services of this ancient institution and still pays annuities of many thousands of pounds. Incidentally London Bridge itself had no direct water supply and the inhabitants lowered buckets into the river for their needs. During the plague it was noticeable that

Bayswater Conduit

people living on the Bridge were more or less free of the disease. This may have been because not many rats lived there or perhaps because the river provided a constantly flushing lavatory basin which was more hygienic.

On special celebrations the conduits in the City and the one at Westminster flowed with wine at the request of the reigning monarch. Needless to say this was approved by one and all!

A successful venture by Sir Francis Drake to take water over 25 miles to Plymouth inspired Sir Hugh Myddelton, a London merchant, in 1609, to plan a new water supply for London from Hertfordshire by way of a 'New River'. Myddelton, a man of wealth and drive, suggested he could cut a canal ten feet wide and four feet deep to run from the pure springs of Amwell and Chadwell to Islington, a winding course of about 40 miles. This great engineering feat was accomplished in four years in spite of great opposition. People objected to the canal running through their private land and the Brotherhood of St. Christopher of the Waterbearers did what they could to stop the project as they saw it as a direct threat to their livelihood. The Company of Water-bearers was rich and powerful and succeeded in bribing Members of Parliament to vote for the plan to be stopped before completion. At that time, Myddelton, who had sunk his fortune into the enterprise, found that his money had run out and it looked as though the whole scheme was doomed. Then surprisingly James I stepped in and offered to pay half the cost if he could have a share of the profits, and this move was called the Royal Moiety. Amwell, in Hertfordshire, derived its name from Emma's Well, called after a lady of that name who bequeathed the well for public use which can still be seen today. The Water House, Amwell Street, Islington, on which site the Metropolitan Water Board stands today, was built on the site of the Round Pond in the parish of Clerkenwell (so named as it was the well where the Livery Company of Clerks met and performed plays). This became the man-made reservoir which stored water brought by the New River. The water was then distributed to private houses and conduits about the town by buried pipes made out of wood, stone or leather. According to Michael Harrison in his book *London Beneath the Pavement* the principal pumping station was built at Stoke Newington and the Round Pond was only done away with

Copenhagen House, Islington. Built 1650

in 1914. In 1862 a statue of Sir Hugh Myddelton was unveiled by Gladstone at Islington where the canal finished. The first power for pumping was suppled by windmill in 1709 but later a steam pump engine was used. This source of water represents about an eighth of London's water supply today.

There were many private companies supplying water in the nineteenth century, competing against each other to provide a better service for the somewhat bewildered consumer. Among these was the Hampstead Water Company which under one of its directors, William Paterson, founder of the Bank of England, ran water to the City. The York Buildings Waterworks were the first to use steam power for pumping by an engine invented by Thomas Savery in 1712 – raising water by fire is the way they described it! The Chelsea Waterworks Company was the first to introduce sand filtration for London's drinking water. Eventually all companies were amalgamated under the Metropolitan Water Board.

During the nineteenth century thousands of people living in the London area died of cholera and typhoid. Dr. John Snow first isolated the germs of cholera and found them to be born in water polluted by sewage. He published pamphlets to this effect but Parliament and the Civil Service turned a blind eye to his discovery. When the next epidemic of cholera broke out Dr. Snow noticed that in a certain area of Broad Street and Cambridge Street six hundred people had died of the disease within a few days. He went to the area and found a pump in the centre. He then went from house to house inquiring whether people had used the water from the pump and in every case he found that people had died after drinking the water. He then had the pump water analysed which showed that the water had been infected by sewage which had seeped through the thick brick walls of the well. At the same time many water companies were supplying drinking water straight from the river Thames which had become polluted to a high degree. One of the water companies, Lambeth, moved higher up the river where the water was not polluted and supplied their customers from there. The result was that the deaths from cholera dropped dramatically from 130,000 to 37,000 within a year. Although Londoners had drunk polluted water for centuries cholera was unknown in Britain before 1831. The disease stems from the East but no one can tell why it was unknown in London before this time. The disease was stamped out with the formation of the Metropolitan Water Board in 1902.

The thrifty Victorians had a system by which they could tell if water was being wasted in any one house. During the night a group of men employed by the Water Authorities would tour the streets listening for running water beneath the pavement. If a house was using water throughout the night the family would be called on the next day to explain why. Perhaps a tap had been left running or a pipe leaked – whatever the cause the owners would be made to rectify the wastage. Meters were also introduced in some areas.

Early in the twentieth century hydrants were installed in the streets to supply water for washing the roads and for firemen fighting a blaze. Drinking fountains for public use were introduced and also numerous horse troughs for working horses. Ornamental fountains began to grace parks and gardens and people enjoyed seeing clean water gushing everywhere. The fountains in Trafalgar Square were particularly popular with tramps and people sleeping rough as they provided a convenient early morning bathroom – until the police caught up with the users.

Although the sewage situation was bad in London and the smells unbearable at times it was not until members of the Houses of Parliament found that their new premises had been built over a particularly virulent sewer, the sickening smell of which prevented them from attending the House, that at last something was done. Acts were passed to improve the problem in London and the rivers which had been open sewers were turned into closed sewers. Organization to empty cesspits was set up and the problem of what to do with human excreta was discussed earnestly in the House. At that time no less than 185 sewers discharged into the Thames and at high tide the scum would flow back into the streets bringing filth and disease. A plan to turn sewage into manure was tried but although many thousands of pounds were spent on the project it was found to be unpractical. Another suggestion was that methane gas could be produced from sewage to provide power for industry but this was turned down. Someone suggested carting the waste to Newhaven-on-Sea and dumping it off-shore. What the inhabitants of Newhaven had done to deserve such a fate is a mystery. Finally the idea that brought action was to strain and purify the sludge and put it to sea in hoppers to be emptied in some remote part of the ocean and this is still carried out today.

The whole system of London's sewage disposal was the brain child of one man – Joseph Bazalgette, Engineer of the Metropolitan Board Works. He drew up plans in 1855 to build tunnels underneath the new Victoria Embankment that would take gas and electricity pipes and cables as well as main sewer pipes. The rest of the river Fleet was at last filled in and became a large main sewer which now runs underneath Farringdon Street and New Bridge Street.

Sewers housed all sorts of rubbish in days gone by, including dead dogs and cats, offal from slaughter houses, old crocks, pans and many lost articles and the shoremen, dealt with in a preceding chapter, made a good living by scouring the underground passages. Waste from breweries and gas-works produced obnoxious gases which blew up parts of the tunnels from time to time or asphixiated people caught underground. Up to quite recently a wire basket was dropped through a drain with a gas detecting paper in it which would change colour if gas was about. All men working below ground were issued with safety lamps which glowed red if gas was near on a par with the miners. The man-hole covers served more than one purpose. Whenever it started to rain a man who had been appointed watch while his mates were cleaning the walls of the sewers, would clap the heavy iron cover down on the pavement thus warning the workers to hurry to the surface. There was a real danger of drowning and well into the last century it was a common sight to see sewage regurgitated up through the drains when there was heavy rainfall. These days the river acts as a relief sewer if rain causes the sewage works to overflow. Pigs were kept and fed off the sludge on the walls of the sewers years ago and even during the last war the sludge was cleaned and purified and used to grease rolling stock, and yes, you've guessed it – to feed pigs!

Since the use of detergent the problems of sludge have worsened, but still the sewer walls are cleaned and disinfected regularly. In the mid twentieth century there were more than 400 miles of drainage pipes in the London area and over 2,500 miles of small bore pipes. Two sewage works, one North of the Thames at Beckton, and at Crossness, south of the river, handled 400 million gallons of sewage and rainfall in one day. The old rivers that still run underneath London are remembered in such names as Westbourne Grove, Shoreditch, Houndsditch (where dead dogs were thrown), Conduit Fields on Hampstead Heath, Brook Street and of course Fleet Street.

The gas age developed during and after the Napoleonic War. Like all wars it increased man's power of invention and on the Continent, especially in France, experiments had been going on for some time to produce gas light and heat from coal. Attempts had been made in the previous century to obtain gas from coal but as most of these had ended in explosions the projects had been discouraged. But progress cannot be halted and at the beginning of the nineteenth century a German named Friedrich Albrecht Winsor (changed from Winzer) had experimented on the Continent with others and was the first man to organize gas street lighting in London. He bought a house in Pall Mall and saw the necessity of showing the public this new invention and therefore arousing the interest of the manufacturers. He was a very good showman and advertiser and realized just what the new system of lighting wanted. On King George's birthday on 4 June 1805, four months before the Battle of Trafalgar, gas pipes had been erected along Pall Mall with burners. At sundown these burners were ignited with tapers by a man who must go on record as being London's first gas lamplighter. People flocked from all over the Metropolis to witness and marvel at the clear steady light that the gas jets produced. The gas came from two coal carbonizing furnaces in Winsor's house. By 1807 Pall Mall was the first street in the world to be lit entirely by gas and Winsor applied for permission to develop a scheme to light the whole of London by gas. At first his project was dismissed as being too expensive but in 1812 the Gas Light and Coke Company was granted a charter for lighting the Cities of London, Westminster and Southwark. Winsor was dismissed with an annual pension of £600 because he was too dynamic and progressive to work with. Later his pension was anulled and he went to France where he died in poverty in 1830.

The nineteenth century saw also the introduction of gas for lighting and cooking and inevitably, as with the water companies, there were many private concerns all vying for the customer's patronage. The digging up of streets and the laying of pipes went on willy-nilly and if a consumer was persuaded by another company that he could be supplied with cheaper gas it was common practice for his pipes to be dug up and discarded and the new company's laid in their place.

For a while the water pipes were still made from wood but it was found that in London's damp soil the wood rotted after about twenty-five years. Also they leaked, not being able to stand the pressure of water as supplied by the new pumping stations. The real danger began when gas pipes were laid and the gas infiltrated the water pipes, causing tainted and polluted drinking water. To reduce water pollution gas pipes were made of cast iron or lead jointing – although copper was sometimes used in private houses, but as the gas was not properly purified this sometimes resulted in explosions. This explains why so many old geysers with copper piping blew up in the early days. The Metropolitan Paving Act passed in 1817 decreed that all water companies should lay pipes of cast iron but it was not until around 1850 that the last of the wooden pipes was seen. The tearing-up of road surfaces all over the capital proved a danger to pedestrians, especially at night, and subsidences were frequent.

But the gas industry had been established and soon gas pipes were being laid all over London to supply streets, factories and private dwellings with gas. Gas meters – a penny in the slot – were introduced at first. In 1815 the Guildhall was lit with gas. Rat-tail burners, the first kind of jets to be used, could still be seen in a shop in Fleet Street called Ye Olde Segar Shop as late as the last century. Gas mantles were produced much later and gave as much light as a powerful electric arc.

Although London as a city port has not as many bridges as perhaps other river ports, it abounds with tunnels. In fact the British workman was building tunnels under the Thames long before the French, those experienced tunnellers, had even thought of driving a subway under water. The celebrated engineer, Marc Brunel, himself a Frenchman living in England, noticed that the small timber worm or Teredo could burrow into ships' timbers using its own shell as borer and protector at the same time. He then set about inventing a machine shaped like a shield which could be used by workers burrowing deep into the subsoil but at the same time giving protection. The first river tunnel took nineteen years to build and during that time the water poured in many times and lives were lost. Nevertheless it was a great achievement and was finished in 1843 and opened to the public accompanied by a joyful peal of bells. Fifty thousand people flocked to Greenwich to pass through it in the first 24 hours – paying a penny for the privilege. It was declared one of the wonders of the world and a dance was named the Tunnel waltz after it. Later the Shield was developed by a man called Greathead who used compressed air to power it and in doing so completed the work in a much shorter time. More tunnels were built under the Thames nearer the City with good results and these early borings were later used for carrying main sewage pipes, electric cables and gas-mains.

During the mid nineteenth century the traffic jams in London were unbearable – much worse than they are today. The large railways were in the process of being built but had no connecting line between them. A man named Charles Pearson suggested a plan to alleviate the traffic problem by building a system of underground railways to link the main stations. The problem was not so much to build the tunnels as to create an engine that would not emit suffocating smoke or fumes underground. A number of inventions, many of them useless, were put forward for consideration. The Metropolitan Railway chose locomotives modelled by Gooch which were run by steam, which was not passed into the atmosphere below ground, but into a receiving tank where it was condensed until it could be released in the open air. On one of the trial runs Mr. and Mrs. Gladstone were 'taken for a ride'. The first 'cut and cover' railway was opened to the public in 1865 and ran from Paddington to Farringdon Street. The rush of passengers was so great that the doors had to be closed. The money for the underground railway was put up by the main railway companies and was not wasted in spite of many legal claims from private citizens that the subways had damaged houses and other property. The project flourished and prospered. The Metropolitan Railway provided its passengers with the utmost comfort – there were three classes of travel and restaurants, bars, toilets and waiting-rooms on the stations. The carriages were completely roofed in and the first-class compartments were partitioned off. The lighting was of the very latest design – a patented system of compressed oil gas which gave off a bright iridescent light. This put the main railways to shame as they were still using oil lamps. By degrees the subways were extended and in 1872, after ten years, they were carrying 44,000,000 passengers per year and by 1884 a complete circle had been built linking all the main stations.

But the time had come to think of deeper tunnels and the Victorian engineer began to plan a network of tunnels deep into the bowels of the earth to transport passengers around London. The problem was to find a source of power which would not cause air pollution and it was fortunate that at that time electricity was making its début on the London scene. The electric lamp, as invented by Swan and Edison, was already being used for lighting. The old Gaiety theatre in the Strand had been lit with electric light since 1877 and electric arc lamps had been installed to light roads leading to the Mansion House. The novelist Sir Rider Haggard was the first private citizen to have electricity installed in his house. Colonel Crompton, a name closely associated with the electric lamp, arranged to have the Law Courts in the Strand lit with the new power. London's first generating station was underground, beneath the arches of Cannon Street Station, and at first underground wires were used. However these were found to be too costly to insulate so overhead cables took their place. The skyline was cluttered at one time with wires going in all directions. Later, as underground communications improved, the electric cables were earthed once more using the trench subways.

It was not long before the electric motor and lift to carry passengers deep into the earth were invented and the system of tube stations as we know them today had come into being. The first electric underground railway in the world was opened to the public in December 1890 and the Prince of Wales, later to become Edward VII, was there to perform the ceremony. He was the first to ride with other VIPs in the train. The track ran from King William Street to Stockwell, which was a rural suburb in those days. The coaches had no windows and were therefore dubbed by the public 'padded cells'. The guard had to call out the names of the stations when the doors opened. The next to be built was the Waterloo & City line running from Waterloo to the Bank. One of the first underground stations, Hawksmoor Street, was built in the crypt of St. Mary's Woolnooth church and the directors paid the Bishop of London £25,000 in compensation. The first truly modern tube was opened in 1900 again by the Prince of Wales, and it ran from the Bank to Shepherd's Bush and was known as the 'Tuppenny Tube' because of its uniform fare for any distance. All coaches had electric light and windows and it was a great improvement on all other models. Within three years of opening it was carrying as many as 140,000 passengers a day. The running of the first escalator evoked much interest when it was shown at the Earl's Court Exhibition in 1911 and it was not long before the tubes had developed the new invention for their own use; the advantages over the lift were obvious when a large number of people had to be catered for.

During the war the underground stations served as effective air-raid shelters except of course when they received a direct hit.

When a bomb hit a water-main at Clapham Common many people were drowned because the underground was completely flooded.

Today over 250 miles are covered by London's underground railways. An iron aqueduct carries the Westbourne river above the platforms of Sloane Square Station. Escalators carrying up to 9,000 people an hour at speeds of 100 to 145 ft per minute are installed at over sixty-five stations. The longest is at Leicester Square and is 161 ft. Oxford Circus is the station with the most escalators – numbering 14.

A chapter dealing with the history of London transport would not be complete without a mention of the Regent Canal. According to Herbert Spencer in his book *London's Canal* the idea was put forward in the Regency period to build a waterway to link the Grand Junction Canal at Paddington with the river Thames at Limehouse. Nash, who was later to lay out Regent's Park, and Rennie, who was to design the new London Bridge, were both keen on the scheme and Rennie put forward plans. They were turned down on the grounds that the project would be too costly and not viable. The idea was rejected by people who resented a public waterway running through their private land and the Watermen too, were against the scheme as they thought it would threaten their livelihood. At last Parliament approved a plan put forward by John Nash and it is thought that Nash put as much as £1,500 into the scheme, under assumed names, as the limit of shares was curtailed to £100 per person. At first the canal was thought to be a success and the quiet village of Paddington was transformed into an important transport terminus. But it soon floundered financially, partly due to the fact that one of its directors, Thomas Homer, embezzled a large amount of funds to pay his debts (he was later caught and transported) and partly to the fact that the large railways were being built and the one at Paddington became very important. Although Nash knew of the railways he thought, mistakenly, that the canal would benefit from them. In the event, the railways proved to be its financial downfall. The boatmen, on the other hand, were pleased with the project as it gave them the means to deliver building materials by water to the various stations under construction.

A story concerned with the Macclesfield Bridge on the canal is worth repeating. In Victorian times it consisted of three brick arches mounted on iron columns. Early in the morning on Friday 2 October 1874 a steam tug had in its wake five barges travelling away from the City. The names of the barges were Jane, Dee, Tilbury, Limehouse and Hawkesbury. Mostly they were carrying sugar, grain and general cargoes, but the third, the Tilbury had five tons of gunpowder, ready for blasting, on board. When the third barge went under the bridge there was a terrific explosion and the barge, bridge, trees and houses nearby were blown to bits or collapsed. The other barges were severely damaged but luckily the men were not hurt. A gas main carried across the canal in the structure of the bridge was broken and flaming and this caused many houses to blow up in the area. After this disaster the dangers of carrying explosives without special protection were urgently debated in Parliament and in June 1875 the Explosives Act was passed. The bridge was rebuilt and some of the iron columns were used again and the defaced stone was turned the other way so that it faced the bank and not the river. From that day it has been known to boatmen as 'Blow Up Bridge'.

When the zoo was moved to Regent's Park in the mid nineteenth century the grounds included part of the canal. After the war Lord Snowdon designed and opened an aviary which was built over the waterway. In 1929 the Grand Union Canal Company was formed and with government help a million pounds was donated to dredge and improve the water link between Limehouse and Birmingham. In 1947 the greater part of the British canal system was nationalized and the Regent Canal is now controlled by the British Transport Commission.

The horsedrawn tug vanished in the mid fifties and was replaced by the diesel-driven small craft. Although the canal was not a commercial success it did and still does provide a quiet backwater, historic and scenic, for the public, where private or commercial boats can go as they please.

Chariots and carts were in evidence in Britain at least three centuries before the Roman invasion and the ones used by Boadicea when fighting the invaders were in some ways better designed than those used by the Romans. All chariots and carts had two wheels and the British chariots were drawn by two horses yoked together by a pole wide enough for the driver to stand on and were furnished with a seat, which the Roman chariots did not have. Wagons, with four wheels, were used for processions and the transport of goods and this mode of transport remained without alteration for centuries.

In Tudor times the poor cadged lifts in goods wagons and the élite sometimes travelled by horse litter – a kind of stretcher contraption on poles to which horses were harnessed back and front. Both Catherine of Aragon and Anne Boleyn travelled to their coronation in horse-litters while Mary Tudor rode to hers in an ornamental wagon with a canopy, drawn by six horses.

The first coaches were made in Kocs in Hungary in the fifteenth century and the word coach is taken from the name of this town. They were very uncomfortable with no springs or padding. About two hundred years later a Frenchman designed a coach which was hung on poles suspended by leather straps. This reduced the jolting but tended to make the passengers feel sick! As time went on the wagons grew longer and heavier and tended to make already rough roads almost impassable. Parliament passed Bills stating that wagons were not allowed on the public highways unless their wheels were more than 9 inches in width as it was thought that wide wheels would flatten the road surface. At one time there was a law which allowed wagons with wheels broader than 16 inches to go through turnpikes and toll-gates free of charge. Stage wagons went from London to various parts of the country and later coaches were introduced but as they were much more expensive the poorer classes continued to travel by wagon. The first coaches were badly sprung, with wooden shutters for windows, and carried six passengers inside and more outside. More-comfortable coaches came on the scene later, carrying four inside only and an armed guard outside for protection against highwaymen. Mail coaches were dispatched from London to all parts of the country, to a strict timetable, loading at the General Post Office in Lombard Street.

Hackney coaches were first plied for hire in London in 1625. The term is said to stem from the French *haquenée* which means a slow pace or an ambling nag. Chaucer in his *Romaunt of the Rose* says 'he had in his stable an hackenay'. Drivers later took to waiting in the streets for customers and in 1634 a certain Captain Bailey had the idea of parking four Hackney coaches by the Maypole in the Strand. Others followed this idea and it was not long before London was littered with Hackney coaches. The sedan-chair made its appearance at about this time, probably in an attempt to lighten the coach traffic, but this idea did not last and the number of Hackneys continued to increase and were then used by sightseers and tourists to see the sights of London.

In 1820 Hackney cabriolets or cabs were introduced from Paris, using old disused carriages and only one horse. At first they were open and chaise-like, with only one pair of wheels and were therefore prone to accidents. Soon safety measures were introduced by Parliament and only coaches with four wheels were allowed on the road. Steel springs, padded seats and glass in the windows all contributed to the comfort of the passengers. Two-wheeled, horse-drawn cabs with the driver's seat raised behind were known as 'hansoms' after the inventor Joseph A. Hansom. The hansom in summer had a canopy to protect the enamel paint on top of the vehicle as well to give shade to the occupants. These canopies were made by the cabbies' wives in the manner of the canopies of the gondolas in Venice.

The last rally of the horse-drawn coach with all its trappings was at the coronation of George VI. They were lined up after depositing their passengers outside India House where a coronation dinner was being held. There were at the time only about half a dozen coaches left in London and this gathering was their swan song. Nowadays of course coaches are only used on State occasions or for the Lord Mayor's Show.

The horse-drawn omnibus was first introduced to London by George Shillibeer 'de Paris' in 1829. He was a funeral director who had worked in France for quite a few years previously. The vehicle was drawn by three horses, with twenty-two passengers inside. The first route was from Paddington Green to the Bank, and surprisingly a library of books was at hand in the bus to occupy the passengers on the journey. In 1857 the bus developed a 'knife board' and thirty years later it had a 'garden seat' – the uncovered upstairs, which was introduced by a man named Captain Molesworth. The London General Omnibus Company was formed in 1859 and was stationed at Highbury in the early days.

If the introduction of the horse-bus was a boon for foot passengers, it was a death-trap for horses. The average life of a strong horse pulling buses was four years. The strain of constantly stopping and starting, often on bad and varying road surfaces, proved too much even for the fittest strain of horse. The animals frequently slipped, breaking limbs or injuring themselves internally, and had to be shot on the spot. Although the omnibus companies fed and cared for their horses, giving them one rest day per week, after four or five years the beasts were sent to the knacker's yard. The railways too owned a large fleet of horses during the nineteenth century and although they were well cared for, they too were of no use after a few years. The weather also shortened the life of the working horse in London and according to W. J. Gordon in his book *The Horse World of London* (1883), dry roads brought slippery surfaces and wet and icy roads were also hazards. The animals suffered from colds, sore throats and fever in the damp climate and wet harnesses chafed and produced sores which quickly became infected. Pickfords, the removal people, used a large fleet of horses in those days. Many animals, especially those privately owned, were ill-treated but gradually education showed that it was not in anyone's best interests to ill treat a working animal.

There seems to be no doubt that it was due to the efforts of the members of the Automobile Club of Great Britain, later the Royal Automobile Club when it gained royal patronage in 1907, that the motor-car was at last accepted as an alternative mode of transport by the government and public alike. Although the first self-propelled vehicle made its appearance on the roads as early as 1770 – namely an engine propelled by steam and built by Captain Nicholas Cugnet of the French Artillery, a model of which can be seen in the museum of the R.A.C. in its Pall Mall headquarters – it was not until the 1880s that vehicles moving of their own volition were to be seen on roads on the Continent. These machines were due to the inventions of Gottlieb Daimler and Carl Benz, working independently. In this country steam coaches invented by Hancock had been run on roads as early as 1829 and in 1832 the London and Paddington Steam Car Company had been formed, but the Locomotive Act of 1865 put an end to further development. It stipulated that the speed limit of a mechanical vehicle was to be 4 m.p.h. and that a man should walk in front with a red flag to warn pedestrians and horse-drawn vehicles of its approach. It was also law that in each county a separate road licence had to be obtained. Motor enthusiasts in Britain and on the Continent were appalled by the attitude of the English Government. Late in 1894 the first road race from Paris to Rouen had taken place and this stirred Sir David Salomons, a prominent motor supporter, to action. The following spring he sent out thousands of invitations to people all over this country and abroad to come and see a show of horseless carriages at his estate at Ely Grange, Tunbridge Wells. People who owned mechanical vehicles were asked to bring them along although there was no British design. Sir David himself owned a $3\frac{3}{4}$ h.p. Peugeot and Mr. F. R. Simms, later to establish the R.A.C., brought his vehicle which he said could double up as a fire engine in an emergency. The story goes that Sir David drove over to the exhibition early in the morning in a horse brake. Removing the horses he placed a large placard on the brake which read 'Horse-less Carriage – made in England'. Many of the newspapers the next day reported with a measure of pride and elation the development of the English motor car and remarked on the clever way in which the engine had been concealed!

This event together with other pressures forced the government in 1896 to repeal the Red Flag Law and replace it with the Locomotives on the Highways Act, known by all as the Act of Emancipation. That same year, the Motor-Car Club was formed by Frederick Simms and the London to Brighton run was organized to celebrate the liberation of the motor car. The Motor Car Club had premises at Whitehall and it was from here that the run officially started. Everyone who owned a vehicle was invited to take part and quite a few came from the Continent. Before the commencement of the run speeches were made and the red flag was formerly torn up amidst cheers from competitors and onlookers alike. The contingent of twenty-three vehicles drove through London as slowly as they could to create as much public interest as possible. Thousands of people lined the route and marvelled at the splendid and unusual pageant. Because of the lack of garages, taverns along the route had been instructed to be ready to supply water. After a stop at Reigate for lunch those arriving at Brighton were told to gather in Preston Park so that all who had finished the run could parade together through the streets of the town. It is interesting to note that since that time a gathering of cars has been called a car park after that first assembly. Why Brighton was picked as the destination is not clear although the Mayors and their Corporations of Brighton and Reigate were very interested in motor travel and were present at the dinner held in Brighton at the end of the run. Their health was toasted by the organizers and it was clear that the co-operation of these bodies was much appreciated by the Club. Brighton was beginning to become a popular holiday resort patronized by the royal family; also had a very successful bicycle factory and it is probably for these reasons that the interest in road travel was promoted in the town.

In June 1896 Frederick Simms, having bought the Daimler patent, together with his friend the Hon. Evelyn Ellis, demonstrated to the Prince of Wales the Cannstatt-built Daimler. This demonstration took place in the grounds of the Imperial Institute and one of the tests in which the Prince participated was to be driven up a narrow wooden ramp with a gradient of 1 in 10. Prince Edward was very impressed and showed great interest in the new machine and all that it promised for the future. Mr. Simms, supported by many influential friends, founded the Royal Automobile Club in December 1899 and translated the constitution from that of the French Club that had been formed earlier. Frederick Simms financed the project from his own funds at first but in time, as the club grew and prospered, others were persuaded to put their money into the venture. After leaving Whitehall the Club was temporarily housed in Piccadilly before moving to a site in Pall Mall where it can still be found today. In 1900 the 1,000 mile trial for motor vehicles was made from Hyde Park Corner and this proved to be a convenient starting place as the number of competitors grew. According to Phil Drackett in his *Book of the Veteran Car* there were a number of well-known names competing, such as Mr. Herbert Austin driving a Wolseley, Mr. J. D. Siddley driving a Daimler, the brothers George and Frank Lanchester with a Lanchester and the Hon. C. S. Rolls in a Panhard. Mr. S. F. Edge drove a Napier and the one lady driver, a Mrs. Bazalgette, proudly completed the course in a Benz Ideal. At the end of the tour the Hon. C. S. Rolls gained the gold and Mrs. Bazalgette the silver medal. The route covered towns and cities all over Britain and thousands of people turned out to see the exhibition of new road transport.

The Brighton run was revived in 1922 and called 'The Old Crocks' Race' by the *Daily Sketch*. This name has stuck with the public much to the chagrin of the competitors. Since then the race has been held annually on the first Sunday in November, except for the war years. The number of entries now stands at roughly 300 and it is surprising where all th old cars have come from. Some have literally been dug from the ground, others rescued from rubbish dumps or found rusting away in old sheds and garages. Some have been bought for a few pounds and are now worth thousands of pounds. In 1963 the oldest four-wheeled British petrol-driven motor-car made its début. It was said to have been built in Walthamstow in 1894 by a plumber, Frederick Bremer, who had access to Benz patents and built the car in his spare time. The oldest car ever to take part was a Hammel from Denmark built in 1886, and like all other very old entries it was allowed to start earlier than the rest. Another surprise was in 1971, the 75th anniversary of the Act of Emancipation, when the entries included a 1900 Daimler, originally owned by Edward VII, which was entered by her Majesty the Queen. It made history as the first car owned by the royal family to take part and was driven by Mr. Evelyn Mawer, past President of the Veteran Car Club who had taken part in every run since 1947 in his own Oldsmobile.

Many well-known people have taken part and will take part in the London to Brighton Run. Past participants have included famous racing drivers such as Pat Moss and her husband Erik Carlsson, and Graham Hill driving a car for Oxfam with Dora Bryan sitting beside him. In 1968 Princess Grace and Prince Rainier of Monaco took part, riding in a 1903 De Dion Bouton. They crossed the finishing line at Brighton soon after noon and said that they would like to take part again. In 1972 the run was sponsored, for the first time, by Unipart. This was a very welcome sponsorship as the battle against ever-rising heavy costs, had become a great worry to the organizers, who still operate under the direction of the R.A.C.

The R.A.C. played an important part in guiding the Government to introduce legislation to licence cars and later to stipulate that a driving test should be passed. They fought many legal battles for the motorists in those days and encouraged garages to open along main roads. Inns and hostels which had lost favour were brought to prosperity once more with the new and ever-developing form of transport.

Air travel has of course revolutionized communications and transport during the last century but there is not room for me to touch on the development of the air terminals that serve London. But I would like to end this chapter on a high flying note, namely to record the story of man's first air flight over London. It was achieved by an Italian, Vincent Lunardi, at the end of August 1784. He used a hydrogen balloon, 33 ft in circumference, and a crowd of 20,000 people, including the Prince of Wales, watched the ascent from the Artillery ground in Moor-fields. Lunardi had arranged to take a passenger, a Mr. Biggin, but it was decided at the last moment that this gentleman was too corpulent, so Lunardi took up a dog and a cat instead. It was said that the cat suffered so much from the cold that the aeronaut made a special landing in a corn-field at South Mimms to let the animal off. A countrywoman found it and, we are told, sold the cat for a good price to a wealthy gentleman who had watched the balloon flying high in the air. Lunardi ascended once more and eventually landed near Ware in Hertfordshire, witnessed by Nathaniel Whitbread. The Lunardi Stone, surrounded by railings in a meadow at Standing, records the feat of the man who became a national hero of the day.

9

Leisure and Pleasure

It is fairly easy to find the division between sport and entertainment. Sport has consisted of competitive activities from early times, influenced by gambling, and in many cases has included the participation of ordinary folk. Entertainment, on the other hand, whether it be cruel, cultural or comic, is given to the population by certain sections of the people. The professionals, such as the players in miracle, mystery or morality plays, conjurers, musicians, or dancers, entertained a privileged audience, and the criminals, heretics and martyrs who ended their days on the scaffold, in the lion's den or at the stake, gave pleasure to the masses, as did the wrongdoers who endured torture in the stocks, pillories and on ducking stools.

The miracle and mystery plays which took the Bible stories and lives of the saints as their subjects, were first performed by religious houses in English for the benefit of the illiterate who, although compelled to attend church services, did not know or understand them as they were conducted in Latin. The Bible too was printed in Latin until it was translated in the fifteenth century. Therefore entertainment in English was a great joy to the rank and file and became so popular that the guilds took up the idea and gave not only religious but secular performances; also, they had an eye for business and saw this as a good opportunity to advertise their wares. The Lord Mayor's Show is the last link with ancient guild entertainment and advertisement.

During the sixteenth century playwrights began to write and produce plays for themselves, the greatest of which were Ben Jonson and William Shakespeare. At that time it was thought that Jonson was the greater of the two. Their plays could be bought in St. Paul's Churchyard and in the bookshops on London

Bridge. At first acting was performed on a raised dais in public taverns and no scenery or costumes were used. Even when theatres were built, such as the Globe, Southwark, where Shakespeare's plays were performed, there was no backcloth and nothing to indicate a change of scene except an explanation by the narrator. The platforms were often called apron stages as they extended out into the audience. At an inn called the Belle Sauvage on Ludgate Hill at about this time a showman named Banks had a famous performing horse called Morocco. The horse had once climbed to the tower of Old St. Paul's and his master was so proud of him that he had his hooves shod with silver. Banks toured Europe with his horse and eventually came to Rome. After seeing the clever antics of the animal the people were so frightened that they thought the horse bewitched and had Banks and Morocco burnt as heretics.

During the eleven years of the Puritan régime all theatres were closed, but when Charles II was crowned theatres and entertainment in general flourished once again. During his reign Charles issued two Letters Patent giving authority for two theatres to open in London and to hold the sole rights to present the spoken word in the capital. One was for a theatre to open in Covent Garden and the other in Drury Lane. The Theatre Royal Drury Lane was the leading playhouse at this time and it was here, during a performance of *The Indian Emperor* by John Dryden, that Charles first set eyes on Nell Gwyn who was starring in the show. Charles changed the format of the English theatre, introducing curtains, scenery and footlights in the form of candles and lamps – which was the vogue in France at the time. The playwrights then had to adapt their plays to take place at one venue so as to avoid changes in scenery which would have been too complicated.

Sadler's Wells in Islington has a unique beginning. From the fourteenth century Islington had provided the backcloth for the clerks of the City who performed their plays at Clerkenwell, the adjoining village. A piece of land was bought by Mr. Sadler, who in the course of excavations discovered an old well. As the water was fresh and clear he opened a water-spa and tea-gardens which became very popular and put Islington on the map. At first it was called the New Tunbridge Wells but changed to Sadler's

Wells soon after it was opened. Street entertainers flocked here to amuse the patrons, many of whom came from Court circles. It was patronized by the nobility from 1683 to the beginning of the nineteenth century. In 1733 Princess Caroline and her sister were frequent visitors and the place became well known as a venue for hypochondriacs.

Canonbury Tower was built at Islington in 1520 and is 40 ft high. It was built by the Prior of St. Bartholomew's before the Dissolution and contains the original panelling. It is one of the oldest buildings in London. Today it serves as a repertory theatre. Due to patronage by the upper classes other businesses started up in Islington. Many pubs and taverns were opened and gave rough entertainment to the clientele. Collins music-hall was opened here and was one of the first 'halls' in London! The waiters gave turns, a chairman presided over the show and the audience participated. Previously, the Sadler's Wells had opened as a brick built theatre in 1765, and theatre-goers were escorted through the streets by link boys with flame-torches to avoid footpads. During the last century Sadler's Wells became the home of ballet in England, due to Dame Ninette de Valois, a pupil of Diaghilev who may be described as the father of modern ballet. In 1956 the Sadler's Wells Company became the Royal Ballet and now performs at the Royal Opera House, Covent Garden.

The Theatre Royal, Drury Lane was opened almost immediately after Charles II had issued his two Letters Patent but the one destined for Covent Garden was not built until 1732 when the proprietor, John Rich, acquired the Letters Patent. Because of the Patent, Rich was allowed to use the name Theatre Royal. The theatre produced shows of music and drama and was burnt down more than once in the early days. In the mid nineteenth century The Theatre Royal Covent Garden became the Royal Italian Opera Company, and many Italian operas were produced there. The royal family were very interested in opera and gave patronage to the theatre which then became the venue for the fashionable leaders of society in London. Until the Second World War, with the exception of the years of the First World War, opera was performed at Covent Garden during the London 'Season' and it became established as the entertainment of society – 'evening dress was indispensable in the stalls and boxes'. During the last

Canonbury Tower

war the opera house was used as a dance hall but reverted to a theatre in 1946, when it became the permanent home of the Sadler's Wells Ballet Company.

There was no obvious connection between the theatre and the market at Covent Garden and when the fruit and vegetable market moved to Nine Elms in 1974, the market building was purchased by the Greater London Council and converted into a fashionable shopping area – which perhaps compliments the Royal Opera House in a better way than did the market!

During the latter part of the nineteenth century music-halls were springing up all over London and were in general favoured by the working classes. Charles Morton, 'the Father of the Halls', opened many music halls in London and the Provinces, encouraging the poorer classes by putting on turns that they could appreciate. Londoners, with their sense of humour ever near the surface could laugh at their predicaments when they were mirrored in comic songs and witty ditties as performed by talented artistes. George Leybourne was one of the all-time-greats and was discovered by Morton. At one time Leybourne was earning as much as £120 a week which was a great deal of money in those days. He often performed in more than one 'hall' during the course of an evening and Morton arranged for a carriage pulled by four white horses to transport him from one theatre to another. This of course established his image in the eyes of the public and was good advertisement. Leybourne's hit song 'Champagne Charlie' has never been forgotten and the wine merchants at the time provided him with free champagne at a cost to them of £20 per week. Leybourne lived beyond his means and wrecked his health; he died at the early age of 42.

The nursery rhyme 'Pop goes the Weasel' was written by Charles Sloman and sung as a music-hall ditty in such places of ill-repute as the Cyder Cellars and the Coal Hole. The lines 'Up and down the City Road, In and out the Eagle' refer to the Eagle tavern which replaced the gardens of the Shepherd and Shepherdess when the City Road was built in the East End in 1825. Later it turned into the Grecian theatre which was easily distinguished by two stone eagles set on pillars on each side of the entrance. The Eagle was finally demolished at the turn of the last century but its memory is perpetuated in the old nursery rhyme.

Marie Lloyd must be accepted as the queen of the music-hall. She sang many songs which have entered the traditional stream, the most popular being perhaps, 'Don't Dilly Dally on the Way'. Her real name was Matilda Wood and she was born in 1870. When she went on the stage she changed it to Bella Delmere but did not gain success so she changed it again, to Marie Lloyd, and in doing so changed her fortune. She was heralded as the foremost comedienne of her day and every song she sang became a winner by the measure of her talent and sex appeal. She married three times but never very happily – one of her husbands was Alec

Burley, the coster who ran family entertainment, and in 1912 at the height of her fame she was pointedly left out of the cast of the first Royal Command Performance owing to her coarse humour. Marie was a big-hearted woman who did not give up easily, and she often performed in great pain during the last years of her life. She collapsed while playing at the Crouch End Hippodrome and died in 1922 at the age of 52. Her house was found to be the house of a pauper and there was not enough cash to pay for her funeral. It was paid out of public funds and thousands of people attended the event in London. Music-halls in London and all over the country draped their fronts with black crêpe paper and half the taverns in London adorned their mirrors with the same. Artistes wore black neckties – something they had not done since the death of Edward VII.

Madame Tussaud's has been established in London as a permanent place of entertainment since it was housed in Baker Street in 1835, and later moved to its present site in Marylebone Road. The making of wax effigies has been a popular pastime since before Roman times and Madame Tussaud's Waxworks are world famous. She was born Marie Grosholtz and from the age of six lived with her uncle, Dr. Curtis, in Paris and helped run his waxwork show. At the age of seventeen the young Marie made a portrait in wax of Voltaire which can still be seen today. During the French revolution Dr. Curtis and his niece were forced to mould death masks in wax of all those who were guillotined. When her uncle died Marie inherited the business and married Monsieur Tussaud, an engineer, in 1795. She had three children and came to England to promote her waxwork business, leaving her husband to look after the Paris establishment. Monsieur Tussaud squandered the capital and the waxworks had to be sold to pay his debts. Marie Tussaud decided to stay in England and for thirty-five years toured the country with her waxworks, helped by her children. She never saw her husband again. She gained a permanent site in London before dying at the age of eighty-one in 1850. It was her custom to sit at the entrance and take the entrance fee and today the wax figure of this extraordinary lady can be seen in the foyer. Madame Tussaud's has the reputation of making wax replicas of people without asking their permission. This is remembered in a limerick published in Punch in 1919:

There was an old woman called Tussaud,
Who loved the grand folk in Who's Who, so,
She made them in wax,
Both their front and their backs,
And asked no permission to do so.

Another great place of entertainment in London cannot be ignored and this is the Albert Hall. It was built from 1867 to 1871 as part of the memorial to Prince Albert and was designed by General H. Scott. It stood on the site which at one time housed Gore mansion, in which the hostess entertained Thackeray and Dickens. It is one of the most popular halls in London and can hold up to 8,000 people. It is in the form of a huge oval arena surrounded by tiers of boxes and galleries and its roof consists of a shallow metal and glass dome. Encircling the exterior below the dome is a frieze which illustrates man's progress in the arts and sciences throughout the centuries, a theme very near to the heart of Prince Albert. The Albert Hall is used for a wide variety of events, from the 'Proms' and other classical music concerts to activities of all kinds including boxing and wrestling. Many rallies are held here, the most well known perhaps being the British Legion Service held in November to commemorate those fallen in the two world wars.

Fireworks have provided an entertaining spectacle enjoyed by both rich and poor from Elizabethan times onwards. They were first used in religious festivals but the Queen ordered displays to be enjoyed by everyone. In London the Thames was the natural venue for pyrotechnics as the water showed off the fireworks to the best advantage. After the discovery of the Gunpowder Plot, 5 November was made a public holiday and it was not long before fireworks and bonfires were part of the celebrations. Up to the beginning of the nineteenth century the only colours produced by fireworks were the flame colours of red, yellow and orange. Then potassium chlorate was introduced to the mixture to make it burn with a much greater heat and produce varied colours. Barium salts give a green flame, strontium red, sodium yellow, and copper with chlorine gas gives a blue light. Years ago barges were used on the Thames to bear set pieces, which floated downstream giving maximum coverage for the crowds on both sides of the water. Bridges, too, were often used to anchor large firework pictures. During the eighteenth century, especially on Guy Fawkes Day, firework displays were at the height of popularity in the capital. George III and his family watched from a specially constructed dais on the river bank while the watermen in their barges presented wonderful spectacles. Among the more memorable pictures were St. Paul's Cathedral, the Tower of London, portraits of the king and his family and of course Guy Fawkes himself, complete with lantern and gunpowder barrels. In addition to the fireworks huge bonfires were built in Lincoln's Inn Fields, regardless of the danger to property. Up to two hundred cart-loads of fuel and over thirty guys contributed to the scene.

Pleasure gardens sprang up all over London advertising splended displays of fireworks – the most famous being at Vauxhall Gardens. Later the Crystal Palace spectacular superseded this, staged by C. T. Brock, 'the father of the British firework'. The Crystal Palace displays lasted from 1865 to 1936 when the building was burnt down.

London has had its share of street entertainers, groups of players and buskers of every sort, all of whom used their talents to ward off starvation when no other work was available. Many were musicians and the instruments used varied from the human voice, the penny whistle or the violin to the well organized German band which was so popular in Edwardian times. The 'one man band' was very successful and he played as many as six instruments at once by means of elbows, head, feet, mouth and hands – not forgetting knees. Cornets and accordians, and of course the barrel organ with the traditional monkey, were common sights and dancing bears could be seen in the streets of London up to 1908, with the eye of the R.S.P.C.A. upon them. Many were out-of-work music-hall artistes; nigger-singing and dancing troupes were common as were the pierrots until the popularity of the seaside resort became apparent and pierrots found success there. Dancing in the streets was common, especially by children – who could resist giving a coin to a child who danced beautifully? Other routines included clog dancing – Charlie Chaplin started as a child performer in such a troupe in the late nineteenth century. He was employed as a stooge by the troupe who were of German nationality, and he and his mother and brother were very poor. Often he had to queue at the free soup kitchens.

Boxing to music was another attraction – to the strains of the hurdy-gurdy two men dressed in fancy clothes would give an exhibition match moving in time to the music. Sometimes a Scotsman in a kilt would dance accompanied by another on the bag-pipes. The Irishman provided a stream of uncensored jokes and was the poor man's comedian, as was the 'felt hat manipulator', a clever impersonator who could mimic anybody in the public eye by just altering the shape of his hat. The fire-eater commanded an audience as did the juggler and the acrobat. Men ate pebbles, glass and nails for the public to stare and wonder at. These were skilled entertainers busking outside theatres hoping for a chance to perform inside.

In the early days birds with gaily-coloured plumage were kept in cages on top of barrel organs and were used as fortune tellers. At the side of the cage where the bird seed was usually kept were packets of slips of paper each with a fortune printed on it. When the money was paid the side was drawn out and the bird hopefully pecked at the papers thinking that seed would be underneath. When it became disillusioned it let the paper drop and this was the fortune handed out to the one who had paid to 'have a go'.

The bottle carrier must have been one of the rarest and most exciting sights. The act consisted of two men – one athletic carrying the other sitting on a bottle balanced on the top of his head. The top man also carried bottles under each arm. There was only one street act to perform this feat in Edwardian times and in fact a placard was carried stating that the men held the world record for bottle carrying. This was never disputed. A strange sight in modern times in London would be to see the man who travelled around showing his collection of 'Happy Families'. This consisted of a large cage which he dragged around the streets in which were housed all sorts of animals. For instance, cats, hens, magpies, tortoises, hawks, dogs, rats (sewer and white), ferrets, monkeys, jays, starlings, hedgehogs, pigeons and so on would be shown living together in close proximity. This was made possible by training the animals and birds when young and also by showing them kindness and patience and giving them enough to eat. At night they were housed in a stable together and never harmed one another. At one time there was only one Happy Family in London and this brought the crowds, the owner earning as much as £1 per day, a great deal of money in those days. The first man to do this was John Austin who came from Nottingham to London to make his fortune. Austin stayed in London for thirty-six years and in that time attracted many thousands of people including members of the royal family. Others copied his idea and when Austin died he was taking hardly enough to feed his animals.

Human freaks were a great attraction not only at fairs but in the street. It is said that Charles I had amongst his subjects the oldest, Thomas Parr, the greatest, William Evans, a porter who is said to have grown to 7 ft 6 ins tall, and the smallest, Sir Geoffrey Hudson, a dwarf who was served in a pie when nine years old and only 18 ins tall to amuse the king. Evans could put Hudson into his pocket which he frequently did. Fleet Street was notorious for the macabre. One 14-year-old child was displayed in a shop, never having grown out of the baby stage. Giants and dwarfs were commonplace and a dwarf without hands, feet, legs or thighs could shuffle a pack of cards, write and thread needles, presumably with his mouth. In 1702 a contortionist could be seen who could literally tie his body into knots. In 1812 the Lord Chancellor put a stop to many of these sights, quite correctly proclaiming that they degraded the human race.

With the coming of State education in 1871 the standard of literacy amongst the masses steadily improved. Common folk began to take an interest in such buildings as the British Museum and the Natural History and Victoria and Albert museums of Kensington. Incidentally the British Museum was established by an Act of Parliament in 1755 and was the collection of scientific books and manuscripts left to the nation by Hans Sloane the wealthy eighteenth century physician. Sloane made his fortune from a rich marriage and an early appreciation of the value of quinine. The Museum was built in the fashionable part of London called Bloomsbury, but owing to a wealth of gifts and contributions had to be redesigned and enlarged by the architect, Sir Robert Smirke, between 1823 and 1850. The museum houses a variety of valuable pieces and is responsible for the National

Library. This came about after a collection of priceless books was bestowed on the nation by the book antiquarian, Robert Cotton, when he died. In 1880 the Natural History Museum was opened in Cromwell Road to take the overflow from the British Museum. Even so many exhibits are stored and are only on show occasionally, due to lack of space.

Prince Albert planned a series of museums in Kensington with the help of profits made from the Great Exhibition. The South Kensington was opened in 1857, and was dedicated to science and art. Later, because of lack of space, the science section was moved to the new Science Museum close by. In 1899 Queen Victoria laid the foundation stone of the Victoria and Albert Museum and in 1909 Edward VII opened the building.

Towards the end of the nineteenth century free libraries came into existence and free newspaper libraries also. For the first time books were available to the poor free of charge, and this in itself was an added incentive to learn to read. At first it was thought foolhardy to open a free library in the East End but the one in Bethnal Green proved so successful that soon others were opened in the poorer quarters of London. The slum dwellers did not abuse the privilege of taking a book home to read but treated the new development with a respect that was not always present amongst the richer classes. This move helped foreigners with their language problems – the first help they had received. The Shepherd's Bush library was the first to have a ladies' reading room. Libraries for hospitals were provided by public subscription as the life of a hospital book was short in those days, for many were burnt after being in contact with those suffering from infectious diseases. Although Mudies in New Oxford Street had been open for quite a number of years, it served only the fashionable community and the subscription was high. In Edwardian times the London Library in St. James's Square catered for the researcher and for an annual subscription of £3 a member could take out ten volumes at a time. This together with the British Museum and the Guildhall library formed the basis of reference libraries as we know them today.

It is interesting to note that W. H. Smith have sold books on railway stations for over a century.

I have talked about the slum conditions of the London poor

in previous chapters and now perhaps I ought to mention how the élite, bent on pleasure, built fashionable squares in which to live. After the Great Fire the wealthy Earl of Bedford bought up large areas of land in London. The first to design a fashionable square was Inigo Jones in Covent Garden. He built a grand piazza flanked by magnificent houses but had to abandon the project in the face of the ever flourishing market. Nevertheless he had set the trend and soon other fashionable quarters were springing up all over the West End. Large houses were built around pieces of land which were used as private gardens and playgrounds. Squares developed along Mayfair and north of Oxford Street, creating a new area known as Bloomsbury. South Kensington was also regarded as a desirable place in which to live. The 4th Earl of Southampton who in 1660 developed the system of land held on lease, laid out Bloomsbury Square as a speculative development. Even today half the land in central London is held on lease. The first of the great squares in the West End was St. James's Square developed by the Earl of St. Albans. Grosvenor Square was started in 1725 on land which had been the country estate of Lord Grosvenor. Its circular garden was designed by Kent with a statue of George I in the middle. Sir Richard Grosvenor had a mistress, the Duchess of Kendall, commonly known as the Maypole because of her great height, and she moved into one of the houses. Since 1960 the American Embassy has more or less taken over the square and the style of buildings has blended in quite well with the Georgian character of the square. Grosvenor Chapel was built in 1730 to serve the residents of the square and was adopted in the last war by Yankee soldiers as their church. Lord Edward Harley and Lady Henrietta Cavendish developed Cavendish Square with the help of John Prince, the self-styled 'Prince of Builders'. Among other West End squares of this period were Hanover, Soho, Bedford and Berkeley. Plane trees were planted at this time to grace these areas and sadly in many cases only the trees remain to remind us of the graciousness and opulence of a former age.

Unlike the residential squares, areas such as Trafalgar and Leicester Squares were built with public money and did much to ease the movement of the London traffic. Trafalgar Square was of course built to commemorate one of the most important sea battles in our history. It was built on the original site of Charing Cross. The Cross was pulled down in 1675 and replaced by a statue of Charles I on horseback sculptured by Le Sueur. The statue is still in the square and a replica of the original cross can be seen outside Charing Cross main railway station. A natural junction of roads was an ideal place to level the ground and build a square – designed by John Nash soon after the Battle of Trafalgar and the death of Nelson. The granite column is over 167 ft high and the figure of Nelson a good 17 ft on top of that. The base of the column is guarded by Landseer's four bronze lions. Other gallant admirals and naval personnel in the form of statues can be seen here and the area is graced with fountains, plane trees and pigeons. It is linked to Buckingham Palace by Admiralty Arch and the Mall. In 1834 the building of the National Gallery designed by William Wilkins was begun on the site which originally housed the royal stables and falconry. This building majestically flanks one side of the square and is one of the finest museums of art in the world. On another side of the square stands the church of St. Martin-in-the-Fields, built by James Gibbs and finished in 1726. The present church is of such a spectacular design that many American churches have been built to the same plan. The site originally housed another church dating back to the thirteenth century which was literally built in the fields. The ancient church is said to have contributed to the line 'I'll pay you five farthings said the bells of St. Martin's', in the nursery rhyme 'Oranges and Lemons'. Its vicar told me of an old legend attached to the church concerning a poor destitute foreigner, about to take his own life. He heard the bells of the London churches ringing out and they reminded him of the orange and lemon groves of Italy and set him thinking about returning to his native land. He forgot about committing suicide and obtained a job as a seaman, working his passage on a boat bound for Italy – and home.

Today Trafalgar Square has its sightseers, dreamers, orators and meetings and is a venue which is used by a cross-section of the community. Every Christmas a tree, given by the people of Norway to Londoners in appreciation of their fortitude during the last war, can be seen lit up and is one of the attractions of the capital over the festive period.

Fashionable weddings were held at St. George's Church, Hanover Square or at St. Paul's Church, Knightsbridge during Edwardian times and before. Flowers became fashionable for the rich at about this time; as much as £1,000 might be spent on floral decorations for one wedding. Since that time other churches have become popular including, St. Margaret's, Westminster. In contrast weddings in the East End around the turn of the century were performed in batches and were called Penny Weddings — for this was the fee charged by the clergy to marry couples in groups, although the actual marriage lines were spoken individually. These weddings were first conducted in Fleet prison and then in churches such as St. John's, Walworth and St. John's, Hoxton. On one occasion in 1754 the Reverend Alexander Keith, incumbent of St. George's Chapel, Hyde Park Corner, married sixty couples at one go. In Edwardian times multiple weddings were still legal but the price had gone up to six shillings. One extraordinary wedding at the beginning of the last century was the famous bicycle wedding held at Notre-Dame de France, Leicester Square. The couple rode to the church together on a 'sociable', a bicycle made for two, followed by their friends and attendants, all on sociables adorned with ribbons and flowers. A huge crowd turned out to watch and the event probably inspired the songwriter to produce the classic 'Daisy, Daisy'.

The food shops and restaurants in London are too numerous to mention in detail but of course they do provide pleasure for the visitor. One that I would like to mention is a tavern named 'Dirty Dick's' in Bishopsgate, because it has a story behind it. Years ago a man named Nathaniel Beatley owned the building and lived in it as a private residence. He also kept a hardware store in Leadenhall Street. His father was a wealthy man and Nathaniel inherited the family fortune after his father's death. He dressed expensively and lived grandly and was engaged to be married to a handsome woman. Just as he was organizing and preparing a banquet at his house to celebrate his engagement, he was brought the news that his fiancée had died very suddenly. This turned his mind and he became a recluse, shutting himself up in the house and not touching anything. He did not wash or change his clothes and they were soon in rags. He left London, shutting up his house and shop, and tramped the countryside living the life of a vagabond. He died in Musselburgh in Scotland. When the house was opened up it was dirty, and cobwebs and skeletons of vermin were everywhere. The place was cleaned up, decorated and turned into a tavern and named Dirty Dick's. Today as well as giving the usual bar service, downstairs in the cellars a small museum can be inspected – housing the largest collection of tickets in London. It has become a tradition that anyone visiting the place for the first time should stick a ticket on the wall of the downstairs room – whether it be a bus ticket or an expensive theatre ticket. Tickets are everywhere, even on the ceiling and tradition has it that good luck will come to the person who contributes to the collection.

London's first coffee-house, so the story goes, was set up by a man named Bowman, a coachman to a gentleman called Mr. Hodges who was a merchant, dealing with goods from Turkey. He had a servant of that nationality named Pasqua Rosee who prepared coffee every morning for his master. Bowman and Rosee set up a coffee house in St. Michael's Alley near St. Paul's Church-yard. They quarrelled and separated and the servant set up another coffee-house together in opposition in St. Paul's Churchyard. From this time coffee-houses became famous as debating clubs being the meeting places for literary men to discuss politics and the affairs of the day. In Tudor times there was a coffee-house called Dick's in Fleet Street and the proprietor, a man named Tottel, was a law printer to Edward VI. The family kept up the tradition of being the official printing house and law publishers to the monarch until Victorian times. As we have seen this is the way Lloyds began and in most coffee-houses newspapers and periodicals were provided for the customer to read. The importance of coffee houses waned during the last century and taverns took their place until the teashop and café came into being.

The London teashop owes its origin to the Aerated Bread Company. This retail shop was situated near London Bridge during Edwardian times. The story goes that the manageress was a sociable being and often invited her regular customers into the back room for a cup of tea. This custom became so popular that she suggested to the Company that it might be a good idea to serve tea as part of the business. The Company agreed to give it a try and the plan became so successful that soon a string of

A.B.C. shops were doing the same. Other companies followed suit such as the Express Dairies, Slaters and Lyons. The London teashop had been launched and provided the luxury of inexpensive meals for the not so well off. Today these eating places have all but disappeared and more sophisticated food bars have taken their place.

Food in the streets is still available, as it has been for centuries. Tea and coffee stalls exist selling hot soup and pies also. Hot chestnuts, cooked potatoes and sausages can still be bought out of doors. The fish and chip van is a welcome sight but sadly the ice-cream vendor who pedalled his cart crying 'Stop me and buy one' has been replaced by the ice-cream van.

There were two worlds of sport in ancient times. The poorer, working classes used the festival days, their only holidays, in which to develop pastimes and sporting activities. The rich used their leisure to develop more sophisticated activities. At first certain games were linked with certain festivals, thus football or camping as it was called was played widely in the streets and countryside from Pancake Day onwards, while marbles, tops, skipping, skittles and kite flying were associated with Easter. Ball games, including stool-ball, rounders and Tip Cat, were played in the fields at harvest time as was leap frog and Prison Bars. Battledore and shuttlecock was played in the streets by children using pieces of cork or wooden weaving shuttles adorned with small feathers to give flying power and bats in the form of wash beaters to keep the shuttle airborn. This was of course the origin of the game of badminton and it was Lord Badminton who promoted it as a recognized sport.

The street games invented by the poor children provided endless entertainment and are as old as mankind itself. Innovation was essential as no money was available. Paper boats were made from waste, and sailed in the gutters. Mud pies were made from heaps of dirt everywhere, ropes for skipping were borrowed wash-lines, rough swords and paper hats were made from flotsam found in the streets and provided adequate equipment for the game of soldiers which the boys played, drilling with an uncanny precision learnt from observing the real thing. The boys played a group game called 'Horny Winkle's Horses' – played in pairs, one sitting on his partner's shoulders. They charged each other with the shout 'Charlie Knockers, one two three' and the pair that were left standing within the group were the winners. Often the girls would make colourful reins for their 'Champions' out of scraps of coloured wool wound round a cotton reel studded with nails – the forerunner of the Knitting Nancy.

Hoops were made from the rings taken from barrels, or old pram wheels, stilts from fishermen's oars or clothes' props, kites, whips and tops were all fashioned from waste material. Barter was rife, two jam jars could buy a bag of marbles or acquire a place in the 'Gods' of the local playhouse. Toys including dolls were carved from wood and the dolls' clothes made out of odd scraps of material. The girls played skipping games in groups, hopscotch or spent many hours playing solo ball games against a wall. Singing games were played endlessly to entertain the infants and many of these are still played today. On the whole the girls did not have so much time to play as the boys. Theirs was the responsibility of looking after babies and younger children in the family and consequently they matured much quicker than the boys.

Guilds had from early days held competitions for their members to find the champion within the Company. Thus contests were held to find the most accurate butcher, the fastest rabbit-skinner, the best sheep-shearer and so on. Other sporting activities developed and the Companies began to play each other for some kind of prize. In this way the idea of having tournaments and leagues developed. The prize of Doggett's Coat and Badge is still competed for by the Watermen of the City. Thomas Doggett, born in Dublin in the late seventeenth century, became an actor and manager of the Theatre Royal, Drury Lane. He was consumed with admiration for the House of Hanover and George I began his rule of England on 1 August 1714. To commemorate the event he organized a race to be held annually on the river Thames between six young watermen who would finish their apprenticeships within the next twelve months, and then would be provided with the freedom of the river. The original course was said to be from Swan to Swan, being the names of two waterside inns at the time. The old Swan Stairs at London Bridge was the starting point and the rowers had to row 4½ miles against a strong current. The winner received not only an orange coloured coat, breeches and cap and a large silver badge bearing the Rampant White Horse of the House of Hanover but £10 also. Others in the race received money according to their placings. Doggett saw every race until he died in 1722, and then left money in the trust of the Fishmongers' Company for the race to be run annually. Today the race is described as London's Oxford and Cambridge Boat Race and is still held from London Bridge to Chelsea. Six skiffs rowed by watermen leave the starting point at the crack of a pistol shot and are rowed through Blackfriars, Waterloo, to the Bakerloo tunnel until the 4½ mile course has been completed. Other races on the Thames between friendly watermen were usually rewarded by teapots for the winners. One boy boasted that he had twenty-two teapots at home all won on the river.

All sorts of small contests were held in the East End from singing birds, dog shows, clay pigeon shooting, quoits and bowls to those held by the costers to find the 'best donkey and cart'. Porters in the markets competed with each other to find who could carry the heaviest basket on his head the furthest distance.

The poor man's sport which was most popular in Victorian times was dog and rat contests. Practically every tavern had a back room where a rat pit had been built. Rats were caught in the sewers in their thousands and a small terrier type of dog was bred to kill them. A number of rats were put in the pit and the dog who could kill the largest number in the shortest time was the winner. When one dog had accomplished his task, the rats were piled high in the corners of the pit and fresh ones thrown in to await the next killer. Although this was illegal the police turned a blind eye, for what better way could London be rid of the vermin that pestered it? Gambling in these dens was rife, and a good ratting dog fetched a high price, although many died from rat bites.

Gambling has been with us since before Christ and when playing cards were introduced to this country around 1465, gambling increased at an alarming rate. It is thought that playing cards originated in old China and were, in the first instance money cards with many suits to represent commodities sold, such as string and paper. When the idea came to Europe a gambling game emerged using numbers up to ten and picture cards. The French developed the four suits which were copied by the English. Thus the 'spade' was taken from the French '*pique*' – because it looked like a pike staff to the English. The 'heart' was simply a translation of '*coeur*'. The 'club' was an innovation of '*trèfle*' and the 'diamond' came from '*carreau*' which means square. Early European cards were hand-painted and too expensive for ordinary use but in the fifteenth century wood engravers used designs stamped on cheap pasteboard and produced a commodity that could be purchased for a few pence. Figures of the court cards are still modelled on the dress of Henry VII and Henry VIII, and hair styles of that era are still copied – the long bob of the men is in keeping with the coiffures of the early Tudor court. The faces of the Queens are modelled on the broad face of Elizabeth of York, Henry VII's Queen. It was not until 1870 that the double-headed variety of cards with corner indexes became the standard pattern. The popularity of card-playing swept the country and soon many games had been evolved. From *Poor Robin's Almanack* we have this verse:

> Christmas to hungry stomachs give relief,
> With mutton, pork, pies, pasties and roast beef:
> And men at cards spend many idle hours,
> At loadum, whisk, cross-ruff, put, and all fours.

All fours became poker, and whisk became whist. And the term cross-ruff is used in whist and bridge as trumping.

Cribbage originated in a game called Noddy and a poem published in 1694, called for some reason Batt upon Batt, describes the old game of Noddy:

> Show me a man that can turn up a Noddy still
> And deal himself three fives, too, when he will.
> Conclude with one-and-thirty, and a pair
> Never fail ten in Stock and yet play fair.
> If Batt be not that right I lose my aim.

Noddy means 'one for his nob' and Stock refers to the Crib or Box.

The game of whist became popular in London around 1730. A group of gentlemen in the Crown club in Bedford Row studied the rudiments of the game and drew up a code of rules which were accepted by the best clubs in London, including the Arlington, Carlton, Conservative, Guards', Oxford and Cambridge, St. James's and Whites. The small volume entitled *The Laws of Short Whist* was published in 1865. Hoyle, an excellent whist player of the era, gave lessons at a guinea a time. Ladies in Edwardian days became very keen on bridge and played it literally morning, noon and night.

An epitaph to a card player said to have lived in the Stuart period, according to Hone in his *Book of Days*, went like this:

His card is cut – long days he shuffled through.
The game of life – he dealt as others do.
Though he by honours tells not its amount
When the last trump is played his tricks will count.

The labouring poor played cards at every opportunity and there is an amusing story concerning a group of Irish labourers who were taken on board as seamen by a captain who had signed off his original crew. The Irishmen had never worked aboard ship and did not know the first thing about sailing or what the different areas and parts of the ship were called in nautical terms. The Master tried to train them but as their intellect was not very high this proved an impossible task. The captain had observed that his 'crew' played cards at every available moment and so developed the idea of naming each part of the ship after a card in the pack. Thus the mainsail became the Queen of Hearts, the rigging the Jack of Diamonds, the mast the King of Spades, the galley the Queen of Clubs and so on. The crew learnt their lessons like magic and the captain ended up with a happy, efficient and willing body of men.

As mentioned the rich developed sports which demanded lucrative support, thus banning the poorer communities from taking part. Snobbishness and class distinction were deeply rooted and lasted in sport well into the last century. Cricket, real tennis, lawn-tennis, polo, golf, croquet, archery, and horse racing were all rich men's sports and were all enjoyed at Ranelagh, in beautiful grounds belonging to an early Georgian house and just half an hour's drive from Piccadilly. It must be considered as the first high class sports club in London.

Archery was the only outdoor sport played by ladies in Edwardian times and was usually played in Regent's Park where the Royal Toxopholite Society was based. Ladies' hockey was introduced soon afterwards. The game of 'ping-pong' was also favoured by the ladies as it was thought too effeminate for the male sex in those days. It was said to have been invented by an Army officer to amuse his children. It was played at first on a large dining-room table with wooden or parchment bats and celluloid balls. The ladies played the game at Queen's Club and often tournaments and international matches were arranged, usually against the U.S.A. No special garb was worn for these matches, just long skirts and long-sleeved blouses, which must have hampered the players considerably.

In Edwardian times an ice rink was opened, using artificial ice, at Princes Club in London and was enjoyed by the wealthy. A Hungarian band played waltzes for the skaters.

Cricket was a rich man's game and the history of Lord's Cricket Ground and the M.C.C. is worth repeating. Lord's was not so named, as I imagined, because of the aristocratic status of its founder members but because the ground was found by a certain Thomas Lord, a Yorkshire man born in Thirsk in 1755. His father, William Lord, a member of the Jacobite cause, lost his land and fortune when Prince Charlie was defeated at Culloden Moor. The family moved to Norfolk where Thomas developed a liking for cricket. He moved to London in 1780 and obtained a post as a groundsman at the White Conduit Club, Islington. His enthusiasm for cricket inspired the formation of a cricket section within the club in 1782 which was sponsored by members of the exclusive 'je ne sais quoi' Club which met at the Star and Garter Tavern in Pall Mall. Members of this club had revised the laws of cricket as early as 1755 and so had a vested interest in the game. By 1786 the cricket section of the White Conduit Club had become so overcrowded that members told Lord that if he could find a more exclusive site for cricket then they would back him. Lord found a suitable piece of land in Dorset Fields, Marylebone, now Dorset Square. The land was bought from the Portman estate and Lord himself personally supervised the laying of the turf. In 1787 the first cricket match was played at Lord's – Middlesex v. Essex. Patrons from the White Conduit Club, including Thomas Lord, Lord Winchilsea, Lord Charles Lennox (4th Duke of Richmond), the Duke of York and the Duke of Dorset, had now formed the Marylebone Cricket Club. The ground prospered and became the main cricket centre in London and the British Isles, taking over the responsibilities of governing the game from the Hambledon Club, Hampshire. After twenty years the rent of the site had become too costly and Lord was forced to look for another venue. He took out a lease on a piece of ground north of Regent's Park and moved there in 1811. This did not last long as the Government decided to build the Regent's Canal through the playing area. Lord moved again to St. John's Wood and the M.C.C. had found its permanent home. It is said that on each occasion Lord took the turf from the original pitch. The first match played here was between the M.C.C. and Hertfordshire on 22 June 1814.

Although I said earlier that the game was confined to the wealthy, the club was not above taking the money of the poorer classes to swell the coffers. The ground was used for many other amusements to attract the crowds. On the first ground in Dorset Fields there had been military parades and balloon ascents and in St. John's Wood amusements such as canary shows, dancing by a troupe of Indians, who were actually allowed to camp on the pitch, and archery contests were common. A spectacular event was a marathon ride by John Joseph Grandserre on his velocipede. With the money raised a tavern was built and in 1838 a 'real' tennis court was built on the site of the Mound Stand. Soon an outside tennis court had been added and in 1875 the M.C.C. and the Tennis and Rackets Sub-Committee drew up the first set of rules for the game of lawn-tennis.

In the eighteenth century all bowling in cricket was under arm and the players used curved bats. In 1828 round arm bowling was allowed and in 1888 over arm bowling became standard. At first the wicket was wide and only consisted of two stumps with a cross bar laid across the top. When in 1776 a match had been lost in spite of the ball passing through the stumps a number of times without dislodging the bail, it was decided to add a middle stump. Creases were at first cut into the turf, and it was not until much later that white markers were used. The score was kept on a tally stick, one notch for every run. The players in the early days wore knee breeches, buckled shoes and coloured shirts – one club sported a daring spot pattern. Football clubs have kept up this tradition but cricketers decided on 'all white' somewhere along the line. Ties were worn until well into the present century and the head gear varied from top hats, bowlers, pillboxes, tam-o'-shanters to the modern day cap. Gambling was popular and as much as £500 would be staked by one person for one match.

'The Ashes' was a tradition invented by the *Sporting Times* after Australia beat England at The Oval in 1882. The paper published an article describing 'the death of English cricket' and stated that 'the body will be cremated and the Ashes taken to Australia.' The actual ashes came from a bail which was burnt during the England tour of Australia in 1883. They are kept in an urn in the Imperial Cricket Memorial Gallery at Lord's, a museum which is dedicated to all cricketers who gave their lives in the two world wars and was opened by the Duke of Edinburgh in 1953. Incidentally Lord's 'nursery end' is so called as it once formed part of a nursery garden before it was acquired by the Club. The famous 'Father Time' weather vane, Lord's landmark placed over the grandstand, was given to the Club as a surprise present by Sir Herbert Baker who designed the stand in 1926.

Today, Lord's is the home of the Middlesex County Cricket Club as well as the M.C.C. and traditional matches are played here such as Oxford v. Cambridge, Eton v. Harrow and Gentlemen v. Players. It is also the venue for the second Test match when the series is played in England.

The Montpelier Cricket Club, one of the strongest in South London, was forced to move from its original site at Walworth in 1844. The area now occupied by the Kensington Oval was at one time a market garden, the land belonging to the Duchy of Cornwall. The Duchy agreed to lease out the land for the purpose of cricket and the Montpelier Club took over and, when the new premises were ready, opened as the Surrey County Cricket Club. The club badge, the Prince of Wales's feathers, is derived from the association with the Duchy of Cornwall. According to Gordon Ross in his pamphlet entitled *The Story of Surrey and the Oval*, it was Lord Rosebery, then Lord Dalmeny, who spoke to the Prince of Wales in 1905 and sought his permission for the Surrey County Cricket to use the Prince of Wales's feathers and the privilege was granted.

Football, our national sport, has been played since Roman times in streets and countryside by commoners on festival days and was relatively unknown to the gentry. It was so rough and created such havoc that it was banned by seven monarchs from 1200 to 1650. While ragged children were kicking a paper ball about in the back streets of most towns, public schools and universities had taken up the game, developing their own rules. The boys at St. Paul's School played on the roof within a wire netting cage. Where the game was played in a more confined space such as this, hacking and kicking was forbidden and other practices, including dribbling and accurate passing, were developed. Most public schools evolved their own set of rules which caused chaos when matches were played in the league. So in 1863 the Football Association was formed and one of its rules prohibited random hacking and kicking. The first set of F.A. rules decided on at the Freemason's Tavern, Great Queen Street, London make interesting reading, and here are some of the finer points:

1. The maximum length of ground shall be 200 yards and the maximum breadth shall be 100 yards, the length and breadth shall be marked off with flags and the goal shall be defined by two upright posts, 8 yards apart, without any tape or bar across them.

2. The two sides shall change goals after each goal is won.

8. If a player makes a fair catch he shall be entitled to a free kick provided he claims it by making a mark with his heel at once and in order to take such a kick he may go as far back as he pleases, and no player on the opposite side shall advance beyond his mark until he has kicked.

10. If a player shall run with the ball towards his adversaries' goal any player on the opposite side shall be at liberty to charge, hold, trip or hack him, or to wrest the ball from him, but no player shall be held and hacked at the same time.

14. No player shall be allowed to wear projecting nails, iron plates or gutta percha on the soles or heels of his boots.

The club at Blackheath objected to these rules and so left the Association and later helped form the Rugby Union. The Corinthians, an early team formed in 1882, was an exclusive club made up of ex-public school and university men. Their home ground was Queen's Club, Kensington. Later it joined with the Casuals to form a well-known amateur football club. Professional football was permitted by the F.A. in 1885 and it was forced upon them because teams paid their talented players secretly to play in the matches. The first F.A. Challenge Cup match, known in those days as the English Cup, was played at The Oval in 1872 and watched by a crowd of 2,000 spectators who paid a shilling for the privilege. There were no goal nets and the cross bars were in fact tapes. There was no centre line or halfway circle and the players wore long trousers and caps. The final was played between the Wanderers and the Royal Engineers based at Chatham. The Wanderers won 1–0. The winning team was made up of monied aristocrats and only reached the final because their opponents in the semi-final, Queen's Park from Glasgow, drew with them, but could not afford to travel to London for the replay. At this time there were fifteen teams taking part in the competition. In 1888 the Football League was formed consisting at first of twelve clubs from the North and Midlands. Crystal Palace and Tufnell Park had football grounds in those days and Crystal Palace was the main venue for the Cup Finals until Wembley was opened in 1923. Tottenham Hotspur won the English Cup in 1901 and goes on record as the only non-league side to do so. Hundreds of people standing on the slopes of Sydenham watched this match played at Crystal Palace. Printers published 'Death Cards' to be purchased by the supporters of the losing side. On a card appropriately edged with black and bearing a picture of a horse pulling a hearse were the words – 'In loving Memory of ———— who died whilst fighting for the English Cup against ———— on ———— at ————.' The memorial underneath read –

> Boldly to the fray they went
> But got beaten to their sorrow;
> They were put to sleep by a better team,
> And the funeral is tomorrow.

Before Wembley the Cup Final was played on the following grounds:

> 1872–1892 Kennington Oval.
> 1873 Lillie Bridge.
> 1893 Fallowfield, Manchester.

1894 Everton.
1895–1914 Crystal Palace.
1915 Old Trafford, Manchester.
1920–1922 Stamford Bridge, London.

The trophy of the present day is the third to be provided by the F.A. The first was stolen, in 1895, while on display in a Birmingham Sports shop after it had been won by Aston Villa. The second was withdrawn in 1910 because replicas had been made of it. The design of the present Challenge Cup has been registered to prevent this happening again. Nine years were lost because of the wars and so in 1981 the F.A. Challenge Cup celebrated its centenary.

The opening game at Wembley in 1923 was nearly a disaster. 100,000 spectators broke the barriers and swarmed over the pitch and the kick off had to be delayed for forty minutes. A policeman on a white horse made history when he tried to control the crowds. Bolton played West Ham and the former won 2–0 and the first goal scored at Wembley was by David Jack. Afterwards the West Ham manager complained that the crowd had cut up the side lines and this handicapped the wingers of his team. After this episode it was decided that all Cup Finals in the future should be 'all ticket' matches and this has not altered.

Although London, like other large cities around the world, is suffering from a recession and a population drift which cannot easily be rectified, it still remains 'the capital with the mostest'. The age of the micro chip is upon us and whether we like it or not there is less work available and more time for sport, pastimes and entertainments. London councils are developing schemes to attract people with time on their hands. For instance the Barbican is developing a large scale project to promote music and the arts within the City. Annually London receives millions of tourists and visitors from all parts of the globe to experience, explore and enjoy such rituals as the Lord Mayor's Show, the Changing of the Guard, the Ceremony of the Keys, or Trooping the Colour. It is these events which bring glamour and excitement and enhance the atmosphere, turning the great Metropolis into an almost magical showplace.

Public Duties or providing the Guard for Buckingham Palace,

St. James's Palace and the Tower of London are normally carried out by a battalion of Foot Guards stationed in the London area. This is called Mounting the Queen's Guard. In recent years when there are not enough Foot Guards to mount the Queen's Guard owing to operational commitments overseas other Regiments assist, as well as the R.A.F. The Queen's Guard is mounted from either Wellington or Chelsea Barracks and the Household Cavalry mount The Queen's Life Guard daily from Horse Guards, Whitehall. In all the troops of the Household Division number 8,000 men.

The responsibility of guarding the sovereign, from Henry VIII's time until the Civil War, rested with the Body Guard of the Yeomen of the Guard and the Band of Pensioners, now known as the Sovereign's Bodyguard of the Honorable Corps of the Gentlemen-at-Arms. During the Civil War, Charles I was guarded by Scots Guards while his son, the future Charles II, was guarded in exile by his Life Guards. The Life Guards are the senior regiment of the British Army. With Charles in France were roughly eighty Loyalists who were organized by Lord Gerard of Brandon into a body of Life Guards, twenty of them on duty at a time to guard the royal residence or escort the future monarch. After the Restoration the Life Guards increased in number and in 1678 a troop of Horse Grenadier Guards was added to each cavalry troop. The Grenadiers were so called because they carried the newly invented grenades in special pouches attached to their uniforms. The officers carried the matches or fusees with which to light the fuses.

When Charles II ascended the throne he lived at Whitehall Palace and this is where the Life Guards were based. At the end of the seventeenth century Whitehall was burnt down and St. James's Palace became the official residence of the monarch, as it is today. Nevertheless the Household Cavalry continued to guard Whitehall Barracks and parade on the old tilting yard, changing the guard practically every day. The Life Guards, the Blues and the Royals make up the Household Cavalry and the Blues and the Royals have long histories of loyal service closely connected with the monarchy. The Blues, known as the Royal Horse Guards, were directly descended from the Regiment of Horse which was raised for Cromwell in 1650. As now, they wore blue tunics and were at one time known as the 'Oxford Blues' after the colour of the livery of the Earl of Oxford who was the Commander in Charles II's time. The Royals, known as the Royal Dragoons, were formed when Charles II married Catherine of Braganza. Part of her dowry was the gift of Tangier to the British Crown. The Royal Dragoons, then known as the Tangier Horses were sent out to defend the newly acquired port against the Moors. After twenty-two years service in defence of Tangier the regiment returned home and received the title 'His Majesty's Own Regiment of Royal Dragoons'. In 1969 the two regiments were amalgamated and now have the title the Blues and Royals. The Life Guards have the standard of the Sovereign bearing the Royal Coat of Arms between the letters EII and R. The Blues and Royals have the Squadron Standard bearing the Rose, Thistle and Shamrock, symbols of the Union of England with Scotland and Ireland. These emblems are between EII and R. Both standards are crimson, the special colour of the Queen's and the Life Guards wear crimson tunics. The Household Cavalry wear breast plates, which were an idea promoted by George IV, and plumed helmets designed by Prince Albert, hence the distinctly German look; they are the only regiments in the British Army to wear armour and their dress has not changed since 1856. The two regiments have 128 horses to maintain the Sovereign's escort and the Queen's Life Guard at Whitehall. The Life Guards have white sheepskin saddle covers and the Blues and Royals, black. The Guards are posted between 10 a.m. and 4 p.m. and the Changing of the Guard at Horse Guards Parade can be seen on most days at 11 a.m. and 10 a.m. on Sundays. The two regiments alternate with each other and the New Guard rides from the new Hyde Park Barracks, past Buckingham Palace and down the Mall before entering the Parade ground. It is a splended sight to see, no matter how many times you have witnessed it. The New Guard meets the Old Guard on the Parade ground and after a colourful ritual in which the mounted sentries are changed, the Old Guard rides back to the barracks. The sentries spend two hours on duty and four hours off. There is also a mounted band attached to the Life Guards and the drum horses are provided by both regiments.

There are five regiments of Foot Guards which guard the royal residences in London: Buckingham Palace, St. James's Palace and the Tower of London. They consist of the Coldstream Guards, Irish Guards, Scots Guards, Welsh Guards and Grenadier Guards. Up to the mid nineteenth century the older regiments had their own uniforms but since then the red tunics and dark trousers have been worn by all the regiments – with certain differences.

The Coldstream Guards is the oldest regiment in terms of continuous service and is descended from General Monck's Regiment of Foot which he formed during the Civil War, under Cromwell. When Charles II came to power the Guards marched from their headquarters in the small Scottish town of Coldstream and formed up on Tower Hill to be inspected by the King. Charles ordered them to lay down their arms and take them up again as the 2nd Regiment of Foot Guards. It is said that not a man moved and General Monck remarked that the Regiment refused to be known as second in the British Army. His Majesty then gave the command 'Coldstream Guards, take up your arms.' Since then the motto of the Regiment has been *Nulli secundus* (second to none). A Coldstream Guard's tunic has buttons in pairs and for this they are known as the 2nd Regiment of Foot Guards. A red plume adorns the bearskin and the official badge is that of the Most Noble Order of the Garter – the highest order of chivalry in the land.

The Irish Guards were formed by Queen Victoria in 1900 in recognition of the bravery of her Irish troops in the South African War. The buttons on the tunics are in two groups of four and it follows that the Irish Guards are known as the 4th Regiment of Foot Guards. A blue plume is attached to the bearskin and the official badge is in the form of a shamrock. This Regiment is the only one to have a mascot to lead then on parade. It is an Irish Wolfhound and the last one, named Fionn, was the seventh in a line stretching back to 1902. Rudyard Kipling wrote a detailed history of the Irish Guards after his son was killed at Ypres in 1915 while serving in this Regiment.

The Scots Guards are by rights the oldest regiment as they were formed in 1642 by Charles I as his personal bodyguard. After the capture of Charles during the Civil War the Scots Guards were disbanded and were only reformed in 1660 as part of the Scottish Army, and later became part of the English army being known as the 3rd Regiment of Foot Guards. In 1831 William IV conferred the title of 'Scots Fusilier Guards' and from that time all members of the Regiment wore a bearskin – without a plume. The title 'Scots Guards' was given to them by Queen Victoria in 1877. Although they are known to be the oldest Regiment they are third in line behind the Grenadier and Coldstream Guards because of a break in their service during the Civil War – and because of this they wear their tunic buttons in threes. As with the other regiments their history tells of a high standard of bravery and courage in every battle fought. They live up to their ancient motto – *Nemo Me Impune Lacessit*, 'Let No One Provoke Me with Impunity'.

King George V raised the Welsh Guards in 1915 when it was decided that all countries within the United Kingdom should be represented by their own regiment. After a period of intense training they took part in the Great War and also mounted guard at Buckingham Palace on St. David's Day in 1915. They are known as the 5th Regiment of Foot Guards and the buttons on their tunics are arranged in fives. A magnificent green and white plume can be seen on the bearskin and the badge is of a leek, the national emblem of Wales. It is the only regiment to have a Battalion Choir.

The Grenadier Guards can be traced back to the personal bodyguard of Charles II when in exile, and were known in 1697 as the 1st Regiment of Foot Guards. To reward their gallantry in the Battle of Waterloo they were renamed the First Grenadier Regiment of Foot Guards. A Grenadier has eight evenly spaced buttons on his tunic, a white plume in his bearskin, a badge which signifies the royal charter surrounded by a garter, and a badge on his collar in the shape of a grenade.

The Changing of the Guard at Buckingham Palace is performed on most days except in May when, for the benefit of the tourist, it is sometimes mounted in Horse Guards Parade. Each Regiment has its own band which plays slow and quick marches linked with that Regiment. The Old Guard from Buckingham Palace and St. James's Palace assembles in the forecourt of Buckingham Palace at 11.07 a.m., and awaits the arrival of the New Guard. After much ceremony and precision marching to music the Captains of the Old and New Guard meet and symbolically go through the motions of handing over the Keys of the Palace. The sentries of the New Guard are posted and the Old Guard marches back to the barracks. As St. James's Palace is still the official residence of the Court the Queen's Standard or Colour is lodged there, and it also flies over Buckingham Palace when she is in residence.

The Colours or Standards of the Regiments originate from serving a practical and necessary purpose in times of warfare. In early days flags were carried to rally troops and to enable those lost in the chaos of hand to hand fighting to find their regiment and reassemble, ready to attack or retreat as the leader thought fit. The Colour was trooped along the ranks and when they returned to barracks or billets for the night the Standard was lodged with the officer in charge. Incidentally the term Trooping means in literal terms 'marching to music'. The last time Trooping the Colour was enacted in warfare was during the Crimean War. The ceremony can be traced back to Charles II's reign when every garrison in the country Trooped the Colour every day. During the eighteenth century the Colour was only Trooped when the monarch was in residence in any one particular town or city. As the ceremony was usually performed in London it became the tradition to confine it to the capital. On the monarch's birthday the Guard Regiment on duty received a special gratuity. To ensure that all Regiments received the same amount of money it was decided to make the birthday ceremony a special one, employing all seven Regiments of the Household Division. Each Regiment has its own Colour with special emblems and Battle Honours printed on it. This was the origin of the ceremony of Trooping the Colour on the Queen's official birthday, one Saturday in June.

The first recorded mention of the Sovereign's birthday being celebrated is an order in the Grenadier Guards' Book dated 30 November 1748. It states: 'Ordered by the Field Officer in Waiting that an additional Guard of a Subaltern Officer, 2 Sergeants, 2 Corporals and 40 Private Men be added to the King's Guard on Friday next being the day appointed for Keeping His Majesty's Birthday.' Later the official Royal Birthday seems to have taken place in either May or June – probably in the hope of a fine day. This was obviously to protect the very expensive gear worn by the Troops. Even today if the weather proves inclement then the ceremony is postponed to the afternoon and if it is still unsuitable then the Parade is cancelled for that year. The birthday of George IV was kept on 7 May 1830 while his actual birthday was 12 August, by which time the king was dead.

Sometimes in the early days Trooping the Colour took place in Hyde Park or even in St. James's Park, but on the whole Horse Guards Parade was the usual venue as it is today. There is no record of Queen Victoria ever taking the Salute in London, according to Lieutenant General Sir Michael Gow in his book *A History of the Sovereign's Birthday Parade by the Household Troops*, but Prince Albert sometimes represented her. An excerpt from Queen Victoria's Journal for 27 May 1845 reads:

'Albert came to breakfast dressed in his uniform for the Birthday Parade, this being the day on which my birthday is officially kept. At a quarter to 10 I drove quite "in cog" with Bertie and Ly Lyttleton, in a small green Chariot round by the Birdcage Walk, to the Horse Guards, where we had an admirable view of the Parade, and without being "found out". Bertie stood at the open window, transfixed with delight, and though it lasted long, he was wretched when all was over. I saw my beloved Albert ride up with Uncle Cambridge, George, Charles and the Old Duke, all the staff etc following us out, but we got away quite easily, just as we came, and saw Albert return loudly cheered by the crowds.'

'The Old Duke' referred to was the Duke of Wellington and it was the last Parade he attended before his death. It was a very impressive affair by all accounts and by their performance and behaviour the regiments taking part and the civilians looking on made it one of the most memorable in history.

Since Victoria's reign the soveriegn, except in times of illness or other commitments, has taken the leading part in Trooping the Colour as our own Queen did for many years, riding side-saddle, and wearing the uniform of the Regiment whose Colour was to be trooped.

I cannot go into all the intricate details of the ceremony which, incidentally, now celebrates Commonwealth Day also, but it is sufficient to say that each movement is significant and represents past military history in one form or another. The Queen's official birthday Parade is held in June and it is watched by her and other members of the Royal family who take up their positions in a room above the Archway at the Whitehall Parade ground.

The Household Division play a large part in the main events involving the Royal Family. Coronations, funerals, jubilees and weddings all call for their brilliant attendance. In July 1981 we witnessed the wedding of Prince Charles to Lady Diana Spencer and the splendour and expertise of those taking part in the procession captured the hearts of everyone. It was in fact the wedding of the world and we must surely be the envy of every nation to be able to put on such a breath-taking spectacle.

Apart from the military apparel, the historic costumes to be found in London today range from Henry VII's time to the Victorian era. The Lord Chancellor's robes date back to the early Tudors, the Yeoman of the Guard to Henry VIII. Elizabethan fashions are to be seen in robes worn by Bishops and City Councillors. The Judge's wig and gown date back to William and Mary, while the Doggett Coat was established after the Hanoverian Succession. The costume of the Lord Mayor and the liveries of the Companies go back to George IV, while the Bank messengers are dressed in Victorian styles.

It is my belief that London possesses a rare commodity in the world today. It is able, through its historic buildings, museums, ceremonies and spectacular displays to present to the world not just one period in history but a reflection of its growth and development throughout the ages. And it is the Sovereign and the Royal Family who are the leading players in this Carnival of the Centuries which epitomizes the pride and prestige of our beloved capital.

Bibliography

Baker, Dr. Ian H., ed. *Barts — 850 Years* St. Bartholomew's Hospital Journal, 1973

Binder, Pearl *The Pearlies* Jupiter Books, 1975

Bone, James *The London Perambulator* Jonathan Cape, 1950

Braybrook, N. *London Green* Victor Gollancz, 1959

Chambers, Robert *The Book of Days* Chambers, 1880

Chatto, William Andrew *Facts and Speculations on the Origin and History of Playing Cards* John Russell Smith, 1848

Clair, Colin *St. Paul's Cathedral* Bruce & Gawthorn, 1960

Drive Publications *Treasures of Britain* 1968

Ekwall, Eilert *Street Names of the City of London* Oxford University Press, 1954

Goddard, Henry *Memoirs of a Bow Street Runner* Museum Press, 1956

Golding, Claud *London the City* Robert Hale, 1951

Gordon, W. I. *The Horse World of London* 1883

Harper, Charles *More Queer Things about London* Cecil Palmer, 1924

Harrison, Michael *London Beneath the Pavement* Peter Davies, 1961

Harrowven, Jean *Origins of Rhymes, Songs and Sayings* Kaye & Ward, 1978

Harrowven, Jean *Origins of Festivals and Feasts* Kaye & Ward, 1980

Hearsey, John E. N. *Bridge, Church and Palace* John Murray, 1961

Holmes, T. *The Great Metropolis* St. Paul's Churchyard, *c.* 1850

Kent, William *London Mystery and Mythology* Staple Press, 1952

Knight, Charles, ed. *London* 2 vols. Virtue & Co.

London Fire Brigade *A History of London's Firefighters* (pamphlet) 1981

Lutterworth Press, *The Changing of the Guard, 1971*

Malcolmson, Robert W. *Popular Recreations in English Society, 1700–1850* Cambridge University Press, 1973

Mayhew, Henry 'London Street Life' taken from *Selections from the Writings of Henry Mayhew* Chatto & Windus, 1966

McCulloch, Rev. Joseph *St. Mary-le-Bow* Pitkin Pictorials, 1964

Metropolitan Police *The History of the Metropolitan Police Force* (pamphlet) 1975

Noble, Dudley, ed. *The Jubilee Book of the Royal Automobile Club 1897–1957* R.A.C. Publications, 1957

Pearson, Margaret M. *Discovering London for Children* Shire Publications, 1971

Piper, David *The Companion Guide to London* William Collins, 1964

Pritchett, V. *London Perceived* (essay) 1962, rev. Chatto & Windus, 1974

Scott, J. M. *The Book of Pall Mall* William Heinemann, 1965

Sexby, J. J. *The Municipal Parks, Gardens and Open Spaces of London* E. Stock, 1898

Simkins, P. and Gibbs, B. *The Guards* Macmillan Publishers, 1976

Sims, George R. *Living London* Vols. 1 and 3, Cassell & Co., 1908

Spencer, H. *London's Canal* Lund Humphries, 1976

Stow, John *A Survey of London, 1598* ed. C. L. Kingsford, 2 vols., Oxford University Press, 1867

Tower of London Authorities *Strange Stories of the Tower of London*

Tydeman, Richard *Without a City Wall* The Church of the Holy Sepulchre (pamphlet), 1972

Williams, I. M. *The Order of St. John* St. John's Gate, London, 1971

Woodforde, John *The Strange Story of False Hair* Routledge, Kegan & Paul, 1971

Wright, A. and Smith, P. *Parliament Past and Present* Hutchinson & Co., 1908

Acknowledgements

The following people have provided invaluable information:

Madame de Baecker, Tommy Sparks, Mrs. Ivy Davey, The Archivist of The Royal Automobile Club, The London Fire Brigade, The London Police Force and Scotland Yard, St. Barts. Hospital, The Royal Hospital Chelsea, The Archivist of The Tower of London, St. John's Ambulance Brigade, M.C.C. Lords, Surrey County Cricket Club at the Oval, The Football Association, The Vicar, St. Clements Danes, The Vicar, St. Sepulchres, The Vicar, St. Mary-le-Bow, St. Paul's Cathedral, Westminster Abbey, The Bishopsgate Foundation, The Mansion House, The Horse Guards (Whitehall), The House of Lords Record Office, The Royal Opera House, Covent Garden.